Doctor Behind the Wire

Doctor Behind the Wire

The Diaries of POW Captain Jack Ennis
Singapore 1942–1945

Edited by Jackie Sutherland

Pen & Sword
MILITARY

First published in Great Britain in 2021 by
Pen & Sword Military
An imprint of
Pen & Sword Books Ltd
Yorkshire–Philadelphia

Copyright © Jackie Sutherland 2021

ISBN 978 1 39901 0 283

The right of Jackie Sutherland to be identified as Author of this work has been asserted by him in accordance with the Copyright, Designs and Patents Act 1988.

A CIP catalogue record for this book is
available from the British Library.

All rights reserved. No part of this book may be reproduced or transmitted in any form or by any means, electronic or mechanical including photocopying, recording or by any information storage and retrieval system, without permission from the Publisher in writing.

Printed and bound in the UK by CPI Group (UK) Ltd, Croydon, CR0 4YY

Pen & Sword Books Limited incorporates the imprints of Atlas, Archaeology, Aviation, Discovery, Family History, Fiction, History, Maritime, Military, Military Classics, Politics, Select, Transport, True Crime, Air World, Frontline Publishing, Leo Cooper, Remember When, Seaforth Publishing, The Praetorian Press, Wharncliffe Local History, Wharncliffe Transport, Wharncliffe True Crime and White Owl.

For a complete list of Pen & Sword titles please contact

PEN & SWORD BOOKS LIMITED
47 Church Street, Barnsley, South Yorkshire, S70 2AS, England
E-mail: enquiries@pen-and-sword.co.uk
Website: www.pen-and-sword.co.uk

Or
PEN AND SWORD BOOKS
1950 Lawrence Rd, Havertown, PA 19083, USA
E-mail: Uspen-and-sword@casematepublishers.com
Website: www.penandswordbooks.com

Dedication

Jack, Elizabeth and Rob came home from Singapore.

This book is dedicated to their memory, and to the thousands of others who returned home, many with physical and mental scars, and to the thousands who did not return.

'When you go home, tell them of us and say,
For their tomorrow, we gave our today'

Kohima Epitaph
Burma Star Association

Contents

Acknowledgements	ix
The Diaries: Notes on the transcripts	xi
Introduction	xiii
List of maps	
Malay Peninsula 1942	xviii
Singapore Island 1942–1945	xix
Chapter 1: Jack Eric Ennis: from Rawalpindi to Malaya	1
Chapter 2: Marion Elizabeth Petrie: from Edinburgh to Malaya	6
Chapter 3: Upcountry meeting and fall of Singapore	10
Chapter 4: Jack's diary – 1942	25
Chapter 5: Jack's diary – 1943	107
Chapter 6: Jack's diary – 1944	174
Chapter 7: Jack's diary – 1945	210
Chapter 8: Elizabeth in captivity, Changi Gaol then Sime Road camp	235
Chapter 9: Homeward bound	248
Chapter 10: Post-war	253
Appendix 1 Captain Jack Ennis – Changi Pathologist	259
Appendix 2 Changi Gaol, Block 'A' Fourth Floor	270
Appendix 3 Postwar Compensation Claims and Correspondence	273
Bibliography and suggested further reading	277
Index of Names	279
General Index	287

Acknowledgements

Firstly to my late parents, Jack and Elizabeth Ennis, for the wealth of stories and the enrichment of their FEPOW friendships. I am also thankful that they valued – and therefore kept – so many mementos which, with photographs, I have been able to use to illustrate this publication.

To my sister Tish and son Jamie, thank you for the extra stories and anecdotes that have helped to add even more to this account of the lives of Jack and Elizabeth.

I am fortunate to have had the encouragement and support of Sir Robert Scott's grandchildren, Scott Steedman, Sarah Petersen and Helena Steedman, and am grateful for their help with photographs and permission to quote from Rob's letters to my parents. Having swapped happy memories - and tears - with their late mother, Susan Syme (nee Scott) I deeply regret that she has not seen the finished publication.

Very special thanks are due to Geoff Gill and Meg Parkes, Liverpool School of Tropical Medicine, who contributed Appendix 1; this adds much value to the context of Jack's diaries. Their knowledge and understanding of the historical and medical background is world-class. For those readers wishing to know more of Far East Prisoner of War medicine, I highly recommend their other publications (details in Bibliography and suggested further reading).

This book would not have been written without encouragement from the late Rod Suddaby, Imperial War Museum (IWM). I was further motivated by meeting two former Changi Girl Guides who in 2006, despite their age, poor health and distance, had made the effort to attend the IWM for the handing-over ceremony of the Girl Guide quilt that they had helped to sew.

For his work in scanning and processing photographs, several of which had literally 'been through the war', I am most grateful to Ivan Young who gave so generously of his time and skills.

I acknowledge the permissions from copyright holders, the IWM and The Scotsman publications, for the use of photographs.

This publication was made possible by the team at Pen and Sword to whom thanks are due. I would especially like to thank Tony Walton, Editor, for his constructive comments and kind words.

Finally particular thanks are due to my husband George who was able to draw on his experience as a former Territorial Army officer and knowledge as a military historian to provide invaluable help in a wide variety of aspects too many to detail.

The Diaries: notes on the transcript

The transcript of the diaries of Captain Jack Ennis in Singapore 1942–1945 forms the major part of this book from chapters 3 to 7, and again part of chapter 9.

The diaries were not written with publication in mind, although from his instruction early in 1942 ('send to Elizabeth') it is clear Jack intended that, should he not survive, his diary would be a record for his wife and family.

Each diary entry is preceded by the date of the entry, for example:

'11 February [1942]
Sisters are to be evacuated. Elizabeth doesn't go.
'25 December [1942]
Shortest half hour of my life.'

The text and notes are written in language that was of that time, and this should be borne in mind however much some phrases might be unacceptable today. Only the most private and personal observations have been omitted. Within the transcript, many acronyms have been explained in square brackets, as have translations of local words. It is hoped that these additions will help the reader without losing the immediacy and contemporary mood of the times.

Where the handwriting has proved unreadable, this is indicated as [illegible].

Names and spellings of people and places are generally as Jack recorded in his diaries. In a very few cases, names have been removed later and marked […] to avoid embarrassment.

Throughout his internment, Jack maintained an interest in the progress of the war in Europe as well as the Far East, and recorded such news (or rumours) in his diary, usually with the sub-title 'Borehole'. 'Borehole Bugle' was Army slang for highly coloured and doubtful rumours of events during the war. He used double question marks – ?? – to indicate some uncertainty, but single question marks – ? – are also used.

The Mess had a hidden radio, perhaps operated by only one or two men, and extracts from news broadcasts, such as BBC or KGEI, were regularly passed on. News also came in from other POWs who had been brought in from elsewhere in the peninsula, the islands or from ships. The Japanese also made copies of the *Syonan Sinbun* available.

Introduction

Crosswords and jigsaw puzzles

Researching the captivity and internment of Jack and Elizabeth Ennis

I always knew about the diaries. Three small black pocket diaries and another, slightly larger, made from brown card and paper, and hand-sewn at the centre fold. In a clear plastic bag, the diaries had lain on my father's desk for as long as I could remember.

Then there was 'the quilt'. Rolled carefully in tissue paper, the patchwork quilt had been handmade and gifted to my mother Elizabeth when she ran a group of Girl Guides in Changi Gaol.

There were also occasional special visitors to our house. 'We were in Changi together,' my parents would say.

Growing up, I remember being told that should anything ever happen to my parents, my sister and I would be looked after by Rob and Rosamund Scott. 'Rob was in Changi,' explained Mum.

In September 2006, the patchwork quilt was presented to the Imperial War Museum. For me, it was very humbling to meet some of the former Girl Guides and their relatives, and to hear of their experiences. Also that year, my father's medical notes were passed to Liverpool School of Tropical Medicine, and I realized a transcript of his personal diaries would complement any further medical research.

Listening to the late Roger Mansell's moving address at the Researching FEPOW (Far East Prisoners of War) Conference 2010 was the final spur for me to act – to transcribe the diaries and make the information available to anyone interested. In Roger's words, 'to honour these men and women by sharing information and giving it away, so that these men and women will never be forgotten'.

And so I began a transcript of the diaries. It has been a slow process, frustrating at times, but often with sparks of elation as seemingly illegible words were eventually deciphered. Jack's handwriting is small, mostly in pen (but latterly in pencil), and his script often flattens out along the line – rather like a tiny spider losing the will to live. Add in a sprinkling of medical terms (words such as lymphangitis, borborygmus and gastrojejunostomy!), references to Apothecary measures and outdated medical procedures, and transcription has been challenging – combining the skills of good detective work with the tenacity required for cryptic crosswords and jigsaw puzzles.

At the same time, I felt the diaries needed to be placed in context, and so began further research.

While transcribing the diaries, often, in an attempt to decipher medical terms or names, I read many books on internment in Singapore – and as I read, I came to appreciate, and further understand, the links between my parents and other former prisoners of war (POWs). While trying to tie down dates, I looked again through the box of old papers – and found documents and letters I had previously missed.

These papers added more colour. They included Jack's Red Cross identity cards, Elizabeth's identity card from Changi, sketches of Jack as a POW, a cartoon by 'Akki', smuggled notes from Elizabeth in Changi Gaol to Jack in Roberts Barracks, letters received by Jack as a POW, postcards he sent back to his mother in London, the formal letter from the India Office informing his mother that he was a prisoner of war, and menus from SS *Monowai* on the return voyage from Singapore.

Many books have been published on the Fall of Singapore and POW experiences in Changi, and even more written about the notorious Burma-Thai Railway. It is not my intention to duplicate any of those works, rather to give a different perspective – of three contemporary but individually unique experiences.

As the Japanese invaded Singapore, Robert Heatlie Scott was at his post as Director of the Far Eastern Bureau, Ministry of Information, and a member of the War Cabinet. After the Fall of Singapore and his subsequent capture, the Japanese identified Rob as a high-profile prisoner. He suffered eight-and-a-half months of interrogation and isolation before being returned to what he described as 'the comparative paradise of ordinary internment'. During this time, he was allowed to meet Elizabeth Ennis, also an internee, who had previously been the Scott children's nanny. On 10 October 1943 (the Double Tenth), Rob was the first to be arrested and taken away as a large force of Japanese and Kempetai [secret police] raided the camp. He was viciously interrogated and tortured. After sixteen months, the interrogators became more and more uncertain of the mass of evidence and conflicting stories they had wrought, by torture, from some fifty prisoners. By now,

Rob's weight had dropped to below 8st. Convinced that he was about to die, the Kempetai sent him back to the civilian camp.

Despite the limited medical aid and rations available, Rob slowly recovered, although it was many months before he could walk again. Elizabeth regularly visited Rob in hospital and at Syme Road camp, Singapore. On 1 September 1945, in a letter handwritten on the back of a faded green requisition form, Rob wrote to Jack, Elizabeth's husband: 'Few things contributed more to my recovery than those visits.'

In 1941, Jack Eric Ennis (occasionally known as John) was a captain in the Indian Medical Service (IMS), deployed to set up pathology facilities in 'upcountry' Malaya. As the threat of Japanese invasion intensified, Jack, along with his unit, was moved back to Singapore. Throughout this time of rising tension, Jack continued to write daily in his diary. From 'the first degree of readiness' on 7 December 1941, his writing vividly captures the escalating severity of the situation in Singapore, the increasing tension and confusion, and the stream of troops, many injured, retreating to Singapore Island.

With a premonition they might be parted, on 24 January, Jack bought Elizabeth Petrie, his fiancée, a small suitcase. In early February, as Singapore was besieged, Elizabeth declined an opportunity to leave. Conditions worsened.

On 11 February, the Japanese launched yet another vicious aerial attack on Singapore. Bombs fell and the streets were raked with machine-gun fire. Jack and Elizabeth had to leap from the car taking them to the Registry Office, diving into a storm drain to escape the hail of bullets. They reached the iconic Fullerton Building safely and were married by Special Licence.

Over the next few days their time together was limited, as both treated and nursed the mounting casualties, often in makeshift hospitals such as Singapore Cricket Club or the Fullerton Building itself. Finally, on 2 March, they were separated to internment camps.

At great risk, Jack continued his diary. The transcript forms the main part of this manuscript.

Every diary written during those years in Singapore is unique, and all are worth reading. I have giggled while reading some (Jack's description of enlivening a theatre production by throwing rice balls on to the stage was not so appreciated by the recipients, as also recorded by Captain Marshall in his diary). I have been heartened by cross-references. Philip Bloom wrote of evenings spent sitting on the rooftop with Jack, looking across towards the lights of Changi Gaol, where their wives were interned. While desperately ill, Captain Ledingham wrote gratefully that, despite the deprivations of their diet, Jack had brought him an egg from one of the hens to supplement a meal that day. I have been saddened by the depression and feelings of hopelessness recorded in another diary, and brought to tears by the tragic death through illness, and therefore the end of writing, of yet another diarist.

At the end of the war, Jack's kindness extended to some of his former Korean guards, as they sought his advice. Amongst the papers discovered only years after Jack's death in 2007, a letter, written in 1947 from a former Korean guard, asks: 'How can I ask you to forgive me for what I did to you during the period of the captivity in Singapore?'

In contrast to the exotic travels of Rob Scott and Jack Ennis, for the first twenty-eight years of her life, Elizabeth (Betty) Petrie had not even left Scotland. As the eldest child growing up in a one-parent family in Edinburgh for much of her young life, she had assumed many responsibilities. It was a modest household, and Elizabeth was taught many skills in housekeeping, sewing and needlework, skills that would later be useful in the 'make-do and mend' necessities of internment. She was self-assured, resourceful, quietly confident and happy in her own company. She also had a strong sense of service, and having been a keen Brownie and Girl Guide herself, became an adult Guider.

In 1940, following a chance meeting with a friend in Edinburgh, Elizabeth took a post as nanny to the Scott family; a rising diplomat, Rob had been posted to Hong Kong, accompanied by his wife Rosamund and their two young children. As Japanese troops entered the Second World War, Rob moved his family and Elizabeth to safety, first the Philippines, then Singapore. When the threat of war escalated, Rosamund and the children left for Australia, while Elizabeth remained in Singapore and returned to nursing.

In 1941, posted to a remote hospital in the jungle, she met Jack.

On 15 February 1942, four days after their wedding, Singapore capitulated. There was no honeymoon; instead, long hours caring for the increasing numbers of sick and wounded in steadily worsening circumstances. Then in early March, Jack and Elizabeth were sent to separate internment camps.

At that time, Changi Gaol housed around 3,000 civilian internees, of whom some 400 were women and children. In this challenging environment, Elizabeth did her best to keep some of the girls entertained and occupied, reading with them or teaching skills such as sewing. Patchwork, using scraps of materials and threads, was one of the activities enjoyed by the girls, and it was after seeing the girls sitting sewing one day that internee Ethel Mulvaney had the idea of what were to be later known as the 'Changi quilts'. It was only many years after the end of the war in the Far East that the heritage of the Changi quilts was recognized.

This manuscript is a record of the internment experiences of my parents, Jack and Elizabeth Ennis, and more briefly, Rob Scott. It is, in the words of Roger Mansell, 'by sharing information and giving it away, that we honour these men and women and they will never be forgotten'.

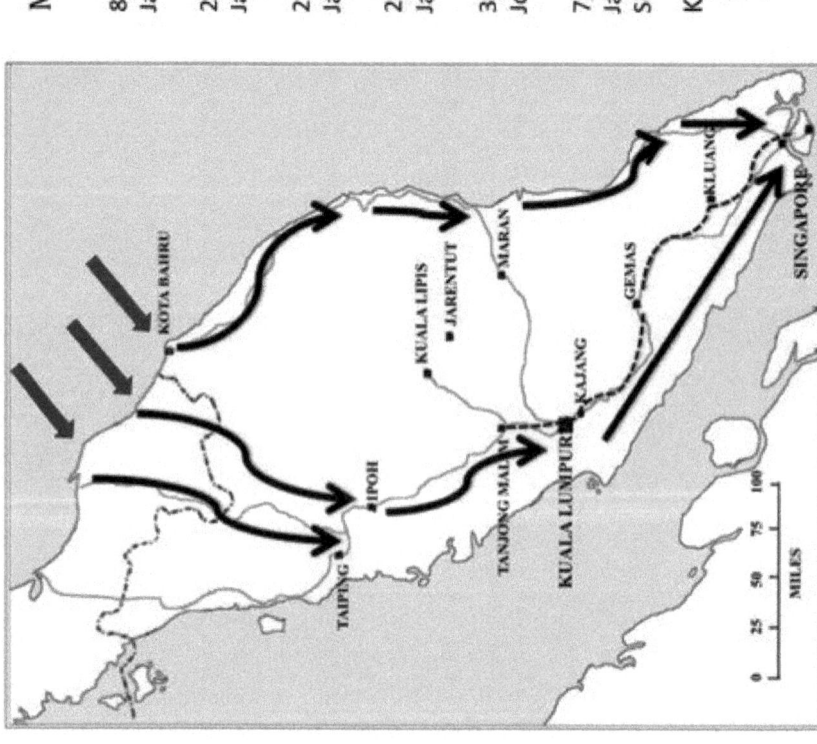

MALAYA 1941-1942

8 December 1941
Japanese invaded Malaya

22 December
Japanese forces reached Ipoh

25 December
Jack left Tanjong Malim

28 December
Jack arrived in Singapore

30/31 January 1942
Johore Causeway blown up

7/8 February
Japanese forces began the siege of Singapore

KEY

⬆ Japanese forces

------ Jack's route

Malay Peninsula 1942

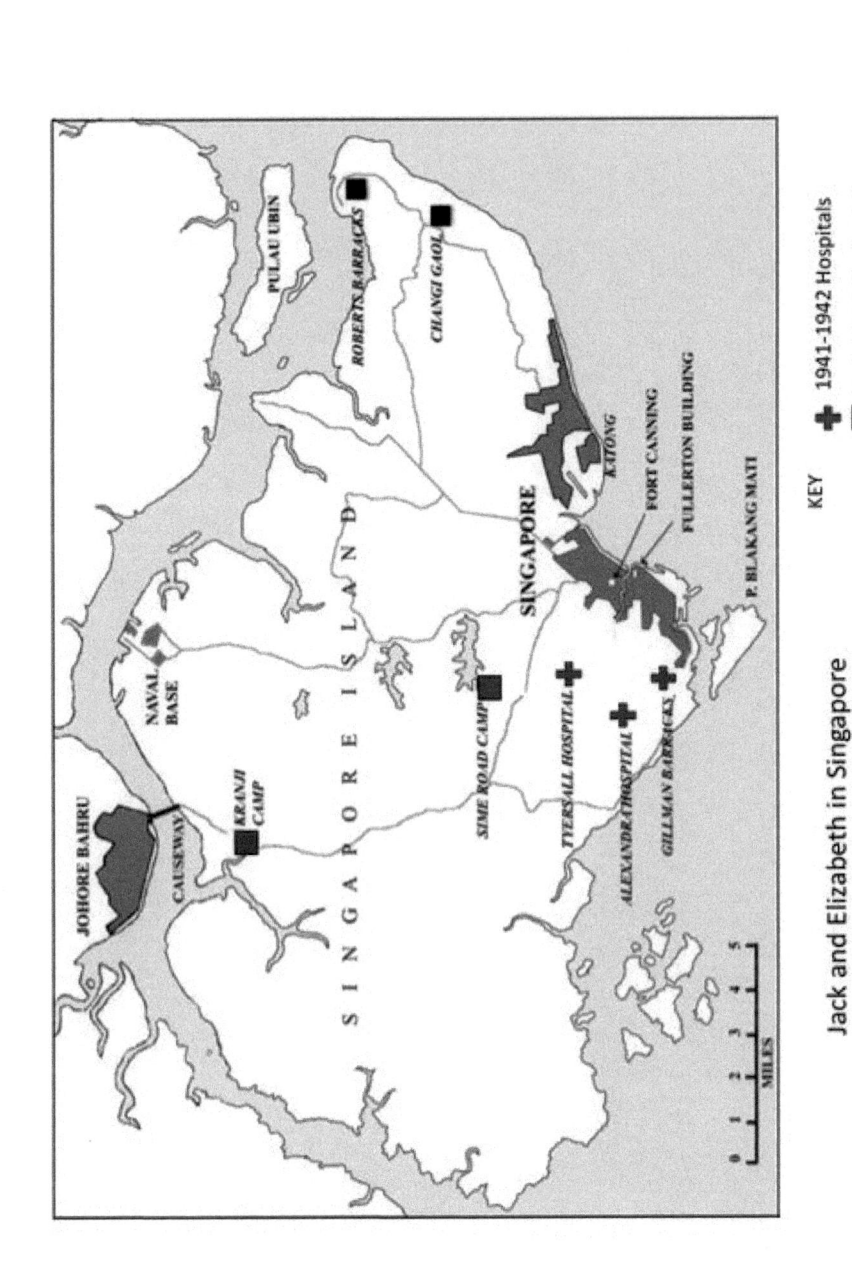

Singapore Island 1942–1945

Jack and Elizabeth in Singapore

Chapter 1

Jack Eric Ennis: from Rawalpindi to Malaya

'The best kind of mind for tropical life is one of an enquiring nature: one which takes an interest in the people and things around; in fact the type of person best filled for this kind of existence is one who has a passion for hobbies of all sorts, and, if a particular hobby should be his life's work, he is all the more fortunate.'
From *Manson's Tropical Diseases* (1940)

Born on 25 July 1911 at the British Army cantonment at Rawalpindi (now in Pakistan), Jack Eric Ennis was the son of Robert James Ennis and his wife Louisa Beetles. Formerly a sergeant bugler with the East Lancashire Regiment, then a corporal with North West Railway Rifles, Robert was now working in a British Government post concerned with railway traffic moving up to the North West Frontier, to the edge of tribal territory on the border with Afghanistan. Louisa had been a teacher in the Army children's school in the cantonment, a large British Indian Army base.

Louisa educated Jack at home until he was 7 or 8 years old, when he became eligible to be sent to one of the Lawrence Schools. At that time there were three such schools situated in different mountain sites in British India and taking in boarders from British ex-Army families. Following his elder brother Stanley and sister Mona, Jack was admitted to the Lawrence School at Ghora Gali (Murree), built at about 6,000 feet on the slopes of a beautiful pine-forested mountainside, some 40 miles from their home on the plains. The Lawrence Schools were run on Army lines (many of the junior administrative staff were seconded from Army units). All domestic needs such as clothing, catering, recreation activities and sports were provided for the 350 boys at Ghora Gali, and equally for the eighty or ninety girls in the partner school. Many of the teachers were Oxford or Cambridge graduates, with some newer science graduates from Sheffield or Birmingham. As pupils reached the end of their education, they were presented for Cambridge exams – and then had to wait six to eight weeks for the results.

Boys were resident for about nine-and-a-half months of the year. Weekends were filled with drill, two church services each Sunday, sports, games and homework, but during the holidays – too short for many boarders to travel back to their homes – the boys were allowed a great deal of freedom. As long as they notified a prefect of which direction they would be heading and went out in pairs, they were allowed to roam the forests and mountains at will.

Jack delighted in this freedom, and, with his love of nature, spent hours observing birds and animals in the forests, climbing the surrounding hills and swimming in the ice-cold pools of mountain torrents.

There were adventures in every season. In later years, he would reminisce about the silent deep snows of winters, and the fun of jumping from upper dormitory windows into the snow – then having to burrow through the several metres of the stuff to find a door and a way back into the building. In summers, there were massive pine trees to climb, then cautiously move to the end of a branch before letting oneself fall back to earth, the drop slowed by the mighty branches and the landing cushioned by the deep carpet of pine needles.

In 1927, after completing his basic education, Jack became a student at the Science College in the school grounds. The standard of education was high: equivalent to BSc in physics, chemistry and biology. Students competed for Government bursaries, and if successful, were admitted to Oxford, Cambridge or, in Jack's case, medicine at his chosen university in the UK.

By this time his brother and sister had already moved to London, Stanley to train in accountancy and Mona to do nursing at Guy's Hospital. His parents now lived in the Swiss Cottage area, where his mother took in student lodgers to supplement her husband's pension.

From 1931, Jack trained at St Bartholomew's Hospital, London, and in January 1937, he gained his LRCP and MRSC (Eng) BSc. In November 1937, he was awarded his Bachelor of Medicine and Bachelor of Surgery from London University. During his student years, he supplemented his income as a demonstrator in the department of biology and later in anatomy. There followed house appointments at St Bartholomew's, London, Prince of Wales General Hospital, Plymouth, and the Hospital for Tropical Diseases, London.

With his growing interest in pathology and tropical diseases, and love of India, Jack applied to the Indian Medical Service (IMS) and, in November 1938, was accepted. At that time, both IMS and Royal Army Medical Corps

(RAMC) recruits were given a two-and-a-half months' training course at RAMC Millbank and Crookham before they were considered fit to look after the health of HM Forces. It was a good course and provided plenty of amusement. For some reason it was considered that doctors must know how to ride a horse – they received a four-week course at Horse Guards Riding School, Knightsbridge. He well remembered the alarming experience of his first lesson with the Scots Greys, although whether the fear was engendered by the huge horse or the ferocious sergeant instructor was difficult to tell!

Jack's duties as a Medical Officer (MO) covered general medical work and the early stages of clinical pathology before being allowed to specialize in the latter. At this time, private practice was permitted in 'one's spare time'. Jack soon acquired a consultant reputation (his success built, in his own words, on 'two new sulphonamides'), although he always found the collection of fees very embarrassing. Unlike many of his contemporaries, who demanded a fee before treatment, Jack treated first. Payment was not always predictable; for example, the Indian poet who paid by writing a poem in Jack's honour, or the trader who paid by delivering one hundredweight of best Syrian dates!

In early 1939, Jack was posted to India. With many young British soldiers, he sailed from Southampton. The doctors on board took turns at duty – often seasickness in the Atlantic, and then the first cases of heatstroke after passing through the Suez Canal. A week after arrival in Karachi, Jack was posted to Jhelum, a large army cantonment of British and Indian regiments.

The hospital there was not busy, mostly dealing with minor injuries and the occasional case of malaria or dysentery. Work finished in the early afternoon, after which officers turned out in white shorts and shirt to attend the nearby 'Club' for tennis, badminton and squash. There was also the opportunity to take lessons in Urdu; a salary increase followed success in each level of tests.

This peaceful and enjoyable life was not to last. With the threat of war in Europe increasing, Jack was sent to Lahore to form a mobile hospital, which was then transferred to Singapore. As he had received more than the usual training in tropical medicine whilst in London, and although still a young officer, he was diverted to take control of the Far East Pathological Laboratory in Singapore in late 1939.

The entire unit of 12 Indian General Hospital (IGH) was eventually housed in a hutted camp at Tyersall Park near the Sultan of Johore's

Singapore residence, adjacent to the Botanic Gardens. The huts were typically wooden with *attap* (thatch) palm roofs, raised on piles of wood or bricks on the sloping hillside. The camp area included the 2nd Battalion Argyll and Sutherland Highlanders (A&SH). They had moved into their Sergeant's Mess with a large stock of beer – next morning their hut was seen to have sunk down on one side!

After being joined in this work by a young RAMC doctor, Jack was detailed to travel to various potential army sites on the Malaysian Peninsula, as far north as Siam (now Thailand). In 1940, he was sent to Kuala Lumpur (KL) to develop pathology services for the Peninsula.

One of these sites was the hospital at Kuala Lipis. A 100-bed hutted hospital was constructed on the east side of the Cameron Range, to take in casualties from the small units that were scattered along the east coast of the Peninsula. This was a very simple type of hospital with two kitchens – Hindu and Muslim – which adjoined each other and fed both staff and patients. With Jack were two British Medical Officers (MOs) and three or four Indian doctors.

As senior military officer (SMO), Jack had various responsibilities apart from the hospital. At that time, Kuala Lipis was a village at the road head and a rail transit station. Duties included control of people and goods (such as livestock in transit as rations on their passage to Kota Bahru) and responsibility for the secret message codes. The latter changed frequently, and often caused unintentional amusement when the correct code arrived several weeks late. With the mobile bacteriology laboratory (Lab), Jack visited the hidden sapper camps distributed along a 100-mile stretch of railway track, often travelling by the Sakai express, by arrangement being deposited at a telegraph pole in the midst of luxuriant rain forest and collected from the same site a day or so later. The train could not stop on an uphill section of track, so Jack was frequently deposited where no path or trail was visible, and certainly no building. Each time the train stopped, passengers would lean out to see the cause; perhaps a water buffalo or elephant on the track. To see Jack, with only his medical bag and small backpack, being left in the jungle caused concern among fellow passengers on the train; one called out: 'I say, old chap, are you all right in the head?'

Meat 'on the hoof' was delivered to the sapper camps in the same way; although on at least one occasion, the goat, tethered just outside the cook tent, was taken by a tiger during the night.

The posting allowed free time for the social life typical of so many expatriates, with tennis or badminton parties, curry tiffins and drinks parties.

In his diary, he writes of driving to dances and concerts in KL, and one can imagine the many invitations a young British bachelor would receive.

He wrote regularly to his mother back in London, to his sister Mona, and occasionally to his elder brother Stanley. He also wrote to and received letters from Olwen Evans, a young PE teacher from Kingsbury, North West London. Possibly having met while Jack had been a student in London, Jack and Olwen had been friends for some time, and Olwen had been a regular visitor to his home. There is no clear record of how long they had known each other, but it was obviously a close relationship. Indeed, from his mother's attitude and behaviour after the war, it is obvious that she, at least, had expected her son to return from India and settle down with Olwen.

Meanwhile, in Malaya, Jack also spent free time exploring the jungle. Even while working, he revelled in the solitude of the rain forest, the bird song, and animal and insect noises. His work often entailed long drives between camps and army bases.

'Left early for Maran today,' he wrote in June 1941:

'It's a beautiful trip, miles and miles of jungle, 109 miles each way. We drove in our 30cwt truck, taking the bends at speed and reached the highway. Lunch at the famous halting bungalow with its historic Complaints Book. Back by 1930 hours, tired and hungry. Jungle is fascinating, forms a wall on each side [of the track] of huge trees, creepers, bamboo and malacca canes. Hidden hairpin bends, the sleepy ferry at Jut across the Pahang River.'

At the end of that month, Jack's life was to change forever. In his diary, the factual entry on 29 June portrays none of the disruption that would ensue:

'29 June 1941

'Two [nursing] Sisters, Miss Court and Miss Petrie, arrived this morning from IGH to "special" Captain Jain who is in the Civil Hospital here with typhus fever caught down at Jarentut. Put them on 8-hour shifts. He is quite bad.'

Chapter 2

Marion Elizabeth Petrie: from Edinburgh to Malaya

Marion Elizabeth Petrie (Betty) was born in Edinburgh on 21 July 1912, eldest daughter of David Craig Petrie, a marine engineer, and his wife Marion Nimmo Boyd, a milliner. There were three further children – Alexandra May, born 18 March 1914; Dorothy Helen, born 1917 but who tragically died of the 'Black Flu' (meningitis) just four years later; and David Craig, born in 1923.

The children first attended Miss Comrie's School, a small local establishment, and when old enough, transferred to Portobello High School. Under their mother's influence, 'the Church' also featured prominently in their upbringing and education. Many years later, Elizabeth still remembered (as a young child while staying on holiday with grandparents in Glenogilvy just north of Dundee) walking the 2½ miles to attend Glamis Kirk, twice a day every Sunday.

Elizabeth joined the Brownies and then the Girl Guides, the latter providing her first experience of camping in a farmer's field near the Pentlands and then later at Cardrona, near Peebles. Her father was often away at sea, and later moved to the USA, so family holidays were taken with grandparents in Angus and Fife, or days on the Lothian coast at Joppa or North Berwick. Occasionally, her mother would take a cottage on Arran, an opportunity for Elizabeth to wander the hills and glens with friends.

An avid reader from a very early age, she would later reminisce about taking a book to sit on the ruined walls of nearby Craigmillar Castle – and daydreaming of adventure and travel. Her interests were wide: Scottish history and legends, songs and poetry, heroes and heroines such as Edith Cavell, Mary Slessor and Florence Nightingale, explorers, travellers and plant collectors like David Douglas in North America, George Forrest in western China and Frank Kingdom-Ward in Burma, Tibet and Assam.

She was a keen gardener and trained in horticulture at Dickson's & Co., Edinburgh. Much of her time was spent in Dickson's large nursery gardens to the south of Edinburgh, and later in the shop, learning to parcel plants and package seeds, often being sent to deliver these to the many large estates which at that time surrounded Edinburgh. Elizabeth was an active member of the Scottish Rock Garden Club, and particularly enjoyed the excursions. In later years, she told of taking the train to Glamis, being met by pony and trap and taken to the castle, home of the Bowes-Lyons, including the young Elizabeth Bowes-Lyon, future wife of King George VI and later the Queen Mother. A tour of the gardens was followed by afternoon tea with the head gardener and his wife.

However, realizing that only the young men of the firm (never the young women!) were sent on plant-collecting expeditions to China and the Far East, Elizabeth changed career. She had been brought up in the Church of Scotland, an active member of Liberton Kirk, and now, perhaps thinking of a missionary calling and the opportunity of overseas travel, she enrolled at the Deaconess Hospital to train as a nurse. This small Edinburgh hospital provided a much-needed medical service to the local community, the overcrowded tenements of the Pleasance, the Cowgate and adjacent closes. After a major extension, the hospital was reopened in 1936 by the Duke and Duchess of York; the children's ward was renamed the Princess Elizabeth Ward in honour of the occasion.

Elizabeth's training began in August 1936, and in November, after the course of lectures, she went on to practical training on the wards. Duties were varied and included spells in different wards – male medical, male and female surgical, gynaecology and three months on the children's ward. Life-long friendships were formed with others in training: Mary Blackhouse, who later became District Nurse in Johnshaven, Aberdeenshire, and Jean Douglas, who later married the chauffeur at Ballindalloch Castle beside the River Spey. Elizabeth also continued with her volunteer work in Girl Guiding and at the Royal Blind School.

Her training finished on 30 November 1939. Her record from Deaconess Hospital simply stated: 'Completed training. Certificate and badge given.'

Her life was now to change direction completely. Elizabeth would recount how, one day when she was walking along Princes Street in Edinburgh, she met a former customer of Dickson's. He enquired how she was doing, and after being told she had recently qualified as a nurse, he asked if she would consider being a children's nanny for the family of his friend, Robert Heatlie Scott.

A rising civil servant, fluent in Chinese and Japanese and with much experience in the Far East, Rob had been on leave in England with his wife Rosamond and their two young children when war broke out. He was immediately appointed Far Eastern Representative of the Ministry of Information and given the important task of setting up the first Far Eastern office in Hong Kong.

No doubt tempted by the opportunity to travel, Elizabeth agreed her name should go forward for the post of nanny, and, shortly after, was asked to present herself for interview. As part of the interview, she was introduced to the children: Susan, aged 6, and 4-year-old Douglas. Many years later, Susan remembered that Elizabeth read them a story after the formal questions of the interview. A few days later, Rob and Rosamond, accompanied by Susan and Douglas, visited Elizabeth and her mother at their home in Peffermill, Edinburgh. The Scotts were impressed with Elizabeth, and she was appointed as nanny.

For a person with a sheltered upbringing, whose previous travels had extended north to grandparents near Glamis, south to more grandparents near Peebles, west to Arran for summer holidays and as far east along the coast as Dunbar (all within a radius of 90 miles from Edinburgh), now was the start of exciting travels. On 6 February 1940, not knowing that she would not return for over four years, Elizabeth left Edinburgh to accompany Rosamond and the two children by train to London. After a month of preparation and packing there, they embarked on the P & O *Narkunda* en route for Hong Kong.

They arrived on 6 April and lived at No.10, Sheko, an isolated bungalow on a cliff top above a beautiful secluded bay.

Elizabeth's duties included the education of Susan and Douglas, as well as supervising their play and free time. She often walked with the children down to the sheltered beach of Sheko Bay. Soldiers based with the Scots battalion on the other side of the bay soon devised excuses to paddle over in their canoes to teach Susan and Douglas to swim – but even at that young age, Susan suspected her delightful young nanny was the attraction! The surf in the bay could be quite wild, so if Elizabeth decided they were not going to the beach that day, a red inflatable ring was hoisted on a flagpole in the garden, replaced by a green inflatable ring on days they intended to go to the beach.

With heightening tension and amidst rumours that the Japanese intended to blockade China's ports and coastline, the British began the compulsory evacuation of women and children from Hong Kong. On 6 July 1940, Rosamond, Elizabeth and the two children sailed to Manila on the *SS Empress of India*.

After staying in a hotel in Manila, they moved to stay with family friends of the Scotts. Lessons continued for the two children, including, for Susan, how to knit. Many years later, Susan remembered with affection how she would struggle to knit a few lines (a brown jumper for her teddy bear) and then, patiently, after Susan had been put to bed in the evening, Elizabeth would pull back the untidy effort, redo the lines and add a few more so that the garment could eventually be finished.

With some of his staff, Rob was moved to Singapore to set up a new office. On 6 August, he was reunited with his family and Elizabeth as they arrived from Manila on the SS *President Adams*.

Family life was to be disrupted again when the Japanese invaded Malaya. On 12 December, Rosamond, Susan and Douglas left by ship for Australia, planning that Rob would join them as soon as he had closed down his office. However, as Rob now sat on the Governor's War Council in Singapore, his departure was delayed.

Meanwhile, Elizabeth was helping in a local school teaching unit when there was an appeal for nurses to join the Services. On 2 April 1941, she joined the Indian Military Nursing Service (IMNS), and was posted to 12 IGH Tyersall Park, Singapore. In her free time she still worked with the 4th Guide Company in Singapore and enjoyed visits to tropical gardens, particularly admiring the profusion of exotic orchids.

On 29 June, together with another nursing Sister, Miss Court, she was sent upcountry to Kuala Lipis, Pahang, on special duty.

Chapter 3

Upcountry meeting and Fall of Singapore

It must have been with some apprehension that the nurses, Miss Petrie and Miss Court, set out on the long train journey upcountry to Kuala Lipis, Pahang, on 29 June 1941. The small hospital was in the charge of Captain J. Ennis, who had a fearsome reputation for 'being a stickler for discipline and doesn't like women'. (Jack later explained that was simply because the Emergency Hospital was set up for men, and no provision whatsoever had been made to accommodate women – even two nurses who had been sent specifically to nurse an extremely ill officer.)

The nurses were met by an army driver and taken to meet Captain Ennis. They waited for him at the hospital, and then, in Elizabeth's words, 'I can remember this car driving up and a very smart officer getting out and coming along, and he came up on to the verandah. And there he stood, in his whites, on the verandah.'

Jack also remembers the scene: 'There she was, neat, very neat, very prim and proper as I expected a nurse to be, and spoke nicely with a nice Scottish accent.'

From their arrival on 29 June, Jack immediately put the two nurses on eight-hour shifts to care for Captain Jain, severely ill with a typhoid fever.

For Jack and Elizabeth, the mutual attraction was immediate and strong – two days later, Jack asked if, in her time off duty, Elizabeth would like to see something of the jungle. It would be the first of many trips into the jungle. As he remembered: 'I took her out, it was evening, and there were palm trees and a big moon. The fireflies were amazing over there.'

Elizabeth agreed: 'I'll never forget the fireflies. We used to drive out – there was a reservoir, and we never spoke, just sat and held hands. We would listen to the sounds of the jungle, and if it suddenly went silent, Jack would quietly start the engine and drive slowly away as we knew there was a tiger close by.'

On 2 July, he wryly noted in his diary that Miss Court was 'rather wild about the late hours' he and Elizabeth kept, but even after going off duty at 10.00 pm, then for a drive in the jungle, Elizabeth would still be 'bright and spruce on duty at 8.00 am'.

Jack's diary for 4 July recorded: 'With Elizabeth again this evening, absolutely delightful, both seem to enjoy the jungle, the river, the insect noises – I do believe I am falling in love.'

The jungle, the moonlight on the river, the fireflies, the orchids, watching for tigers – these remained some of the most romantic memories for both. After the war, Jack always marked Elizabeth's birthday with a gift of orchids from Singapore.

After a fortnight of nursing care, Captain Jain recovered, and on 10 July, the two nurses were sent back to Singapore.

Jack and Elizabeth kept in touch when possible, often by coded messages which, in Kuala Lipis, were translated by the *subadar* (Indian Army officer). One can imagine the confusion created in the office by Elizabeth's telegram which read 'Secret out, be prepared …'!

The secret was indeed out, and on 25 July, shortly after Jack arrived back in Singapore, he and Elizabeth formally announced their engagement at a party in the Indian Military General Hospital (IMGH). The following day a luncheon party was thrown at Raffles for the happy couple. Again, their time together was short, and Jack returned to Kuala Lipis.

Then followed a period of separation with brief meetings in days or weekends off duty. Social life included lunch or dinner at the 'Club', dances, tennis and swimming parties. There was still time – and freedom in Jack's small car – to explore the rain forest, and longer trips to the Cameron Highlands or by boat on the Lipis River.

In late September, Elizabeth was transferred to 20th Combined General Hospital (CGH), Taiping, Perak, with Colonel Rose IMS officer in charge together with Matron Spedding, Queen Alexandra's Imperial Military Nursing Sisters (QAIMNS). Two weeks later, Jack was transferred from Kuala Lipis to Tanjong Malim.

Tensions continued to rise in the north of the country as the Japanese pushed their advances through South East Asia.

Also in September, concerned that any war would be a 'war of nerves' involving the civilian population, the British government set up the Ministry of Information. The staff was drawn from a wide range of government departments, public bodies and specialist outside establishments. In Singapore, the role of the Far Eastern Bureau, Ministry of Information, was to collect and analyze information, then co-ordinate press releases and propaganda. Good relations with the press and broadcasting services were essential, and at this, Rob Scott excelled. His arrival in Singapore as Director of the Far Eastern Bureau had been marked by a leader on the front page of the *Straits Times* on 20 November 1940, accompanied, however, by an acid cartoon from the artist Tretchikoff. Below caricatures of Dr Victor Purcell (newly appointed Director-General of the Malayan Department of Information and Publicity), Mr G.L. Peet (Director of Information and the Press Bureau) and Rob, the 'three wise monkeys' are depicted closing their ears, eyes and mouths to 'evil'. In the foreground, the local press is sketched as a muzzled dog trying to bark, while a poster in the background declares 'No news is good news. By order.'

Normal life continued in Singapore. Had not Churchill himself (in late 1939, as First Lord of the Admiralty) declared that Singapore was a fortress, armed with five 15in guns and garrisoned by nearly 20,000 men?

The Ministry of Information now published regular news items and articles in the *Straits Times*, and broadcast on the radio of the Malay Broadcasting Corporation. The intention was to send out a strong message that would be a deterrent to any Japanese thoughts of attack.

The propaganda machine rolled on, so successfully, that, as Tretchikoff wrote years later, 'Nobody took seriously the reports of Japanese successes for we could not believe them. It was the fault of our own propaganda and we were its victims.'

It was anticipated that Japan would first launch an attack on Thailand and then move to Singapore. As soon as it became clear that Japanese convoys were heading for northern Malaya, a State of Emergency was declared in Singapore on 1 December 1941. The arrival of the battleships HMS *Repulse* and HMS *Indomitable* the following day did much to boost morale; however, the publicity given to the arrival of the two ships was also noted by Japanese intelligence.

By the end of the first week in December, colonial life in Singapore was to change forever. In late December, the Governor formed the War Council, including representatives of the three Armed Forces and Rob Scott. One of the aims of the War Council was to set up a propaganda organization to give more complete and precise information.

Throughout this time, Jack and Elizabeth continued to work in hospitals upcountry. In Malaya, Jack persevered with his diary, brief entries that describe rising tension and difficult working conditions, then finally the retreat to Singapore:

7 December
Everybody standing to, first degree of readiness.
Paddy [Doyle] and I went into KL to see the 'Land Target for Tonight' Picture house deserted.

8 December
6.00 am. Nips declare war. Air raid on Singapore. Pearl Harbor raid, US navy crippled by being caught there.
Later – the two battleships left Singapore at 5.00 am for Kelantan area.

9 December
12.30 pm. *Prince of Wales* and *Repulse* have been sunk by Nippon attack off Kelantan.
I take over British Medical wards at 17 CGH. Work at last. Hospital preparing for casualties.
[On 10 December, the Japanese invaded British-held Malaya, and events continued to move swiftly. The Japanese had landed on the north east coast at Kota Bharu. Convoys of casualties began to arrive at hospitals further south as the Japanese began to fight their way down the peninsula.]

10 December
11.00 pm. Blacks ambulance train coming in from Kelantan front. Few bad injuries, most are fragmented bones and heavily infected wounds. 150 cases arrived. Awful rumours about how the Nips are fighting up there – new weapons, tactics and methods.

11 December
Surgical treatment of casualties. I gave anaesthetics – went all right.

12 December
Fighting in Kedah area began. Convoy after convoy is going north.

13 December
Not doing too well in Kota Bharu area, Japs taken the aerodrome and town. Heavy fighting in Kedah area now Nips advancing.

14 December
8.30 am. Casualties 162 from Alor Star. Bad cases for treatment owing to Japanese advancing.
2.00 pm – 9.00 pm. Anaesthetics for Gibbs operating. Most cases infected.

15 December
Giving anaesthetics most of the day and attending my medical ward of British patients in between. Letting the Lab run itself now.

16 December
Hell of a lot of work.
Trying to empty out all possible medical cases.
One man ran away, (query mental) Wright.
10.00 pm. 360 cases taken by Duncan from Taiping to Sumatra.
Sixty odd left here and one Japanese.

17 December
Usual rushed morning. More and more cases. Medical wards in morning. Anaesthetics until 9.00 pm. Last case three hours, through and through gun shot wounds to the abdomen.
Slept night at office.

22 December
Wake Island vigorously attacked by Nips. Two landings, island falls after about 14 hours fighting.

24 December
Hong Kong falls to the Nip forces. Not good for our morale down here in Malaya with the Nips so rapidly advancing already.

25 December
Left Tanjong Malim at 4.00 pm; truck very bad, won't take the hills at all. Stopped at KL for some suppers, could get very little. On to Kajang arrived about 10.00 pm.

20 CGH were celebrating their Christmas in huts. Found Elizabeth in the former District Officer's bungalow. Feeling pretty hungry, and hope the staff get some food too.

26 December
Spent night at Kajang. Drove into KL to see Brig. Summons and Alford and say I'm going south. Was there in time for a raid. It was not very fearsome, Elizabeth was with me.

KL is very dead and scared already.

27 December
　Left Kajang. Had a good run down to Gemas where parked the night. Sleeping at Roberts Hospital. Lab truck left near the railway station.

28 December
　Left Gemas and head straight down to Singapore, arriving in evening.

29 December
　Up to Fort Canning, nobody seemed very clear up there.
　Job going at Johore B General Hospital??
　Lennox RAMC been sent there.
　Came on to Changi to find an awful mess and confusion.
　Air raid 9.00 pm to 11.00 pm.
　1.00 am. Lt Alagappa is not very keen on taking me into the Hospital, was pointedly rude about it, 'though I am a foundation member of his Mess.

30 December
　Visited town, sent cable to Mother.
　Did some shopping in case there is going to be a long siege of the island.
　Saw Bill Calder, says the boat is all ready in case we evacuate to Europe.
　Dined with Harry, Phyllis [Morris] and Uncle.
　Atmosphere in Singapore is depressing, most people are of low morale already.
　Air raid warning about 8.00 pm. Nothing much happened.

1942

Diary inscription
J.E. Ennis
MB, BS (Lond)
Please send this diary to my wife Elizabeth, if I fail to deliver it in person

1 January
　Called Mother to say all well and safe having arrived down from Tanjong Malim.
　Saw New Year in at Adelphi Hotel.
　Huge Jap bomber formation came over at 11.30 pm last night (54 planes at least). Searchlights held them beautifully.

2 January
   Pte Wharton 'G.'
   Pte Wyatt M.
   Cpl Wheeler
   S/Sgt Cooper

5 January
   270 CGH said to be on their way down and some Sisters to come and live over with 17 CGH crowd.

6 January
   Telephoned DDMS [Deputy Director of Medical Services] office twice today asking about Elizabeth indirectly (20 CGH). Also tried Movement Control – say they will be arriving during the night.

7 January
   Elizabeth arrived in Changi from Kajang.
   Wonderful day, I had been in town and they told me when I got back. She was not to be found in the hospital, but was up in the Mess waiting for me.
   Oh it was good to see you again.

8 January
   Siem Road debacle occurred this morning – what a schmozzle because six old tanks came down the road.

10 January
   'Nor bring, to see me cease to live,
   Some doctor full of phrase and fame,
   To shake his sapient head and give
   The ill he cannot cure a name.'
   M. Arnold

13 January
   Hurricane squadron of 52 planes arrived today and about 25 active pilots for them.

15 January
   Gemas has fallen but it's not in the papers, our forces simply withdrew all the way from Slim River.

Upcountry meeting and Fall of Singapore 17

21 January

Elizabeth presented me with this diary. Went into Singapore, heavy air raid damage in Chinatown area east of Stamford Road.

Met Harty at Raffles Square.

Evening was rather intruded on by other people and strange thoughts.

Good night Elizabeth.

22 January

Severe headache again. Morning tea up at RE Mess. Long talk with Elizabeth in the Duty Room. Took her off duty.

Four alarms.

23 January

Morning was difficult. Noon to meet Elizabeth but gave anaesthetic for Julian Taylor, hernia of Lt Col Litton.

6.30 pm. First sight of Elizabeth.

To pictures, something about 'Wild Geese'. Only made me more tired – to bed early.

Two alarms. Dog fight over us.

24 January

Much work during the morning, irritable and also headache.

Bought Elizabeth's suitcase.

She has to leave at 3.00 pm. Followed to Gillman in an empty car, angry and disappointed.

Elizabeth tried to make up for it, the idea of an early marriage discussed.

She asks Miss Stebbing for a transfer.

No air raid.

25 January

Letter to FCMA [Field Controller Military Accounts]
i. Pay as specialist.
ii. Charge pay of the unit.
iii. Back pay as OC [Officer Commanding] of 12 IGH at [Kuala] Lipis.

26 January

No calls from Elizabeth.

2.30 pm. Brenda passed on a message and I rush into Gillman.

Visit to the Gap as of old but how changed it is. Then we go to Cyranos for dinner, not a good meal but what a change, and we did have a lovely

evening afterwards. Bombs whilst at dinner and again en route back along Tanglin Road.
   Four air raids.
   Elizabeth very homesick.

28 January
   Cabled Mother.

29 January
   Wrote Mother by air.
   Five raids.

30 January
   8.00 am. All troops back in Singapore. Johore Causeway blown up tonight and our siege begins.
   Peculiar sensation that we should be in this mess.
   8.10 pm. Telephone call from Elizabeth.
   Seven air raids today.

31 January
   Real siege now. Malaya is finished.
   Austin is rather despondent about it and the outcome.
   Terrific bombing of Seletar aerodrome today.
   9.05 pm. Elizabeth telephoned – all well.
   Five raids.
   Went to local cinema.

1 February
   News of our siege is broadcast.
   An uneventful day here but much work to do.
   Heavy gunfire along Causeway side of island. May be our artillery?
   Elizabeth's transfer is through.
   Three warnings.
   Second day of siege.

2 February
   Cable to Mother, express (Mother received this).
   Still very quiet here. Air raid after air raid during morning. Few fires started.
   2.00 pm. Into town.

Phyllis [Morris] gone to Australia, safely.
McGavin lost near Kluang.
5.30 pm. Up to see Elizabeth at Gillman, she looks very tired today.
Brilliant moon.
About six warnings.

3 February
Heavy bombing in Singapore today and in docks – convoy arriving
Went in to see Elizabeth, stayed until 6.30 pm only.

4 February
Letters to Lindsay A., Stanley.
New fires at Naval Base started, artillery fire started.
19 IGH got a bomb in Tyndall Park and ?12 killed?

5 February
Dive-bombing and machine-gunning attack near Changi village; planes were low enough – and we didn't do anything about it!
Aren't there any guns in Changi?
Rumble of artillery fire all day.
Fire of oil tank at Naval Base is spreading, great pall of smoke.

6 February
Audacious dive-bombing attack on Pulau Ubin. It was a disheartening sight to see no air opposition and no anti-aircraft fire. About 12 bombs were dropped and machine gunning of neighbourhood.
2.15 pm. To Singapore, some more dive-bombing on south coast.
Met Elizabeth at Milk Bar. Photographs. Met Hewitt.
At Gillman my car smashed into by a runaway, ? an old Morris 14.
Wreckage at Kallang airport.
Raids most of evening.

7 February
Day opened peacefully enough. Dive-bombing on Pulau Ubin as usual. About 1.45 pm at lunch 27 went over and loosed about 100 bombs. All round mess, floor heaved like mad. Hell. T block hit above my Lab, many injured and killed.
Dead and dying all over operating theatre floor, the surgeons tried hard to get on with their job, *dhobis* [laundry men], water carriers, *naik* [corporal] killed.

Sisters stood it well. Kiwi Gibbs was in officers' ward when it all came in.

8 February

Moved the truck round to front of Lab. Many patients moved off this morning. Changi looks a bit of a mess, no water, no lights. WOs [ward orderlies] are smelling already. Indian officers are 'wound up'. Odd aerial activity.

4.00 pm. 27 Bombers over again, I gave the alarm and took Lads and Iris down to the clothing store just in time. Hell of a raid. We had a bomb outside our door, clerk in next room killed; Lt Col H., Bennet and Matron escaped.

We all spent an uncomfortable night.

9 February

5.00 am. Was up, Lab truck was started on its way.

Visit Tyersall then to Canning. Deuce of a flap as Japs have landed in force on north-western sector.

Artillery from Bukit Timah all the time, rumble of guns.

Back to Changi.

4.45 pm. Another big raid. I take a deep trench and it's Selarang this time, IMGH. I go to Tyersall for the night and feel most unsafe. Shelling from near us all night long.

Lurid night on Bukit Timah hill.

10 February

News that some of the nursing staff are to be evacuated from Singapore to Java.

11 February

Sisters evacuated. Elizabeth doesn't go.

Elizabeth and I are to be MARRIED. Special licence from Colonial Secretary and Sir Shenton. Risk bombs and shells. On the way Elizabeth and I machine-gunned at Gillman, twice in big air raids.

Called Mother.

The deed done by Mrs North-Hunt, Registrar General here.

Left Elizabeth at 20 CGH to Tyersall – the Awful Fire. Burned to the ground, everything gone, about 170 patients, all bad cases as well.

It was awful, every hut gone, my truck, one GP left. Still shelling when I got there.

My first night back with darling Elizabeth top of flour store.

12 February

Much shelling all night, terrific artillery barrage over our heads all night. Given and taken.

Early morning air raids ceaseless. Mortar fire began as well.

11.00 am. Went down town to see 17 CGH. It was an awful sight at Raffles Institution, patients lying everywhere, groaning and screaming, shell fire. Food supply poor. Nowhere to shop. Town full of troops walking about aimlessly, disorderly. Pathetic. Adventurous trip back to Gillman.

Night in flour store for protection on our lovely mattress.

13 February

Remaining sisters leave today on the *Kuala* at 5.30 pm.

Ceaseless mortar and shell fire all round us now, seemed right in the hospital.

Left Gillman early, during shelling and mortar, terrific fire at Gap and Pasir Panjang. Fires on all islands. Recce planes over.

Report at Fullerton Building to join IMGH as an anaesthetist. Work overtime.

4.15 pm. Heavy bombing raid, many bombs over us. Fires started.

Elizabeth and I find a cosy room by marine offices. Iqbal Khan [his bearer] sleeps outside the door tonight.

Shelling the town all night.

14 February

4.00 pm. Capitulation of Singapore ?? tomorrow.

Started work at IMGH Fullerton Buildings. Three tables going from 12 mid day, little lunch in the civilians' room at the side, steadily 'til 8.00 pm then broke for supper – then more cases until 1.00 or 2.00 pm on Sunday.

Too busy to see what is going on outside. Anaesthetic after anaesthetic well into the morning of tomorrow. I've hardly seen Elizabeth and stink of chloroform and ether.

Awfully tired when I do lie down and then Elizabeth is absent.

Diary a bit erratic here, time moving so little and confused.

15 February
   Singapore falls to Japanese.
We now have four tables going in the theatre in the censors' offices. Kitchen of sorts off the main theatre where we can get a snack occasionally. I am anaesthetising for Julian Taylor – he takes all the hard cases in the inner room – awful stench of pus and gangrene all over – bodies and dying all round theatre, drip transfusions going on inside the room. One amputation [patient] by me watches the next after him and so on. Water is short, carried up by civilians all the time. Other 'civvies' are getting a transformer and motor working for me in the X-ray room (Major Carlisle) adjacent.

More and more wounded coming all the time. 4.30 pm still anaesthetising when Nips put in their last raid and blew in all the blackout, my patient was half under so I stayed with him, others went into the passages, stretchers with dead and wounded all over, the indescribable atmosphere, hot, humid, foetid, mixture of human discharges and anaesthetics. Theatre floor all slippery. Must call a halt to clean it and get rid of the huge pile of stinking gangrenous dressings that lie in a pile at the entrance of the theatre.

I see little of Elizabeth these days, she is full of her job, so much to do in the wards and constantly making room for more and more cases. The dead accumulate on the outside gallery and I think are dropped in the Singapore River.

Elizabeth, you're magnificent these days, how I must stink at night of anaesthetic and pus.

Our domestic life is little, we're both so tired by night and have to get up at 2.00 or 4.00 am to relieve somebody else in the theatre. We supper together then gossip five minutes, wander back to our room then have a stand-up rub down in a little water in turns, I may go back to the theatre and E on night rounds. Sleep on the floor but it's quite comfortable. Elizabeth wakes up if I turn in during the early hours. Iqbal Khan sleeps just the other side of the screens; he is so good these days.

So quiet, so quiet now with no more banging and blasting going on, end of War for us!

18 February
   'How long is it going to be?'
   Only a few anaesthetics today.

Worried about Elizabeth's duties, she is so sincere too. I fear she is overdoing it.

Had a drink with D. Wallace, physician in ordinary to Sir Shenton T.

It was a rather restless night.

DDMS much about the building now, perhaps living here in his office.

February 19

Rather a boring day, not much work to do, and Elizabeth has so much, I can't do hers and she will not take any advice.

Works much too hard all by herself.

I get a new headdress instead of my old steel helmet.

Oh I wish I had some work to do.

Japs prowling about the place, not offensive as yet.

21 February

Not much work to do today. Several intravenous anaesthetics one after another. Gave out TAB [Vaccine – Typhoid, paratyphoid A and B] during the morning.

I seem to be losing Elizabeth; she is working herself to death and will not take any rest at all, tried to scold her a little.

Gave 0.5cc of TAB as she is poorly by evening and I am as miserable as man can be.

The car has at last been stolen – who? I have the key and tools.

Rumours that we [are to] go to [a] concentration camp.

22 February

Iqbal Khan sent off today, it was a sad blow inside, though so casual on the surface at the door of the operating theatre where I was hurrying in to give an anaesthetic. Elizabeth bid him away, did she say anything to him – must ask later? Promised to hunt him up in India, come what may, E. likes him too, faithful to the end.

23 February

Have to go down stairs for water or get it from the operating theatre.

28 February

We feel we are approaching our parting now, I see more of Elizabeth, what a darling she is, too sincere and good.

Mrs Draper gave us a bottle of gin to try and finish.

We have no neighbours now. P and T [Post and Telegraph] people have gone and so has the barricade of our private verandah.

Visited North-Hunt again and got him an additional supply of digitalis. Took Elizabeth up too. 'Salvaged' some things from Sir S.'s room, cutlery only though.

1 March

Last three days have been happy ones for both [of] us though it is approaching our parting. Elizabeth has been able to spend a little more time with me than with her work which of course I am very jealous of.

2 March

Elizabeth and I slept in Room 21, The Club – too many bugs and mosquitoes for comfort. Our last night – for how long? All packed to go. Awful sick feeling, my diarrhoea adds to the discomfort, Mrs Draper has it too.

A very brief farewell outside Whiteways, too sudden in fact to leave my darling wife behind. Away about 1.30 pm by car at head of convoy of 11 trucks. Japs somewhat difficult near jail, allow us through after parley. Big parade at Changi for Jap inspection, what a collection of British troops.

Hospital is still awful, supper is ok.

I do a post mortem afterwards, died on the operating table from pulmonary embolism.

Sleep on my stretcher.

Chapter 4

Jack's diary – 1942

3 March
 First day of work as pathologist in the Lab to Roberts Barracks hospital. Scrounge the equipment from those who stole it. Walking everywhere, how I miss 'Marion' [his car].
 Diet leaves me rather hungry, drinking more these days too.
 My diarrhoea is a little better, I feel bloated after the rice ration.
 Wonder how Elizabeth is getting on. I do hope they send her out of the country.
 Very tired by evening, my stretcher is most welcome. Am sleeping in the Mess room in Quadrant Road, about 50 MO, two parsons and a Red Cross man called Stuart. Gavin is here too and Stringer.

4 March
 Collected a little more Lab equipment. Commenced work, chiefly malaria films and stools.
 Epidemic of dysentery is beginning and my Lab is right by three latrines.
 I feel a little better, two loose motions only.
 After supper energy enough to go down for a swim. Met Hewitt by the *pajar* [stockade] to tell Elizabeth she deserves some strokes with the rattan for refusing to leave Singapore.
 Tea served is a surprise about 10.00 pm tonight, it was most welcome.
 Wonder what my darling is doing now.

5 March
 All officers remove stars etc and wear one star on left breast pocket.
 Kept busy all day. The flies are an awful nuisance.
 I wear my boots again after knocking out the nails, make a noise stamping round this place.
 Rations quite good today. Rumours of Western troops successes going round everywhere.
 Walked to see Mulvaney, no news of E. as yet. He is most pessimistic as usual.

Stringer and the General still have their staff and are using them about Changi.

6 March
Bathing in the sea is stopped by Jap orders.

Work as usual. It's worsening, as is the dysentery and flies. No rain for days, and it's getting so hot.

We work and sleep to the sound of flies, defecation, vomiting and the rattle of bedpans all the time. Poor fellows, this epidemic is bad.

7 March
Rumours that we have to move out of here to the Hospital area – more discomfort.

No news of E. as yet, I keep worrying Stuart and Roberts, they hold out hopes.

Took a second shot of TAB.

Did a post mortem for Gibby outside the theatre after supper. Fract. femur [–] died on the operating table [–] found a large pulmonary embolism. What conditions, failing light, smell and flies.

8 March
Roberts thinks a message to E. is possible, if only I knew that she was all right.

Supposed to wait until the Tokyo Red Cross agent arrives to arrange plans.

Sent a letter to E. through R., very long and was several sheets, some of it rather depressing.

9 March
All civilian internees are moved to Changi Gaol. Elizabeth must be amongst them too, I feel too awful to think of it, more dismal surroundings couldn't be chosen. God what they are being made to go through.

We are moved out of our comfortable home in Quadrant Road, no place to sleep except the Lab with its flies and Lennox as mate.

Elizabeth, goodnight.

10 March
An awful night spent in the Lab, faeces, smell, flies and dysentery patients, dropped bedpans. I suppose I shall get used to this eventually.

Had Japanese pathologists working in the Lab. Looking at our dysentery cases [–] took away about 100 cultures. Were most uncommunicative and technique was poor.

Vague rumours that Italy might be collapsing.

Elizabeth??

11 March

Diet a bit low today. Had a bath in the rain, it was lovely, but rather public standing outside the Lab and sloshing away – delightful. Clean, and, for a short time, no smell of dysenteric stools, but the flies all crawl about us though half dead. It's the way they are affected by cold and rain.

12 March

Very much the usual day now. Work all day, stools and mrps [microscope slides examination for malarial parasites].

I am off my meals a bit.

Had one post mortem to do, no diagnosis arrived at.

Difficulty about getting water to the hospital is increasing.

Worried about my darling Elizabeth, must be awful in Changi Gaol, no word from her as yet.

Had a bath in the rain – lovely.

13 March

Lovely sleep for the first time in the Lab.

Rain all day, hard at times.

Indian personnel came to collect medical equipment for Japs at civilian hospital. Lab does not lose very much.

Outside rumours are very depressing today. Java and Sumatra have fallen, attacks pending on Emdau and Australia. Rangoon gone.

Still no news of Elizabeth and she is only some three miles away too. [Will] try and see Brig Maj about it tomorrow.

Diet of rice is beginning to get rather tiring.

14 March

Rain predominant today.

Many stray hungry dogs about the hospital, all to be put out of the way.

Pigs have been acquired but in insufficient numbers for us all to get anything worthwhile.

Flies less.

Visited Brig Maj to see if he knew anything about his wife and the women – no luck.

Roberts in, he says E. is still in Katong and well; but I hear otherwise that all females are in the prison. Won't be happy until I see her again.

Medical stores being removed from here to CGH for Japanese.

15 March

½lb of bacon this morning, what a treat! Almost like breakfast of normal times but there is no toast.

I wonder if Elizabeth is getting anything like this.

Dysentery patients move over to the new blocks.

Dysentery outbreak in Singapore town.

Dismantled chassis, being used with manpower for transport.

Post mortem TB meningitis.

Still sleeping in the Lab.

16 March

Uneventful day, much rain.

Saw Roberts and I hear that E. is still down in Katong, wonder if it is true?

Rumours that – ??

Rommel has ceased resistance

Turkey in the War

Russians in Warsaw

Commando raids in Norway.

17 March

Rained practically all day.

Flies were beastly and sat about everywhere, my sodium arsenic trap [having] caused these many casualties.

I wish I could see Elizabeth and get much of my doubt cleared up.

Spent most of the afternoon making a mattress for myself.

On duty.

18 March

Spent a comfortable night on my new mattress.

Memories of Fullerton Building, E. and I together on our comfortable mattress.

Sunny at first then much rain.

Still sleeping in the Lab and getting quite used to it. I do get a good bath here every night. Lennox only does with a sponge down.

We hire out the use of our local lavatory, and Cooper got a toilet roll as payment.

No more news of my beloved Elizabeth.

19 March

Much rain, I love it, others don't. Meals have been good today but I still feel hungry and easily tired.

Find an old chair which I set about to repair for my own use.

Conflicting rumours that Elizabeth is still at Katong not in the Gaol.

Rumour has it that the *Queen Mary* has been sunk.

20 March

Spent some of the day in work and made an effort at repairing the salvaged chair.

Beginning to despair a little thinking of Elizabeth and Mother all day. Feel awfully hungry as does everybody else before meals – blasted rice.

Also getting a trifle weak, otherwise well and thank goodness there is enough of work to keep me occupied.

Dysentery and flies still up. More cases of ankle oedema are appearing daily.

Malaria about the same.

A long think about Elizabeth tonight – how I long for my darling.

21 March

Post mortem. Case of dysentery. Typical.

Scrounged around as usual, always on the lookout for useful 'rubbish', so is Todd in the depot hut.

Somebody lifted my rug from under the stairway, many on the lookout for it, I must procure another one. Extraordinary what a few things one can live with.

Move up to the top of barrack block today, bagged a locker and place on south side.

Red Cross folk give no news at all now, Tokyo mission are here.

Jap vessels move out of Naval Base early this morning.

Rumours – unrest in Italy and riots in Berlin, occupation of Norway??

22 March

Picked up a castaway coconut full of dirt and flies, found it good. Share it in the Lab at tea, a special treat today.

Col. Bennet snaffles one microscope for himself.

Diphtheria scares increasing.

Visit by Rigby, he's going to get his hair cut by Brennan.

Our food ration has been increased by the Japs, still deficient in vitamins.

Strong rumours today
- naval action in North Atlantic
- Chinese forces in Thailand
- Troops in Australia

Nothing of Elizabeth.

23 March

Very bad lunch and supper, the rations have been cut. $1/16$ oz jam/diurn [per day].

Two post mortems today

- Dysentery case.
- Secondary haemorrhage in left thigh and pelvic fossa.

Acquire a new microscope stand to try out on the Leitz.

Rumours full today

- Norway in our hands
- Landings in Denmark
- Paratroops in Amsterdam
- Chiang Kai-Shek in Thailand
- Sicily in our hands and fighting in Italy

24 March

Quite a busy day, Lennox is still off with enteritis, looks weak and ill.

Two post mortems today.

Attended lecture-discussion on Dysentery at 198 FA [Field Ambulance]. Not much gained.

Took the microscope to bits and found it was not so good, to be returned.

Stricter now about passing barriers, must have a Jap present or in a party with a red flag in front, it looks awful.

Still no news from my darling.

Rumours today more pessimistic.

25 March

Time I took out a new razor blade and bit of soap!

Weighed myself today and find I am down to 10st exact, loss of 12lbs only so far.

Report that six soldiers attempting to escape were shot this morning.

Sat and talked with Rigby for a while – old times discussed.

No news yet of our wives.

Rumours of a big Pacific Naval scrap and Japs lost a few vessels??

26 March

Severe tightening up of our boundary regulations, no hope as yet of getting to Changi Gaol to see Elizabeth.

I wish something would happen.

News that Japs are removing food as well as all metal strippings from the island, there can't be much left.

Dysentery up to 1200 today, and no decrease as yet. B. Flanner only isolated.

Two Jap officers have a long sitting with Col. Craven and O'Neale, almost all day.

Storm in the evening and several coconuts fall, booty for those on the spot.

27 March

Hear that General Heath has been allowed to see his wife?? See Bloom and we propose to take action as soon as his fissure permits.

Rations are very poor, I feel miserable on them.

Japs in again, this time for malaria returns etc and collection of slides of 116 cases. Promise to bring in results of collection of stools.

Wish I could find a coconut today, meals are poor, one is automatically on the look out for scraps and leavings on other people's plates.

My lamp is not working too well, this Malonoil is too smoky, must get some paraffin!

Dearth of rumours.

28 March

A pretty busy day in all, no time to see Gawn about Elizabeth, must take action, she is hardly out of my mind all day – only a few inches away and I can't see her.

Very heavy ST [malaria] infection in 'B' ward. Did a post mortem today, Lennox found nothing! It was a query infectious jaundice.

Bennet gave lecture on amoebic dysentery etc, I put up the demonstrations for him.

Jap practice dive bombing over at Naval Base and we hear gunfire this evening coming from that side.

Todd is collecting an awful lot of rubbish at the depot hut. I eat one of his corncobs.

No rumours today.

29 March

We feel 'sundayish' today and slacked. Went to morning service outside my old Lab. It made me think a good deal and I felt sad.

Saw Craven and he is allowing me up to see Brig Lucas for further information.

Slight diarrhoea and bolygmia today, stools look all right and I feel well.

Rigby's patch of ringworm is better. Saw Tim Ward today [–] he looks cheerier and slightly better.

Strange lack of all news and rumours these days.

30 March

Got a pass this morning to HQ, saw 'A' branch about contacting E. He was most rude, vulgarly rude to put it mildly; I doubt I shall forget this bastard of Malaya Command [MC].

Stringer of course came down to Craven about my not going through the proper channels etc etc, said he was doing his best. So this is still Malaya Command; I hope I never forget these people.

Officers from the depot have been posted to wards as 'nursing sisters', Bloom is annoyed about it, others have been posted to SA [Southern Area]. Medical examination rooms already understaffed.

31 March

End one month of internment.

Major has moved into the hut in front of 'V' block.

Sikh guards have appeared over last two days on the roads between areas, and they also want saluting. One has already stopped a sergeant major near the cinema; this is not on our orders as yet.

Rigby posted out today, took two books with him.

Rumour is that Philippines have fallen to Americans and many Japs captured??

- that Navy [have carried out] air raids on Bangkok.
- we are holding in New Guinea alright.

1 April

Bloom saw Lucas today. Apparently the chance of seeing E. is out of the question at the moment, but we intend to keep agitating.

My stretcher has been taken away so I sleep on the floor tonight; it's all right with my good mattress.

Memories of Fullerton and dear Elizabeth, wasn't it fun.

Rumours of a raid on Kiri and fighting there.

Further fighting in Burma, Sumatra and Java.

Dewar IMS back from Singapore and full of stories.

2 April

Morning: Saw battle cruiser and two destroyers going out from the Naval Base.

Tried doing 20 Kahns [test for syphilis] today, not very successful, only weak positives.

I feel off colour and unusually weak today.

?? We hear that the Sisters' ship is lying off Penang and that some sisters (six) are here as POWs.

Gave Captain Neil 5/- [5 shillings] to see if he could collect Elizabeth's portrait; he goes in with a party tomorrow to Singapore.

3 April

Post mortem on a case of diphtheria with compusa mediastinum.

Seven department officers down with dysentery.

Huge evening meal today, a little meat and did we enjoy it all, [but] I get [a] nightmare.

Most people have to pass urine at least once at night; this rice diet seems to affect us all that way.

Gosh we get hungry by evening.

We send in our news about relatives in Changi Gaol.

Elizabeth still in there, gosh a whole month.

?? Air bases leased by Russia to Britain and USA off Siberia.

4 April

Rice, rice – breakfast, lunch and dinner, beginning to get me down.

500 men and some RAMC may leave today for overseas.

5 April

Awoke quite early and went to communion in the old cinema. It was refreshing, but what memories, I could see Elizabeth there, our last show together.

Good meals this day.

Post mortem this afternoon, found haemorrhages, both suprarenals.

I began to use my silver cutlery today cf. Rose pulling his spoon out of his trouser pocket.

Lennox and I divide the big groundsheet, my bit goes under the mattress.

6 April

Uneventful day with good meals. Interviewed a patient who spent about ten days in Changi Prison, his account of women is most hopeful. Vardy told me all about the prison.

?? The civilian men are being allowed to see their wives for one hour occasionally. Told Bloom about this.

Wait until we can hear from some of the AM [anti-malarial] people.

Concert over by Aussy hospital was a pleasant change. Corporal Franks wants news of Naomi Davis.

?? Vladivostok been bombed.

7 April

Breakfast and lunch appalling, supper a little better. Did a bit of digging outside the Mess this afternoon and blistered my hands.

Stuart (Red Cross) gave the men a talk on formation of the Society.

Still thinking out ways of contacting Elizabeth, spoke to Lt. Band, FMSVF [Federated Malay States Volunteer Force] food supplier of the hospital, none of his men go into town. Try RASC [Royal Army Service Corps]?

Still rumour that the officers are allowed into town, I hope so.

Made a find of 2½ gallons of kerosene oil today just outside the Lab in an old steriliser heater.

Lt Col Houston is after some of it already, but it's salvage.

8 April

Light morning but had two post mortems in afternoon

1. Liver abscess.

2. Body of dead Aussy, shot last night outside the wire near Curran Camp – two wounds.

Rained heavily all afternoon.

Meals have been pretty awful today.

Still no sign of hearing from Elizabeth, gosh, how much longer. I am still optimistic though.

?? Jap landings in Ceylon now.

?? Naval battle in Bay of Bengal.

9 April

Had a very busy day altogether. Got post mortem report ready on the incident of found man and went up to SA HQ to give my evidence. Met Lt Col Dunn; they excluded any note about the slip of paper I found in the man's pocket in the mortuary department. Permit 44 Indian Infantry Brigade – back in time for lunch.

Then saw Maynard and we sent in the indent for our cultural requirements that Stringer wants to put before the Japs. Pretty thick indent too.

Lennox busy doing four post mortems so it's been a tiring day Elizabeth. Saw Gibson (Gordons); he promised to try and find out any news of you.

10 April

I am getting mixed up these days, went up to make my report this day.

Malay Command is as bad about this investigation as they have been all along. ?? About five others now found missing and I think the Japs know who this victim of shooting is. We are all to be punished over this.

Neale tells me a yarn that Mrs Rodgers has been seen in town recently with Mrs Bloom.

Boreholes

?? big British landings at Brest.

?? Fighting in northern Malaya now.

11 April

A pretty full day again and I do get hungry after it. But plenty of work soon makes the minutes fly by.

New disease appeared, a sort of epidermic encephalitis. With high mortality, about 17 cases in last week, at post mortem we find nothing.

Kahn reactions today was all ballsed up, overheated the smears so had to repeat the lot.

Eleven Jap naval ships came into the Naval Base today.

12 April

Laughed and laughed today at Vardy's effort at making sandals out of tyre with a bit of string. Suggested that he was to work on the Burma Road.

Made Lennox do a spot of work this afternoon for a change.

One cruiser, six destroyers, cargo vessel, aircraft carrier all went out this morning

13 April

Really the day is not long enough for me to do all I want in it. Did some more digging today.

Much work, and Cooper is loaned to dysentery side while Lt Col MacFarlane is ill.

Massing of Jap Navy off Changi this morning.

I managed to change my boots for better and newer ones.

Elizabeth I am aching for you, my love.

14 April

Two post mortems today.

Officer Cousins with dysentery and pneumonia. Accident case, multiple injuries, from town.

Spent morning trying to clean up X-ray film to mount Elizabeth's picture.

Mess meeting in the evening to discuss trying to get in foodstuffs from Singapore. Cigarettes and tobacco seem to be worrying a lot of people.

First cases of 'wet beriberi' have arrived in hospital.

15 April

Walked over to the top dysentery block with Bloom and we gazed at Changi Gaol from there. Climbed on roof for a better view – gosh Elizabeth, so near and yet so far. And did we gaze wistfully, what thoughts crossed our minds.

FA officers say that it was 43 vessels that passed here the other day, six aircraft carriers, four battleships amongst them.

?? that Russia has been attacked by the Japs at Manchuria.

16 April

Busy most of the day getting slides ready for Bennet's lecture on BT malaria. Had some good slides, also demonstrated the staining.

My boots, new ones, are getting worn in now and reasonably comfortable.

Climbed onto the roof at dusk and saw the prison lights like a huge factory, some brighter ones on the south wing nearest us, ?? women's reading room.

Gawn set up his electric light with a 12v battery, most successful, we sat around it like flies.

?? Laval now leader in France.

17 April

Elizabeth, I mounted your photograph today for putting above my bed, it looks nice.

Got a 'band' and visited Changi village today to see Mulvaney. He is quite optimistic about affairs out here, but so far has not had any news from his wife either.

Talked to a Sikh general on the way back.

Hear that General Keith Simmons has been arrested by the Japs.

Water is on and our flush is working, what luxury this is.

18 April

Lennox did two post mortems and I had two in the afternoon.

John Taylor opened the Changi Medical Society in the old cinema halls; an address on 'Wilfred Trotter', very good too.

Gosh our meals are pretty bad, heard that cook is ill. Won't criticise Mother's cooking when I get back.

?? continuous bombings over Germany.

Russian advances and capturing youths aged 15–17 now.

Exchange of prisoners with Japs.

19 April

Awful depression earlier today and yearning for you, Elizabeth, looking at your picture cheered me a lot.

Took afternoon off for a rest. Did some more gardening as well in the hope that our evening meal will be better, the first two have almost made us weep.

Visited Tim Ward, gosh he is thin; saw Lyndsey of 45 AT Coy [Anti-tank Company] and also Gordon of [the] Argylls.

20 April

Spoke to Neale re contacting Capt Nagusaki, Jap liaison officer, over question of seeing you darling.

Some goods for the canteen have come in, nothing eatable, hear they are to be sold.

Also some Brewer's Yeast arrived in the hospital and there is speculation what to do with it.

Saw Bloom about the letter to Nippon HQ. He is going to confer tomorrow.

Rate of Pay as? POW said to be in A.I.I.432 1940. ? Furlough rates for us.

Found another piece of coconut in nearby slit trench and, of course, ate it.

Pte Wharton sick [with] 'squitters' today.

21 April

Deuce of a gale last night.

Neave told me that Tokyo has sent orders for special treatment of all women and children internees on the island, this sounds good.

Bloom showed me his letter to the Japs.

Demonstration on ST malaria for Bennet.

Colonel Rigby now in hospital with malaria.

Message to G. Graham in town to try and get in touch with E. through civilian engineers.

?? Tokyo been submitted to bombings, and Kobe.

22 April

Soap, bootlaces and polish from the canteen.

Bloom sent off his letter.

Official letter from Bdr Stringer about treatment of women internees.

S/Sgt Cooper now suffering from dysentery as well.

Visited Wharton, he looks bad [and] needed a supply of 'Bromo'.

Food is steadily getting worse but I still feel fit.

Had long talk to Glendenning this morning.

Very little shipping activity to the Naval Base last few days. Wonder what's happening to Kait S.

?? Big British reinforcements arriving in Burma.

Japs said to be leaving New Guinea owing to American air superiority.

23 April

Stanley and Ruth married today

One post mortem today – Broncho pneumonia and BT malaria.

Fair amount of work to do still.

Had long talk with Conrad R. this morning, and also found Hayward up in the ward so gossiped until he fell asleep. Said many nice things about Elizabeth.

Black market appears to be growing to a colossal size, one can get almost anything at a very high rate, $1.10 for packet of cigarettes or .75 for a loaf of bread.

Rumour of Tokyo bombing is very strong indeed.

Had a haircut today.

24 April

Couple of submarines and some small vessels left Naval Base this morning.

Diet is getting a trifle unappetising especially when the rice is cooked badly, our milk and sugar seems to have vanished!

Jap Major General DMS [Director of Medical Services] and retinue went around the beriberi cases today and took away our autopsy specimens for examination. We got on quite well with our 'man' this time, talked more. Whilst we did business, his satellites bartered cigarettes round the corner with patients.

?? Another big naval battle in South Pacific and Yanks doing well.

?? Japs draw back a bit in Burma.

25 April

An Argyll came in medical, said he was fighting until 11 days ago with 200 others and Chinese up in Kluang region, seemed confident that Chiang Kai Shek would be down soon.

Japanese sent in about 100 cases of a yeast tablet in bottles, looks like yeastivite to me. I talked to the interpreter about seeing E., he was not helpful and hurried away, he's rather pro Jap.

Examined several 'yeasts' from outside, folk are experimenting rather un-methodically everywhere.

?? Forces now fighting in Timor and doing well and that we have other landings in Java.

?? Hitler appeals to world about the bombing of Germany.

?? Our forces doing well in naval battle.

26 April

Days of numerous and varied rumours, the RAMC folk from Changi village have today moved in to this area, leaving their lovely garden behind and the facilities of a neglected bit of the wire near a *kampong* [village].

Tim Ward had his leg amputated this afternoon under sodium-pentathol by Paddy Doyle, so far he seems to be doing alright.

?? A big naval battle recently in which both British and Yank navy took part and beat up the Japanese.

That the Russians have begun to advance again.

That bombing of Germany has increased in intensity.

27 April

All sorts of people are trying to grow yeast for its 'B' value but so far none have been very successful. They grow a little yeast and much big [illegible] some pseudo-yeasts, manilia, aspergillis etc. None are of any practical use as yet and should not be dished out to the troops. They think it's great but I doubt if this 2oz of fluid contains 0.1g of dried yeast. Much more experimenting is required, and so far those that have come forward are not very helpful on the subject although they profess to be experts.

Beriberi is certainly on the increase and many cases are dying, the problem is commonly solved by giving us a better diet.

28 April

RBC [red blood cells] 4.56×10^6
HG [haemoglobin] 82%
Weight 10st (with boots).

29 April

My boots are getting well worn in now and fit tolerably well, should be OK in shoe leather for the year.

Seems that the Nip B tablets are only to be issued to 'key' men of Malaya Command by order of Stringer, wonder who these are and who does the choosing. None of the Command people are worth keeping, that's general opinion.

Jap officer stopped a car in the hospital area and got out and whipped a man without a hat because he forgot to salute this occasion.

Change of cook has brought very bad and little food.

30 April

Post mortem on Private Gass.

Meals all day very poor and if it wasn't for the one tinned sardine this evening and a mound of rice it would have been an awful day.

Felt a bit light in the head all day and weak in the legs, but all right this evening.

Duncan Black came in with his gossip, something about all of us being issued with a month's ration of rice by the Nips.

Craven we hear has been put up to full Colonel now in a POW camp.

News of Jerry O'Neil (17 CGH).

?? Japs successful advance north in Burma.

?? New Russian breakthrough of German lines.

1 May

It is rumoured now that sick, inoperably wounded and some medicals might be repatriated. Much discussion as to who might go if it does come off. All think they have an equal right.

News today has been good and bad, we don't know what to believe. Now it's said we have to maintain one month's supply of rice at each unit. The Aussies keep their water bottles full as well. Only one or two small ships come out of the Naval Base these days, more air activity around here too.

Lennox is again ill.

2 May

Second meeting of Changi Medical Society. Discussion on pus below the diaphragm led by de Soldenoff, it was quite a success but later part was marred rather by the rain.

After supper there was quite a strong little Mess meeting chiefly to do with our local franchise scheme and the financing of it, some of us are running out of money and three are out completely. The initial $8.0 has done quite well and our meals the last two days are definitely better, NOT by Jap munificence.

3 May

Frightful day, no end to the work and constant requests for post mortems. Refused some, Mac F did others, and the burial parties took another away before we could do anything.

Six of our MOs have oedema of the ankles and legs so there is a great hoo-ha about beriberi amongst us and the idea of growing yeast is again popular but I am more concerned with figures and doubt their ardour in this line.

I think this is more due to lack of protein than B1.
Rumours are conflicting today that Japs are sacking towns.
Italy has packed in long ago??
No news of Elizabeth.

4 May

'Tis whispered that I may get some news of E. in a day or so.

Saw a Tamil selling stuff over the wire this morning, it was a hazardous affair, and did he look wild-eyed, keeping a sharp look-out and off without bargaining, sack of stuff over his shoulder. Biscuits at $2/- a packet.

Felt pretty depressed all day and sat on the roof to watch the prison lights go out at 10.00 pm. Probably due to excess of work and appearance of sickness in our midst.

Worked out that we cannot provide enough yeast for ward on our rations to stave off deficiency.

Started reading *Out of the Night*.

5 May

Red Cross want to put up a letter about our wives if we agree to sign.

Had an outing in the afternoon and it was really good fun and enjoyable, it was good exercise too. Vardy hurt his mouth with a pole getting a coconut. Middleton lost the flag at one point. M. got thorns in his fingers, Ledingham grew tired and dragged his big boots slowly, I scaled a coconut tree and myself found 15in shells and lots of live ammunition by the gun park, fruit trees in our area. Talked with a Sikh sentry, he seemed very fed up at his treatment.

6 May

Feel all right after yesterday's effort and did a good deal of digging this morning in the potato patch.

We hear that the food shortage upcountry is acute and the outlook here is pretty dismal too unless something can be done about it.

Strong stream of beriberi cases coming in, news the Volunteer crowd are being augmented by others.

?? that our troops are slowly falling back in Burma.

That Corregidor has fallen at last.

That Port Moresby is being constantly bombed by the Nips.

That Hitler and Gayda [prominent Italian fascist Virginio Gayda] have both made stimulating speeches to their peoples (Musso' having run).

7 May

Took my report on 'Yeast' culture up to DDMS. Somewhat cold reception to Garlick by Bill Kennedy who is getting rather 'Stringerish', poor fellow. Hope they'll appreciate what I have said. The lay brigadiers etc around here are pretty ignorant about the subject and have strange delusions that it is easy stuff to culture on any scale.

Get a little more concrete news of our wives in the gaol, said to be a lot of children there, that food is good and that the married folk are running the kitchens so see each other all day. That money has been pooled and men and women go into Singapore daily for purchasing. Hear of a move of 8,000 Aussies out of the island in the near future to some place overseas.

8 May

Improvement in the food said to be down to a new Nip Food Controller.

Injection vitamin B1 down to 15 ampoules but then augmented tonight by 500 amps suddenly sent in, easing the situation for a short time only. Two cases allowed to die today for lack of B1 supplies.

Black market is flourishing; one fellow sets up shop under the tree just outside our mess, prices are said to be coming down because the Aussies are likely to be going away, but prices are still pretty stiff eg. $3.6 for jam, $-for ten cigarettes etc.

Colonel Ross is in dysentery ward again; he is suffering from anaemia too. Kingston (food officer) has gone down with it today.

?? Burma has at last fallen to the Japs.

That Corregidor has also given in after holding out all these months.

9 May

Elizabeth and I are still no nearer, though we did on our scrounge walk today by 11th Division get within ¾ mile of the prison and I looked closely at it, saw nobody outside, nor sign of life within. Middleton head of the party again, we even went down to the sea through lovely coconut groves. I secured one lying on the ground, threw sticks at other ones but our lack of energy couldn't bring anything down. At 137th Regiment met 2/Lt Scott (Denis) of Fullerton Building. Fancied he was looking very well, promised to give a message to E. if the opportunity came. Feeding arrangement over at this place was excellent; of course they can concentrate all day on their diets.

Felt very hungry at the end of our tramp but otherwise well.

10 May

Much work as usual, no respect of Sunday by the sick on wards. Walked out in the afternoon to FMSVF and saw Mac of the Gold Mines, he's a cook for the unit, then out to Straits Settlements Volunteer Force (SSVF) where saw Len Marsh of Selbourne, he's lost much weight and grown a fine beard as well. Long gossip, no news of Harty or as to his whereabouts. Also saw Harrison (of SSC) [–] everybody looking so undernourished and wasted.

David and MacFarlane are in the FMSVF Officers' Mess, see them another time. Chat with Lillico up at the Dist. Centres of SA, he looked well and in good condition, had drawn the plan to go as MO with British troops going overseas, now cancelled.

?? A sea battle off the Solomon Isles and we are doing quite well.

11 May

Second letter.
Note sent.

Opened usual dull day but ended with excitement. Vardy told me at 6.30 pm that Mrs Corndins was being transferred to the prison; I rushed off, got a band of my letters and legged it up to old Corny's flat in SA. Wrote a small note too for Elizabeth in case the big letter was stopped and Mrs C. took both – wonder when I'll know if these got through all right. Wish I could hear something from E., it'll do me a world of good to see her neat writing again. I think Mrs C. was taken in after dark in a car with blacked out lights.

We hear that blackout is again being enforced on the island.

Went to the Monday night concert, it was very good and I went to bed feeling more pleased with life than for a long time.

Good luck to my courier.

12 May

On duty again.

Did a post mortem this morning, most unsatisfactory as there was nothing found.

In evening Stringer came round and visited the Lab. Talked to me about E. He didn't seem to know much about Mrs C. being taken away, no reason thereof, asked how Japs came to know of her being up in the camp. About question of visiting we are no nearer he tells me.

In the evening talked to young Chapman and found I had some oedema of the legs but felt quite well. Reported to Vardy.

News is very cheering today.

?? Japs lost two aircraft carriers in sea battle near Solomon Isles.

?? Chinese are pushing southwards again in Burma area although we have had to withdraw.

13 May

Looked over by Vardy, my reflexes are OK, but I've morning oedema and my BP is 102/42. Ordered to lie up and am put on 24 Jap. tablets daily. Feel a bit blue about it, who wouldn't if one is to last out this internment.

The Aussies, about 3000 of them for overseas, left early this morning, took a CCS [Casualty Clearing Station] with them, bound for some other place where food is better. If most can be taken from here, it might ease the serious food shortage which is threatening Singapore and is already evident upcountry from the reports I hear.

Blackout has been ordered in the town and is evident in the streets. Still see your lights, Elizabeth.

14 May

Feel OK, the tablets caused quite a diuresis, I'm too restless to be a good patient, fidget all the time, want to get back to my Lab and work. Vardy threatens me with the officers' ward, [but] after seeing Smyth return I am certain I'll rather stay here, [as] the food is apparently really bad in there.

Place is full of rumours good and bad.

?? Jap landing in proximity of Calcutta.

?? Germans launched a vigorous spring offensive and driven Russians back in Kerch peninsula. We are doing heavier bombing than usual.

Sitting on the roof tonight at sundown saw prison lights come on, and then all of a sudden they were switched off.

No lights in the streets now.

15 May

Out of the Night [by] Jan Valtin has got me, it's an awfully absorbing book, almost finished it now. Read up the trypanosomiasis and leishmaniasis as well.

Feel much better BP 110/50 now so I am a little improved. Some oedema present in the morning.

16 May

Notable for lecture by Maj Gen Heath on the Malayan campaign, chiefly apologetic affair and the captain of Singapore dismissed in a few pathetic words – keep for record. Provoked much discussion afterwards and we thought Heath purposely went over time so that he could not be questioned.

Went down and ate coconut with Morris afterwards in the hut.

?? Penang and Gemas have been bombed, and so has Saigon.

?? Landings of some strength in Sumatra and fighting hard.

?? Germans advanced in Kerch Peninsula area but Russians held them elsewhere.

17 May

Bloom is the happiest man in the camp; he's had a long note from his wife, mention of Elizabeth in it to say she's well. Made me feel awfully jealous, wonder why my darling couldn't get a note to me. B. was ill with diarrhoea but he has recovered now. Mrs B. says that only seven regular officers have their wives in the prison [including] Mul', Bl., I, de Moubray, Hewitt.

Hear that Heath now taken to Changi Gaol, not for questioning, but to see his wife who is about due now?

K.S. smuggled out the letter to Bloom, four pages of writing.

Walked to FA roof to have a look at the distant prison lights and think deeply of my own Elizabeth. Chatted up top with Roy Maynard [of] AMS [Anti-malarial squad].

18 May

Austin Best, looking fat and well, came over to visit us this even[ing]. Says he's living comfortably, I [plan] to visit him about the weekend!

Says that SA are to be removed as most of the troops are on fatigues in Singapore, also maybe the Nips want to do some fortification? They certainly go about more armed these days.

I am allowed to work half day now but feel could do the whole easily; start with a most interesting post mortem, query carcinoma of the prostate and secondaries in the lungs.

Still very little shipping in and out to the Naval Base but aircraft are a bit more active.

19 May
Third Note.

Visit from George Graham at River Valley Rd camp [–] he took my note to try via the Bishop. He had no news from Singapore.

Still some slight oedema BP 110/60. I do feel much improved with the rest, still on tablets 24/day.

?? Rumours that Gemas has been bombed is increasing in intensity, and troops in Singapore have to take cover when unidentified aircraft fly over, [but] as far as I know none has been seen yet.

Blackout in the Straits appears to be less and a number of field lights are now visible. Prison only has lights until 8.30 pm and then extinguished.

Went to an interesting history lecture over at the FA Mess this evening.

High Nip official visited the camp areas, host of cars and flags with fully armed sentries posted, keeping an eye on the crowds; they look efficient.

Attend Julian Taylor's lecture on 'Fistula', fair.

Graves is down with dysentery, saw him this morning and had a long talk.

Rumour that we all may have to be leaving this area and maybe go up to Johore.

?? More fighting in New Guinea and bombing heavy by both sides.

?? Anthony Eden in House of Commons said to have stated prisoners in Malaya are being fed and well looked after, I wish he was here on this incident.

?? Position in Burma is improving.

21 May
Took a ⅓ share in a 3½lb tin of margarine.

Went to a very good after supper lecture on 'Banks', rather humorous and enlightening, learned much about a cheque.

?? *Prince Eugene* been torpedoed off Trondheim but not sunk.

?? American aircraft carrier *Saratoga* been sunk.

?? Gamais has been bombed.

?? 75,000 Germans have been killed on the Kerch peninsula.

?? Mannheim has been bombed to hell following Stuttgart.

22 May
Very little oedema and I feel quite energetic.

Interesting post mortem on Captain Marryat, osteomylitis R humerus and supp arthritis 8-9 TV.

This evening we had a bit of meat or steak, oh boy was it a tough bit, but good.

Kingston brought me a sample of 'lime juice' that eroded the Lab floor – test it on the patients?

4.30 pm. We get a lecture from Gavin acting as Stringer's mouthpiece, various complaints about the dirty wards, inattention of patients, diets, officers' complaints.

Saw Bloom, but we still have no news of our 'Heart-throbs'.

?? Seremban and Penang been buzzed by us Borehole.

23 May

Examined by the family doctor again and passed fit [with] BP 115/72. Having eight tablets daily for the last three days, I've a tremendous appetite as well.

Official information received that those QAIMNS caught in Sumatra are definitely in Changi Prison, including Miss Davis, Frank's girlfriend.

We are informed that four combatant officers are to live in the hospital to look after the interests of patients as there are so many complaints and insults hurled at us in the remainder of Changi.

?? Eight large towns in Japan have been bombed, planes encountered very little resistance.

24 May

Visited Austin Best in SA today. He lives in comfort and a very lazy life too, says he's given up the practice of medicine, dabbles in German and does his cooking. Trying to keep his tummy filled off the black market.

Also went down to Changi Village and looked Col. Strachan etc up in their country home. They scrounge fruit and vegetables from all over the place whilst on duty.

?? Another naval action and more Japanese losses.

?? Japanese advances in Yunnan province.

25 May

Uneventful except for the long meeting with Brigadier Stringer in the hut – it was chiefly in the nature to pacify all MO in here as we are getting a bit fed up with outside insults.

Points

1. Singapore did not capitulate because of a breakdown in Medical Services rather of ammunition, (??) water, food etc.

2. We have worked continuously before and after at a heavy pressure.
3. Outside units made a mess of this place from the start, and we have turned it into a hospital.
4. Men are doing a full day's work with no extra ration or any pay.

Long talk with 2/Lt Calderwood (police) A&SH told me much about the prison and life in there, hear there is no ration issue but all has to be purchased. Feeding not good.

26 May

On the roof, what a glorious red sunset, Elizabeth can you see it, your grey walls away on the left, a tinge of red above them.

Saw Denis Scott again, said that his party went by the prison and he saw lots of women waving from the bars. There couldn't be much space in there if what Calderwood says is right, if only the Japs would allow them out just a little.

Home and Mother seem almost a myth, apparently they don't yet know whether we are dead or alive; gosh, how she must be worrying about her youngest. Hope Lloyds is still sending some money.

?? 60–70 Jap ships have now been sunk in the action.

Still rumours of fighting in Sumatra and Java.

Japs seem to be intent on attacking Australia.

28 May

The new post mortem room and mortuary is now ready for use, it's better equipped than one the RE [Royal Engineers] would fit up in peacetime.

– first used by Macfarlane.

Attended another economics lecture, excellent. Also have time up there to sit and gaze at the prison lights, for the brief period that they are on these days, and try and wonder what Elizabeth is doing.

News is scarce, more troops leaving the island at the weekend and taking a few medical people.

Rained like mad today so it's lovely and cool.

31 May

?? New Guinea is almost out of Jap hands now.

- Another Naval action going on and this time much nearer to us, going in our favour.

- Cologne blitzed by RAF [with] 1000 planes last night.
- Libyan show started up again and forces are south-east of Tobruk.

1 June
Fourth Note
Saw Bangs today [and] he met MO to the female internees, who gave news that you are well Elizabeth, wonder if you have been a patient or as a nurse[;] his name sounded like McMahon.

Sent my single page letter to B. hoping it will get through sometime.

Mrs B told Bloom in her letter that all the women are suffering from 'Changi menopause' as they term it[;] what about you, darling?

Meals have been extremely poor all day and I hear that the ration for the week is down too.

Attended a history lecture up at FA Mess, gazed the whole time at the lights, they seemed to be on a long time tonight, much after 9.00 pm, for I called at the concert party on my way back. Quite good, cheered me up somewhat.

2 June
Last night I noticed the lights on late and tonight they are on again till 10.00 pm.

Our hospital bitch is attracting all the dogs for miles around and they sit and yodel when the bugle calls are sounded, especially at night.

Visited 11th Division today and had a chat with Glendenning and Wharton, also called on Stratton – C, he is much thinner and looks rather forlorn, he arrived in Changi without even a razor. They live under poor conditions there, [with] hovels and broken down Malay houses. Numerous Japs along to inspect the 15in gun.

Bought pair of sandshoes $1.65, bit large but should do.

?? Three Nip 'subs' got into Sydney harbour and were sunk there.

?? Cologne has been heavily bombed.

3 June
Prison lights were out early tonight, all other lights on as usual.

Attended a lecture on 'Australia' up at the FA Mess, hurried back owing to storm threatening.

Survivors of an escape vessel brought back from near Banbors Island[;] 40 at the start and 20 died from exposure and malaria including Rear

Admiral Spooner and Air Vice-Marshal Tucker[;] those brought in are absolute scarecrows, lived on coconuts for weeks. All are very heavy BT infectious.

?? Essen has been severely dealt with now.

?? Libyan battle is going in our favour.

No further advances on the Burma front.

4 June

Day is not long enough really to finish all I want to in it. Relaxed and went to concert in SA – 'Two girls' in it and they were awfully good, stimulated an appreciative audience a good deal (Graves and Vardy quite restless on retiring to bed, and I dreamed of you, Elizabeth).

Hellsabuzzin a farcical play staging a runaway from Changi University held in the open-air cinema down in the village; we marched down, hot and sweaty. Met Tom Hind (Mersing) and David (Lipis). How folk have changed! Place was full of beachcomber-like officers, all kinds of dress and headwear to say nothing of beards and moustaches.

It is now said that all troops except medical are moving from Changi.

?? Andaman and Nicobar Isles have been retaken by us, may be some confusion over their names.

5 June

Usual day but wound up by attending 18th Div concert in our Hall. 'House Full' was no exaggeration; I took my box seat 30 minutes early. Col Rose was by the door resenting all intruders obstructing his view, [and] gave me a bit of coconut (as sweets).

Violinist (Denis East) of London Philharmonic Orchestra was star turn, a beautiful tenor, bass and baritone as well, piano accordion and comedian.

?? Libyan battle is ending in a victory for our side, tanks in a minefield and bombing.

Heydrich (Gestapo) has been assassinated in Czechoslovakia, not dead yet.

6 June

?? Bremen has been severely dealt with by RAF.

Huge convoy of troops British and American, including armed divisions, have landed in India.

7 June
> Fifth Note

Took the afternoon to visit Lads at his quarters amongst RASC folk. They seem to have a second hand idea too that MO and orderlies are funding off the patients in the hospital, but of course have no definite evidence. This other complaint too had no basis, no medicine for patients – well there is hardly any of many drugs; of bedding and nets, this place started out well but much has been pinched and by out-going patients too.

Lads gave me tea and biscuits, very good too[;] we visited Rigby, Best been sent to hospital with dengue, Rigby not keen on having the Loyals, they feed well and there's little work to do. Left my note with Lads to pass on to his pal (with hopes).

?? Jap convoy intercepted near Midway Island.

9 June

Whilst at breakfast, five bombers flew over, the first we've seen for months.

Japs want the names of all those who have relatives in Changi Gaol[;] maybe we get somewhere this time?

Also been asked to sign form allowing Brig Lucas to draw our 'pay for May' at $25 diurn. All kinds of rumours as to what is going to be deducted before we get hold of the cash; and the canteen is getting so well stocked too.

Saw Bangs today, he has had no luck so far, but my message he says has been passed to you, Elizabeth.

?? Naval action from Midway has carried on to and passed Wake Islands.
Rangoon and Akyab being bombed by us.
Emden has been heavily bombed.
Japs beaten up by Chinese at Changsha.
Refereed a hockey match at 18th Div.
Attended the good concert again.

10 June
> Duty

At breakfast as soon as it was known that Rose would not be down his portion was divided out – but he appeared. What faces, just to ask for a biscuit.

Hopes soar high of visiting the gaol for Japs have asked for names of those who have relatives in it.

Vincent B. up from Singapore [–] he may get my (your) portrait this week with a bit of luck.

George G. sent word that my letter through him shall be through in a few days with some civilians who are being returned to the gaol. B. very kindly gave me a tin of sardines for some Irishman on the occasion of his next trip up here.

One man brought in dead from Singapore, electrocuted at a mains cable.

11 June

Uneventful night, it's quite a change to sleep on a sprung bed again, sheets of the duty bed but always smell a trifle, but my own pillow helps.

Post mortem on last night's body, the person died of choking in his own vomitus. Huge crowd in the mortuary including Kennedy and Wolfe. He arrived from Singapore with the two pictures of Elizabeth, lovely, but the mouth is a trifle spoilt, took these over to put up in the morgue, $2.0 to pay Nancy.

Another Nip Colonel inspected this hospital this evening whilst I was having a haircut, asked if we did post mortems as well in the already overcrowded Lab.

Exciting Mess meeting re cigarette ration and our contribution out of our allowance (of $7.50). Padre Daniells was a nuisance and Middleton (Breathaway) was annoyed because his amendment didn't get a hearing.

12 June
Fifth Note

Lads returned my note to E. [as] no luck by his method. River Valley Road trucks were in so I sent the note down to George G to hand over to a civilian when they are being returned. Stone the MO was running a small black market as soon as he arrived, selling to ORs [Other Ranks]. What an officer!

Spelling Bee in the cinema was d*** good fun. Star turn was Bloom who missed all three words that were put to him. Dewar let his Depot Mess team down too: he missed 'vaccination', what a roar from the audience. Pte Wharton and his team did brilliantly well, beat up the Depot team.

13 June

We are all dished out our allowance, officers at 25C per day. i.e. $7.75 for last month but $\frac{1}{30}$ went towards the hospital, and $4.00 to our Mess Fund. All paid except Daniells and Stewart who only contributed $2.50 – the cads.

Paid Nancy $2.00 for the pictures, all square now. The canteen has a huge crowd pushing around it; nothing of much was left after it all. Cigarettes are selling at a high price again with the increase in funds which has come in. OR get 10C/day, hope this does not mean general reduction in our rations.

Daniells and Cruickshank rude to each other about the sub' to Mess.

14 June

Quite a slack morning, visited Best at tea time and also the anti-malarial folk, but Col Strachan was not in. They had received a letter from Jack Field, gathered that it was rather despondent in all, over-crowding was getting them down. I hope it's not the same on the women's side.

B. wanted to complain much about the hospital and his four days in it but hadn't much grounds in fact. Peanuts in SA have had a huge sales, now there are none left and finally only selling at a [illegible] lb pkt each. We have none in our canteen that is sold out of foodstuff. Aussy lecture on POW camps in Australia was very good [–] married folk are allowed to live together there and food good.

?? An offensive started in Burma.

Yanks lost the aircraft carrier *Lexington* off Midway Isle.

15 June

?? Nip losses at Midway Isle was 54 ships, 2 aircraft carriers and 150 planes.

400,000 Yanks landed in India up to now.

Nips try attack on Aleutian Islands [off Alaska] but are beaten off with losses.

16 June

Saw Bangs today and he says his note has gone in all right so darling you should know that I am well, if only I could get a note from you to say that you too are well.

Saw Maj White from Caldicote Rd camp, [who] promised to take and try and send off a note for me, also a list of names of all the females in the prison.

Post mortem in the evening – Left frontal lobe abscess following a frontal gunshot wound.

18 June
   Sixth Note (letter)
   Feeling awfully fed up and depressed today [as] Mulvaney, Bloom, Heath, de Moubray and others have all had letters from their wives but Elizabeth doesn't seem to have bothered as yet, wonder what is wrong; naturally can't help thinking that time makes one forget. Evil thoughts to write down.
   Talked with M. who is up from Keppel Harbour, Ethel says food is not good, slight improvement now. Makes one think lots of things. Elizabeth why don't you write me a line?
   Gave M. a letter that he promises to get in in a couple of weeks and also maybe a reply out. Smythe and Nancy are detached to proceed upcountry with a party on Saturday (2000 men).
   POW letter cards have been reported seen today in 11th Div area.

19 June
   Seventh Note
   Had two post mortems first thing this morning, and, after the first, Houghton came up for a note to Elizabeth, to go in a letter to Sgt Jenkin's wife (? via the Bishop)[;] scrawled one hurriedly, very brief, asking for a reply as soon as possible. I'm getting impatient now.
   Lennox is laid up with an infected bee sting and lymphangitis; he has so much crusted dirt about him that I am not surprised.
   POW cards have been distributed today to all but the MO as there are insufficient, not allowed to send any to our wives. Vardy is wild as we as usual have been left out and seem to get the worst deal in everything eg. canteen goods.
   Spelling Bee, won by Aussy Officers, it was very funny and entertaining, our representatives got to final – by luck.
   ?? Vladivostok bombed by Nips.
   A Nip General has been taken in Java by guerrilla bands.

21 June
   Much work in the morning and another post mortem. V. Bennet was up and said that G.E. had sent in my note to Elizabeth all right so that another certain – and still no reply from her, what is wrong?
   Dr W. says you deserve a jolly good spanking afterwards, but that even won't atone for the long privation now – must be some difficulty in the prison.

Later – visited 11th Div, met Mitchell Gledding etc, heard that de Moubray had got a reply from his wife, so my letter must have got in all right, and yet there's no reply yet.

Hear that Spedding is definitely in there, from Sq. Leader Fairway.

?? Churchill over in the USA again.

Hitler made a speech.

Tobruk is in a bad way, heavy fighting south of Sollum.

22 June

List of enquiries from females in the gaol. J.F. Draper Block 4 (cousin) was asking after me, and also after Mulvaney. I wonder if it's really E. who wants to know.

Another 500 left this morning for upcountry, more medical stores went up, and I think QM Rahill this time.

A lovely rainy day and nice and cool as well

23 June

Saw de Moubray, [who] gave me some of the female gaol news, not too bright there. They only have enough money for about six weeks more she says. Why doesn't E. write and let me know a little, it's beginning to get to be an obsession.

White was up today, still hasn't brought that 'list'.

Did a post mortem on a ? encephalitis after supper, finished by lamplight. Walking down the slope met two Nip guards, wanted all lights out, threatened a fellow with a lighted cigarette at the point of the bayonet.

Blackout everywhere, said to be a practice only, hope it's not as it's indefinite.

?? Tobruk we hear has fallen to the Germans, after the Italian Naval success in breaking up our convoy to it.

Russians in Kharkov, but Germans have about taken Sebastopol.

24 June

Dewar tells me that Elizabeth's name is not on the list of female internees, and so does Bangs[;] having had no letters worries me the more, where could she be now – wish I knew! It's like writing to a blank wall. I have an awful sinking feeling inside and despair.

Rumours that women and children may be repatriated on our 'letter' ship.

More aerial activity around here now.

?? Three Jap ships sunk by Yank sub in the Malacca Straits.

25 June

?? Been given out on BBC that Nips may now allow our names to go home [to inform relatives they were in captivity].

?? Some exchange of female prisoners.

26 June

HG 94%.

Attended celebrity concert, it was quite good[;] John Foster a new tenor functioned this evening. The violin was off, East lacked resin for his bow.

News came that cholera has broken out in Singapore, severity is not known. We are rather frustrated. I hope the folk in this gaol are alive to its seriousness.

600 troops were returned quite suddenly from one camp in town, said to be turned out for Nips who have come in.

Large Nip convoy said to be now in Keppel Harbour, 50–60 boats. Much more activity these days. 4 large flying boats have appeared recently, enormous craft [with] 4 engines.

?? Nips are not doing so well in Java.

Bremen has been heavily bombed.

London bombed again.

27 June

Visited III Corps and saw list that Dewar referred to. Mrs E. is not on it, but I was informed that it is not complete – thank goodness. Thence to see old Cornelius, he hadn't heard from his wife, but others whose notes she took have had replies so Elizabeth you must have had at least one note from me, short as it was. Wonder if my long letter was delivered? Saw James L. at the District Centre, playing bridge all day, tells me that Duncan Black was amongst those gone upcountry.

C. told me that Mrs Reid and some other women have been upcountry to Tanging Rambutan but have since arrived back at the gaol.

Lecture today by an officer who escaped from Norway after the BEF [British Expeditionary Force] had left.

Received $2.50 Amenities Fund.

28 June

More of our troops from town in last night. This starts all sorts of optimistic rumours of course, or is it down to cholera?

Discussion with Maj Maynard AMC [Army Medical Corps] re our diagnostic facilities and submitted a further indent to the DDMS for sending on. Various restrictions on food etc have come into force as from today, orders of a sort from Malaya Command.

?? We are out of Libya now and fighting within Egyptian border.

America ready to start offensive. Churchill been there again.

29 June

This blackout is a nuisance and stricter than ours ever was, and is enforced at the point of a bayonet. We had a gramophone recital on the roof last night but the Nip guards had everybody turned off the roofs after sunset until further orders.

Four large flying boats have been very evident all day, four engines and rather slow. Went up to 3rd Company to see the list they have there, but Elizabeth's name is not on it, so I am still left very depressed. Talked to West (45 AT Coy).

?? Churchill delivered a rousing speech predicting a quick and sudden end of the war.

We have evacuated Marsa Matruh.

Terrific fighting at Sebastopol.

400,000 Yanks in India now.

1 July

Note from E.

Woken whilst still dark by roar of planes over us but it's only the big flying boats. Later, about 9.30 am there was some gunfire south of us. Two large fires over towards Naval Base later in the day. Two Nip fighter planes have appeared today, they look good and fast.

Visited SA and looked at more lists of internees['] names, E.'s was still absent, walked back awfully fed up. But – joy of joys, there was a note from darling on my table. I delayed to open it, did everything else first, then sat down to a first read of it. Wonder which of my letters she has received, can't quite make out. Hers must have been dated about 28th. Bloom got one too and so did the others. Oh I feel good, Elizabeth, must thank you quickly for this.

2 July

Blackout ceased last night, the lights were on in the gaol, but we had none. I sat down and wrote some reply to E.'s note by my screened lamp in the Lab last night. Exceptionally dark night last night. Cruickshank worrying Ledingham in the dark, he hit Col. Bennet under the shower by mistake, a good crack on the backside, slipped away as soon as he saw he was not seen.

Huge fire blazing away in the direction of Johore, explosions at intervals, hope it's a bit of sabotage.

?? Libya bad. We are pushed right back 90 miles from Alexandria. Huns pushing on with armoured columns.

'No confidence' vote in Commons.

American raid on a Jap occupied island.

3 July

Official message came through from Elizabeth and again I'm glad. Raises hopes that we might see each other – in time, at present it looks though it's infinity away.

Saw Mulvaney, he's had no more news and hasn't had success in getting my letter off as yet. His camp is rather tight these days being by Keppel Harbour. All Nip convoys are well guarded he says. Very little shipping in or out of Naval Base. No vessels through for days.

Two neat fighter planes are whizzing about our skies, they are fast and manoeuvrable. Looked in at the concert, not a very good show, came back and finished the note to Elizabeth.

4 July

Had 'limed' rice [rice dressed for seed] for lunch yesterday, it's awful, just couldn't face it, would have vomited immediately. I think that food is deteriorating again, no meat for days, and then only 4–5oz at a time.

5 July

Visited 11th Division. Lovely walk down. Glendenning is still worrying about his health, says that he 'casts his scrotal skin about once a week'. Long talk with de M., explored possibilities of getting in notes, he wasn't useful or wouldn't tell me the means.

Hurried back late for supper and then attended a very good lecture by an Aussy Sgt Oberman RAF who was in a torpedo-carrying Wildebeest ([one of] 12 [in squadron]) attacking the Nip vessels off Emdau where they were effecting this landing there. Hopelessly outnumbered by fast fighters including ME109s [Oberman was mistaken as although German ME109s were evaluated by the Japanese in 1941, none were flown in combat].

Shot down off Mai Win and hidden by Chinese for next two months. Saw some atrocities during his freedom.

?? Counter attack commenced in Libya.

- Sebastopol has fallen. Elsewhere fairly stable.

6 July

Eighth Note

Capt Davis in from Riverside Camp, held out hopes of getting through a note so sent my first reply. Quoted Scottish verse in this one.

My scrotum has started itching a little but no scaling as yet and it's not too bad. Some folk have raw peeling skins. It's a fairly common complaint and we think is an early P-P [Vitamin B3] deficiency.

Vardy's story: of Chinese fishermen paying entrance fee of $50 to a society, last few in American bills, sold his fish to crew of a submarine off his *pajar*.

?? Guam, Wake and Timor are once again in Allied hands.

Libya, the battle is raging. We have pushed them back a little.

7 July

My scrotum is definitely worse, awfully itchy. Pitt and others have had theirs for weeks. Frankland's cleared on Marmite. We are to start on rice polishings tomorrow, see if that helps at all.

Had a siesta for a change and then watch 'A' team play 13th AGH [Australian General Hospital] in the league soccer. We won 3–1, it was good fun and vigorous match. De Soldenoff almost threw the ball back into our goal on one occasion.

H. Gibbs' story – Nip officer's yarn about bombing of San Francisco, New York and Chicago. Says our man 'Now no more bullshit.'

'Oh yes,' continued the Nip, 'that too has been levelled.'

8 July

Bombers much in evidence today in formation. 27 and 21 with 30 fighters escorts, flying north-east. The 21 came back after 1 hour. Flying boats also about and we saw anti-aircraft fire in direction of Kallang.

Robson, up from Singapore, says some Chinese heads have been stuck up on poles near the Airport and Rochor Canal bridge.

Commenced taking [illegible] of rice polishings daily. My scrotum is awfully itchy now.

?? Germans in Libya are being bombed like mad, they are defensive now and we offensive.

Russians driven back in the Kharkov sector, also push towards Moscow.

9 July

Blachan [dried shrimp paste] for lunch, gosh the room did smell, I expected 'bluebottles' in at any moment. Still it carries down a lot of rice. We get so hungry these days that anything resembling food apart from rice is appreciated.

10 July

Moved over into the new Lab today, it's not a bad place at all. Except that we have no lavatory for ourselves now, it's a serious problem, the outdoor latrines are awful things to use. Flies and their larvae on the seats. Lots of our [illegible] clients also miss this nice clean W.C.

JB went there and found patients using it, much to his consternation and embarrassment.

Our room is at end of 'L' block and we have more workbenches, a sink, washbasin and electric light plugs. Convenient as I sleep on the floor up above. Wharton and Wyatt sleep in the Lab.

Staff is now

A/S George, Cooper, Houghton, Wharton, Wyatt. Latter is off the post mortem business.

11 July

Plenty of light in this room and a good view of the main road and the hospital road. Can watch at the Nip 'big shots' go by without looking down on them, they don't seem to like this latter very much, but won't mind us. The Skin Ward is next to us; Hamilton Gibbs does his extension outpatients at the other end.

13 July

Ninth Note

Walked over to see Gibson in the afternoon and gave him the note, understand he has quite a regular contact through the man. Didn't tell this route but acknowledged her first note. Quoted 'toorie' in this.

The fishing *pajar* lights are on again so I suspect Bangs will start up his business again and open up another avenue.

?? Germans only 50 miles from Alexandria, war in a bad way there.

Russian front news still depressing.

14 July

Attended the usual history lecture, on to Alfred now and his time.
Bloom delivered E.'s letter.

July 15

Elizabeth again – 2nd.

Tenth Note

Note from E. via River Valley Camp written about the 26th, enclosed in a letter to B.

Saw Bangs at teatime and gave him a note, also enclosed was the message for Scott's wife. Had a long talk with Bill Kennedy, life in general, he's very pessimistic. GOC [General Officer Commanding] gave a lecture on Norway campaign; it was as chaotic as the Malayan affair. Our War Cabinet must be pretty awful.

?? Big tank battle in Libya about 125 miles from Alexandria.

Gandhi very ill ?? on his death bed.

An Indian been admitted to the War Cabinet.

Russians have held the German advance across the Don.

16 July

New Razor Blade

Great excitement, Nip order that colonels and above are to be shipped overseas, probably to Tokyo. Of course Craven and Bennet have put in for exemption as essential here. Brass hats galore are passing back and forth up to the control office, an awful stir. Joe B. sat with a look of utter dejection at lunch. Being S., has to go.

Our canteen supply is poor, have had five coconuts on order three weeks now, all I get this evening is two duck eggs.

Hair cut today.

17 July

'Hoo hah' continues – now McFarlane is included and also Harry M., said to be three parties altogether. Col G apparently not to go, other two still on the list.

Saw Richards. Hear that civilians are down from upcountry apparently for transfer to the prison; possibility of repatriation of them has cropped up again. I hope so, E. will then go. Some difficulty about the mail service just now, temporary I believe.

Went to 11th Div. show in our cinema hall – only fairly good. Two violins and a jazz drum.

Pretty dismal news this evening.

?? Russians very had pressed and still retiring. Voronezh surrounded. Hun columns going on.

Timor heavily bombed by Yanks.

Gandhi said to be demanding immediate home rule in India.

18 July

Atmosphere upstairs last night was very depressing, the 'going aways' and the news combined to depress.

All day people have been wondering of further developments, Wyatt and Wharton are down to go from the Lab staff, our two useful junior members.

All kinds of rumours also flying about – ? repatriation of civilians and sick.

We are losing Pemberton, Gibbs, McConachie, Bell, Harry M., Julian Taylor and Bennet.

Much visiting between camps, many cars going back and forth.

J.T. gave an excellent talk of 16th–17th century France, extremely humorous, and of their history.

19 July

Brass hats passing back and forth, other MO been warned to be ready. Julian T. is off the list and Benson is filling the vacancy. J.B. looks awfully upset at being rooted out.

Visited SA to see the full lists of civilian internees, of course E. is on, quite a thrill to see her name. Currid, Harty also there. At the same time heard a vigorous anti-Nazi lecture by S/Maj Rose, the German lecturer, followed by Brig Jamieson who was weak by comparison.

Five huge flying boats going round all the afternoon, pity none of our craft about to bring them down.

News in general is better times, so we are cheerier than yesterday

Returned from SA with Victor Dewar.

20 July

Brig S. 'Swan Song' in the old cinema hall, not very good, couldn't help feeling sad, it's probably the end of his service. He dined in our Mess afterwards.

Again to SA, saw Colonel R. who is to go as well. Medical inspections this morning including rod culture smears from rectum onto LLBSA plates and blood smears from mrps.

General feeling is against going away, although ?? more food and better climate, but one can place no faith in Jap behaviour when they are hard pressed or for that matter even as we are here.

21 July

Your birthday Elizabeth, remember. Big variety show in the cinema and Captain de Gray gives his farewell history lecture.

Finished *Return to Malaya*, must have Elizabeth read this book later.

Mother is 65 years [old] tomorrow – dear Mother, and I have not been up to expectation for her!

22 July

No further change, draftees are still being examined. Wharton down again with his dysentery, relapse, so he's not going. Rigby has his malaria again. Gen. Heath also down with a fever.

Had a big farewell dinner, including sweets and coffee. Bennet gave poor speech as goodbye and we all rushed off to the concert of two plays *The Monkey Paw* and *The Dream* by SA players. Both were awfully well done and we enjoyed them. Withers played as Axel Munthe.

Anthony Eden in the Commons said in a reply that no news had come of Singapore prisoners, but of Hong Kong no further atrocities but medical facilities poor and death rate high.

23 July

Excitement has died down, period of rumours continues and folk are getting a little strained over this waiting for departures.

Fracas with Graves over some 'rudery' on his part to the Lab, must say I had my own back rather obviously. Little things like this rather spoil a day. However we found a person's cerebral spinal fluid later containing some highly suggestive diplococci – ? Spotted fever.

Lecture J.T. on French History. Mulvaney was in, seen no ships in the harbour as yet, in fact Singapore is said to be blockaded successfully.

?? Russians pushing Huns back in southerly Sector, and are expecting Jap attack in the east, where they have 4½ divisions ready.

Rangoon been heavily bombed.

Another attack on Aleutians been repulsed.

24 July

Hear that six civilian men are to accompany the party to Japan. Also that gaol has been punished on rice and water for seven days because of all the correspondence. A dim female in there gave the service away by mentioning it in an epistle of hers. The B***** Japs. We'll get square one day.

Bought three coconuts today from the Aussy canteen, very good too, shared down in the Lab.

Clinical Meeting of Changi Medical Society, turned out quite a success, too many cases shown and interest in food spoilt it a bit.

Dutch Officers from Sumatra relate awful stories of the treatment of Australian nurses by the Nips, and killing on the beaches they came up at Palm Bay.

25 July

Eleventh Note

Epistle acknowledging receipt of E.'s two, sent this morning by Mathieson who was up after a long time. Two pages, but one incomplete.

Met Maj Sullivan in the medical store, he thinks his wife, a nurse, and a Miss Jenkins, [have] been brought back from Sumatra, both thought to be in the prison. Wants me to try and get a note to E. asking for news, he promises to get it through.

Big flying boats are very active this evening, brilliant moonlight.

?? Huns on outskirts of Rostov but Russians holding elsewhere on line.

40 bombers over England, seven were brought down.

Allied talks over Pacific situation and Gen. McArthur moves HQ to northern Australia.

26 July

New Nip Maj. General arrived to take over Singapore. Visited the POW camp area, about 25 cars with pennants flying, guards and a machine gun. Several Nip naval vessels are in Keppel Harbour and also passed through to the Naval Base, including two large transports ?? for the going away parties.

Two Red Cross ships in Keppel harbour, one discharged wounded to the civil hospital.

?? from Burma.

?? Russian position, no change.

Nip invasion of New Guinea repulsed with heavy losses to them in ships and men.

Pamphlets dropped over Emperor's Palace in Tokyo by a plane.

Chinese in Canton area pushing back the Japs.

27 July

If our Air Forces knew what a bag there is to be had of naval vessels and aircraft around here at the present time!

Hear Sir S.Thomas and five other others including Gen McCrae are also in the party for Tokyo.

I feel a definite improvement in this scrotal itchiness after seven days on Vegemite, scaling is certainly less.

Up on FA roof tonight watching the lights, hear that Stratton-Christenson is married, wife and daughter living in Quetta. He never let out any of this to Elizabeth at that time!

28 July

Celebrity concert tonight.

Reg Rennison – Piano

John Foster Haigh – Tenor

Denis East – Violin

It was a lovely programme in spite of the very modern electric lighting going off twice, and being replaced by *sandang* [hanging] lanterns. The piano was a bit off colour, notes sticking etc. Rennison very deliberately picking muck off the keyboard.

29 July

12th Note

In this acknowledged receipt of both notes and also asked after Miss Jenkins and Nancy Sullivan. Gave the note to S. for ultimate disposal.

Austin Best has taken up residence with us in 'A' Mess; he's awfully fat and flabby.

Wish I could get more eggs; they are really good to eat, awfully appreciated by me these days.

?? German drive towards Stalingrad is progressing. Russian situation is critical.

In Libya after an artillery duel we are developing an opposition.

Nip landings in New Guinea are being fought back successfully.

30 July

Duty

Hear that sudden personal searches are frequent in the gaol these days and they do not allow them to do any local purchasing. Money too is awfully short.

1 August

Few of us took a flag out, joined Ross at 11th Div. thence down through *kampongs* to the sea. Bought some pineapples off Javanese. Pemberton and Ross had a swim, Garlick and Vardy were scared of Nips the whole time, then to Laycock's house. Magnificent garden of flowers, Vardy collected a lovely bunch. Gardenias in profusion. Up a road towards the gaol, Chinese stall where we bought dates, drinks and were presented with about 35 good bananas. Nips came down towards us so off we went about 10 yards, feeling very guilty and expecting to be called back at any minute for a face slapping. P. walked off with the glass in such a hurry. Back to the beach, ate our fruit, watched the Malay boys swimming, a real holiday. Back along the coast through coconut grove. Malays gave us fresh coconut milk and the young meat.

Whilst there, General P. and others passed us on their way to the beach for an evening stroll. Back through Selarang very tired, thirsty but pleased with life. If only E. could get out for a bit, some sun would do a lot of good.

3 August

13th Note

In which I acknowledge that two [illegible] that I sent you [illegible] Elizabeth, and talk of old times.

Walked over to SA in the noon and saw Pigot for delivery, he was quite confident of success, had to hurry back for work and to see 13th Div [stage] *The Dover Road*. It was almost as good as home theatres, stage and electric lighting, good band. Decorations of a lounge were perfect, cast too was awfully good. The clothing wanted in nothing, and the two women, one hardly thought of them as two males acting the part. Euston had grown his hair long, waved and blond, looked very beautiful and feminine. Their acting too and carriage was so feminine. Elizabeth ought to see this play of A.A. Milne's. We'd both profit maybe of it! Fun.

4 August

Verbal message

Missed seeing MO Tyrrell last evening but saw him after tea today and he promised to tell Jack D. all about me so Elizabeth should know, also said about the last note. Tyrrell had to be taken back by one of our ambulances rather late as Nip transport did not arrive. He had supper with us.

X-ray machine is now repaired, I understand, but requires some replacements. Tyrrell seemed pessimistic, things in the gaol are very tight, they had only collected $19,000 at the start.

?? Heavy bombing in northern France and Belgium. Dusseldorf particularly.

American reinforcements to Libya, in air strength.

Nip battleship torpedoed in Sourabaya harbour.

Bombing of Hong Kong, Fuchow and Hankow.

5 August

Rumour about today that all our postcards have at last arrived in England – wonder how true it is. This is at least the third time that we have had this news.

Nips seem to have quite a number of fighter planes round here, apart from the large number of bomber planes.

?? Russians are holding Germans in Rostov front. Heavy losses both sides.

Heavy bombing of northern France and Germany continues. Saarbrucken bombed too.

Churchill over in Moscow.

?? Heavy bombing of Alor Star, Sungai Petani and Butterworth [and] also places in Sumatra.

6 August

Life is getting very routine; we all seem to be waiting and waiting. Never a thought that we are likely to be on the losing side in this war, the end seems so far distant. Often wonder when E. and I shall be together again and the world at peace. Here in this camp we eat, I get my shower, sleep. Nips never worry us, yet never a sight of E., so near too.

About 6.00 pm called out to interpret for Lt Col Pearson who has been stopped for saluting a Sikh guard incorrectly, so says the guard, but our gate sentries think otherwise; however after much argument P. was taken away to the prison office in 18th Div area and locked up. McLaughlin went along, [and] eventually they offered to release him in exchange for me as I had asked the sentry's number and name.

7 August

Went to bed with a most uncomfortable feeling. Gathered some of my rubbish together and expected to be called for by the Sikhs any time[;] fearful thoughts as to what kind of punishment they would try to inflict. Pearson was brought back about 9.00 am, none the worse [for] his night out. Fed well, given a couch to sleep on and apologized to for the detention. Capt Dillon of the Sikhs is at present ill, lucky for P. this was so, [as] their treatment of soldiers outside the wire and others is cruel and depraved[:] tying to trees full of red ants, screwing of the head in a wood vice or flogging, or beating with iron bars. Ordinary smackings are nothing as handed out by the Nips. They're certainly having their good time now.

8 August

?? Americans have commenced an offensive, taken an island near Timor, fighting in Solomons and British New Guinea and up north. Also in the Aleutians.

USA Navy said to have sunk 18 vessels in a sweep in north Pacific.

Libyan situation is static again, maybe we are pushing a little.

13 August

At last ELECTRIC LIGHTING, but only in the hospital area, after weeks of expectancy.

14 August

Thus fiddling about with lights and water all day. Whilst visiting Tim Ward in P2 lights flashed a moment and then out. Engineers conducted a long test and found they were at 440v instead of 220v. Rather disheartening. After the first blaze of lights last night the expected happened – half of all bulbs had to be given today.

Overseas parties had rectal smears taken again today; now think that 'B' and specials will be the first lot to set off.

After concert went up to the mortuary and MacGregor's home, it was decorated for his pal's birthday. Tablecloth and all. Three course dinner.

15 August

Of course the lights are off tonight. Apparently a Nip engineer forgot to switch on at the substation last evening and went back to Singapore. Gaol lights came on as usual.

Rumour about that women and children and men over military age may be repatriated shortly from Singapore. I do hope this is so, but would so like to see Elizabeth again, even five minutes before we get so far apart. Also to give her advice about financial affairs. When will we be together again? Say that 1500 are to be taken, including parties from Hong Kong and Shanghai, 600 from this prison. Also that doctors in the prison may be released to work in town.

Fire in town tonight, said to be a sabotaged oil dump. ?? Chinese doings.

16 August
Six months in prison

Lovely cold morning, beautiful sky before sunrise, quite a nip in the air as we stand around waiting to say goodbye and good luck to our colleagues, Harry M., Tom O'Donnell, Rigby, Gibbs, Bell, who are leaving us for Japan. Trucks arrived by 8.00 am and off they went, 56 men and baggage on two trucks. Our trucks, which we so carefully used to avoid overloading, one Nip 'superior' soldier to look after the party. Special party left at 10.30 am. Generals in cars, brigadiers in a bus and colonels on top of their luggage on trucks just like the men. Col. Bennet went off today with a pile of luggage. Austin B. is very peeved that R. should go off without returning his $60.

Watch a game of soccer in evening and then the 'lights' from FA mess roof. Electric lights on again.

17 August

After supper went over to 11th Div then a quick walk down to the beach and back. It's annoying how near the prison lights appear from their *padang* [playing field] [–] could almost recognise you inside, Elizabeth. No news for ages, wonder what is the matter.

Somebody even told us today that the Nips smack the women's faces for minor offences, just as they treat BORs [British Other Ranks] – could it be true!

There'll certainly be much to repay when the opportunity presents.

?? Yanks have launched an attack in the Solomon Islands and are doing all right

Riots in India and the Congress leaders have been put in prison.

Churchill in Moscow still. The German drive towards the Caucasus is still going on. Russians doing alright elsewhere.

18 August

Saw Maj Sullivan today; the message to E. was delivered he says but we still have no reply to go by. We all still think that many from Sumatra have been brought back here.

A dysenteric patient brought back from party 'D' and Specials says they have all (1400) been stuffed into the hold of a 3000-ton vessel below hatches. No sleeping accommodation and no smoking allowed below. They were all stripped and sheep dipped as well, clothes sent off for disinfection. General P. complained and 400 officers and men were transferred to another vessel, again below decks.

Saw *Devon Road* at our hall. It was every bit as good as the first time. Two 'women' excellent. If only there was a bar at the intervals, we might not think that we were prisoners.

19 August

The new Maj General GOC of Malaya came on a tour of inspection. Many precautions taken, nobody allowed to look down on him from balconies or windows. His first tour has not left a good impression. Watched the cavalcade drive passed the Lab, sitting by the microscope window, these men have swept all before them so far – the b******s.

34 cases of diphtheria now since there has been no antitoxin available[;] three have died already, wonder how many more [–] certainly is increasing. Repeated requests to the Japanese have failed to bring forth any response, although huge stocks were left over in Tonghin at the time of capitulation.

We get an issue of sweets (4½oz), jam 1lb, soup mix 1lb each from the South African Red Cross – all the way from a country which is free. When will we be out of this place.

20 August

Hear that the civilians have been given a ⅙ share of the Red Cross supplies, wish that more would come for them, and that the women and children are taken away.

Goodall and Nardell went down to the gaol for interrogation re their knowledge of Swilling and Chittagong[;] very simple questions asked about terrain etc, obtainable in any good atlas map of the country.

Maj White there too, got beaten with his own stick for standing up late when a Nip General passed by him. Indians about the place were most obsequious.

24 August

Saw Graham this morning whilst I was on my way up to do post mortems on two more diphtheria cases, one faucial and one scrotal. Jibani been in hospital for last two months with a detached retina, Allogypia, Loganadia, Chatterjee and several others we hear have sneaked on us. All the camps in town are more or less closing down, 10,000 to be back by the end of the week, [and] civilian camp is also packing up to return to the gaol.

[Hear from] Strachan, again, that civilians may soon be repatriated from here, hope this is so. Elizabeth must get out of this awful hole.

25 August

Fourteenth Note, 2 pages.

Met George G. up today and delivered him the goods, also a verbal to Jack D.

Any numbers of fellows are coming back from the working parties. They look awfully ragged and unkempt and in appalling general condition too, just don't seem to care a damn about themselves. Most of the pellagra cases too are from camps where the food was supposed to have been good, plenty of meat and vegetables. Another 15 diphtherias are in from town today bringing the total in 'S' block up to about 140 cases, including scrotal and skin cases (20 or so). Still no antitoxin available, and Taylor seems to be doing better now, has had a total of 17,000 units.

11th Div concert party in our cinema tonight, quite funny for a change and I enjoyed the show[;] perhaps it was the good meal tonight.

26 August

Good rugger match down on the *padang*, Hospital vs. RE, turned a bit vicious in the second half. After supper met Tom Cranshaw at Aussy match then to a lecture by an Aussy taken recently in a ship south of Colombo, captured by two surface raiders who were just returning from the neighbourhood of the Cape where they had been sinking vessels ?? 20. Also said that Australia was flabbergasted when Singapore fell so easily, as they had been told all kinds of lies as to its strength and air support.

Ate one of the pineapples with C. Cut the smaller one but it was too raw to eat.

?? News this side is optimistic but in Russia situation is really critical.

27 August

Maj Anderson, lecture by Aussy MO on the medical arrangements of Japanese in Malaya: one large town hospital of 2000 beds at Singapore, later at KL, and ahead of this only 12 MO to a regiment. [Japanese] don't care much for casualties until fighting is over, all is done first to attain their object. Used 75,000 men to fight in Malaya and a reserve of 75,000 at Singapore. Lived on the land as they came down, each soldier cooks his own food. Carried a water sterilising outfit and prophylactic quinine gr Tv/diurn.

Very little transport, cycle or walking. Piss and shit all over the place, poor personal hygiene. Communal hot bath is relished, so all have scabies. Feet are bad too, poor foot wear. All troops well camouflaged, also carrying 'B' tablets. E is getting them in town. Regular VD treatment, no one is allowed back to Japan if they still have positive WR [Wasserman reaction – test for syphilis] at the end of their tour of service abroad. Troops which were here came from Manchuko area, to Indo-China, last six months in Thailand undergoing vigorous training in jungle warfare preparatory to this invasion. Their camouflage was awfully good, said they could easily see our men in khaki.

Had to go up this evening to office to fill in a form for Nips – Nationality, Name, Rank, Unit and state of health at the time. Wonder what this is for now!

Nips have sent in two lots of anti-diphtheria serum, sufficient for four or five cases on full treatment. No more cases have died; Maynard suggests mainly 'mitis' infection. More scrotal cases in from Singapore.

29 August

Captain Phillips of 'B' Mess, owner of the red spaniel with 'ball disease', has disappeared with two Eurasians, assume an attempted escape.

30 August

The area commanders called to the 'Council House' in the morning and told that everyone has to sign a form 'On our honour that we will not attempt to escape etc'. Gavin told me about it after tea and anybody who wanted [to] is to go up to the office and do this signing tomorrow. There is an ACI [Army Council Instruction] against it so we must refuse[;] anyway the chances of escape are so remote as to be out of the question. Capt Phillips, Perrera and other Eurasian have been caught already and are in the Sikh camp awaiting punishment.

Attend lecture by Markowitch on 'Canada', a lovely place. Elizabeth we must try and visit it sometime, our first good holiday etc!

All Aussies, except one who is on a crime report, have refused to sign the form.

31 August

Terrific arguments all over the camp as to the pros and cons of signing parole. Ultimately I believe no one has signed in the area except one Aussy who is on a crime report – all sorts of conjecture as to the result of this, [they will] probably reduce our rations on account.

Tomorrow we have the first roll call by Japanese and are all wondering what else they might want to do at the same time. We stand in alphabetical order, Allen first on the list. Parade at 8.15 am tomorrow, rather early!

Looked over at the lights from the roof, blue floodlights on as well. Oh darling I hope you're still well in there and not too unhappy.

Talked anaesthetics with Gawn.

1 September

Bad day. Up in utter darkness, hasty breakfast and then to Roll Call parade. Our own check seemed alright, waited two hours then Nips arrived, counted us three or four times. We sat down at intervals, eventually very restless and didn't even stand up as they passed and re-passed. Their old SMO [Senior Medical Officer] Major looks like Sleepy ([of the] 7 Dwarfs). They counted and counted, sometimes less, sometimes more, eventually went away with a count of 13 more than we ought to have in our area. Lunch at 3.00 pm. Maj Gen Shimpei Fukuye IJA [Imperial Japanese Army] was here himself and a host of others. In some areas they simply asked how many on parade. No discharges or admissions to hospital. Awfully tired by evening, but we had a cinema show in our own mess, it was all comics, Chaplin in *The Count* and *Tarzan's Son* also some of *Popeye*.

2 September

Dawns a horrible day for us prisoners. 11th Div SA [and] 18th Div all troops moved into the Selarang blocks around the square. We were under orders to move as well, all to be in by 6.00 pm including patients. Col Cameron put up a special appeal so Hospital allowed to stay, but 'A' party and certain other officers, Gawn too, had to go over and didn't get orders until 5.00 pm. All went over, like the retreat from Moscow or worse, baggage taken over on anything, even dragged along the road, or rolled down the hill. Old men, officers and all sweating along to get in by time – [plus] eight goats, few dogs, fowls. Continuous weary stream after lunch, bicycles, prams did good service; to say nothing of 'Changi trucks' [chassis of dismantled truck used with manpower for transport]. Single men loaded to capacity. Believe they have to fit in 1000 to a floor and the square is packed already. How will they cook and [organise] latrine arrangements! No regard for epidemic diseases etc[;] sure many will die in next few weeks.

3 September

Order about the move came about 4.00 am in quite a hurry. Said to be a reprisal for failing to sign parole, we wonder! Area Commanders attended the execution without mercy of 4 BORs who attempted to escape some time back. Two were patients from hospital and taken out from here. Sikhs did the shooting very badly too. No Geneva Conventions have been observed this day, sheer brutality everywhere.

Nobody is allowed out of or into our area, no discharges. What about food, fire etc?

Capt Phillips RAMC and two others are awaiting the penalty.

Austin B. gives me *Good Housekeeping* to read.

Everybody very quiet, air of depression and expectation, folk don't seem to like passing between blocks. Sikhs are raiding the vacated areas, lifting food chiefly. We can see the roofs at Selarang absolutely crowded, even a tent pitched on one. Two camps from Singapore brought up patients and good 'Boreholes'. We get delivered full ration (½ meat) at the hospital.

4 September

Spirits up a bit this morning. Work as usual. Admissions come in from town. Mulvaney from Keppel Harbour, they heard about the Selarang 'Black Hole' last evening. Patients from Singapore allowed in this evening. Neill says there are 17,000 in 5½ acres, 357 to a floor, remainder in square where latrines are being dug, food cooked and everything. [Just like] 'Woolworths' on a Saturday night. Our food should not have come in; ?? Capt James, interpreter, got it through and has been put away by the Japs for punishment. They saw Craven gave him 100 cigs, said 'You good boys now' and gave 480,000 U anti-diphtheria serum. Col Holmes, Commanding Officer (CO) Troops and others had conference today and result is we are all <u>ordered</u> to sign the form.

?? Burma offensive has started with two days [of] bombing, then advance. Solomons and New Guinea almost in American hands now.

Russians push back Nazis in the Stalingrad action.
We have commenced an offensive in Libya.

5 September

2100 hours signed under IJA Order No. 17 and orders from Col Holmes 'I, the undersigned, do solemnly swear on my honour that I will under no circumstances attempt to escape'.

So to bed wondering when the others will be released.

Slept on Gavin's spring bed last night, it was bad, too soft, and oh! Was I bitten with bugs, reminded me [of] last day at Fullerton. They even set about crawling up my net. After lunch the big trek back to former areas began, everybody was certainly in high spirits and pulled back with more vigour than when they went. Back came the trolleys, trucks, sledges, ducks, goats and dogs. Men certainly seem more together and united with the officers than ever before[;] Nips have done what MC failed to do in years. None of them looked the worse for the three days 'Black Hole', though rather dirty and ragged, full of yarns.

6 September

Visited Selarang in evening, looks like a poor gypsy camp, square full of deep trench latrines and rubbish. Only two water points for all, a medical inspection room and first cooking by Aussies. Four machine-gun points just outside the building's drains that form the boundary. Top floors can see the gaol ever so close (Elizabeth, you're not so far away darling – maybe in one of the rooms I'm looking at now.) Nips began to clear stragglers out by 6.00 pm.

Saw Young RAMC and he said he'd see Mackenzie FMSVF and let me know in a few days about the position!

Arm bands and flags are in use once more but we don't like to go about as much yet. Parties going over to Selarang to help clear up the mess today. Returns too have been coming in, and things are settling down again. Gavin is wearing a Red Band.

7 September

More of these scrotal cases are coming in from Singapore than ever, also numerous multiple paralyses which clear up on Vegemite or Marmite. Skin infections with KLB [Klebs-Loeffler bacillus] are getting more frequent and are characteristic in appearance.

3rd Corps are moving from Temple Hill area over to Selarang today, and all those barracks are going to be occupied by Nip troops.

Sikhs are beginning to do a lot of nasty work again, stopping BORs for the slightest, or even if they do not commit a fault. They are bastards and suitable treatment, I hope, will be meted out to them later. The ones on guard near us are 'shitting' in the grass by the gun park, dirty swine.

9 September

Great excitement caused because I found a case of dermal leishmaniasis, tip of nose. He had left India in November 1941 and had the lesion for the last four months. Scrapings were absolutely full of parasites, better than the book picture, all the GPs flocked in to have a look, hardly room to move in the Lab.

Strachan scored a success too, a difficult case of BT malaria diagnosed, four parasites in two [illegible] and this was his fifth rigor. He's a relapsed case from Dec. '41. He's typical of several such cases we've had to diagnose although they run temperatures to 104–105° four to five times before a positive. Most down to poor immunity through lack of proteins and vitamins as well, no antibodies being made.

12 September

Height, weight, age, chest measurements, of all MOs taken today by the IJA. We are considered fit too.

Vardy took my BP [–] 80/40 again and go onto the Nip B tablets again. 24/diurn for about 10 days. I do feel pretty worn out these days without much effort either.

Afternoon. About a battalion of Nip troops marched out to the vacated barracks in SA. Looked recruits, Chinese and tall hefty Mongols, a very slovenly lot, carrying our rifles too. Only one or two officers. They goose-stepped past the police at our gates. Sikhs seem to think they are going to be taken upcountry to fight ?? [in] Indo-China.

Mah-jong again tonight, am learning the game quite well.

13 September

Max P. and Bangs went on the usual walk today but met a ? Lt Col 2nd i/c POW who was rather annoyed and sent them back to the camp limits, and no more going out again for strolls. The 'Apes' said flags were only to be used for working parties and not for recreation purposes – we know that! Bands of course we have used individually between camps, and flags supposed to be for an officer and party of ten for work outside. This seems quite a good idea, as does the wires between areas. Only wish we could get up to the prison with a flag.

Walked to Selarang again, and looked at the prison closely, also the low building where you must be Elizabeth, can't look out from there at all.

14 September

3rd Corps and some of SA seem to have settled in very comfortably up in the Gordons' barracks, lots of room and fresh air. They seem to have a lot of spring beds although the order to hand them in to the hospital has been repeated several times. They have taken them away from us MOs otherwise I should have had one a long time ago. Folk outside are always ready to criticise the hospital but never very co-operative. Officers in particular, as patients, are dreadful and seem to expect normal diets and even the very best of drugs. Latter are running very low now and there seems no hope of reasonable replenishments from anywhere. Very little obtainable in Singapore and that is expensive.

17 September

Fifteenth Note, two pages

Wrote a letter to George G. and sent him another enclosure. The previous one has gone in with folk from there who have been re-gaoled.

Not feeling too well, easily tired, somewhat light-headed by evening, and oedema of the legs once again.

The Red Cross vessel *Tutuka Maru* came in yesterday with Nip repats on board. They visited our areas passing through in buses and cars[;] wonder if they looked in at the prison too to see conditions there. Rumour that there are a few letters, cigarettes, clothing and useful cats also aboard the ship. Wonder who'll get them, not enough for everybody here!!

Elizabeth, hope they send you away soon.

18 September

Meeting of Changi Med. Society.

Cases shown were:-

    i. Eye lesions, spots on cornea and loss of vision – ?? Vit A deficiency.
    ii. Spastic diplegia – ?? B_2 deficiency.
    iii. Scrotal dermatitis – typical cases treated with Red Palm oil.

iv. Oriental sore – my case with microscopic specimens. Few knew anything about the condition.
v. Surgical cases.
vi. Pellagra – a very unique collection of cases, and rare, yet most are just common diseases which we are trying to cope with.

Very few RMOs [Regimental Medical Officers] attend these meetings, [but] it would do them a lot of good as at present they haven't any idea what prevalent diseases are filling the wards, [and] treat their scrotums with fungicidal ointments, stronger and stronger. They do little to try and co-operate with those of us who are working in the hospital. Some exceptions.

19 September
Post mortem by Lennox last evening on a case of spastic diplegia – ?? B_2 deficiency, brain L. lobe shows numerous dotted areas of demyelination in the optic and motor radiations, ++ occipital pole. Man's first complaints were visual and right-sided so fits in perfectly.

Vardy brought me in a case to see – larva migrans on the foot. Very pretty picture too, better than the book, usual treatment advised. He hadn't seen a case before.

I feel awful again, oedema ++, BP 90/40, so am prescribed Okamatu tablets once again, a whole bottle too.

Red Cross vessel has sailed again, on its easterly course. Stores were unloaded by the people at Mulvaney's camp.

Mona married at home [and] becomes Mrs (Ivor) Davies.

21 September
Had a pretty awful night with my sore throat and cold. Throat is not as bad this morning, but the nose is fairly 'running' and I am using handkerchiefs galore. Do a throat smear too but find nothing suspicious.

Saw Vincent B. up from River Valley camp, [who] says the civilians are still there waiting to go back to the gaol.

22 September
Woke up feeling not too well, went down to lunch and almost collapsed, [so] back up to bed. Acute vomiting and malaise are the chief symptoms so to bed and a rest.

Post mortem on Best's case of spastic diplegia, the brain showed large numbers of degenerated areas in the white matter, more advanced than in last case of the 19th. Again marked in the occipital and motor radiations. This is a new disease on us.

Painful feet by the hundred have also appeared, [which] fail to respond so far to Vegemite, or rice polishings. It's a most crippling affair and getting more prevalent than balls [Burning feet syndrome].

Sikhs and a Nip brought in an unconscious man with an obvious fractured base of skull [–] result of a blow from rifle butt. Nip said 'He no good, I stab' drawing his bayonet, [with the] man lying on the stretcher at reception room.

23 September

Signed for a loan of $2.0 from the Command Paymaster. This is supposed to be an advance on the 'pay' which it is rumoured we are going to receive at the end of this month.

24 September

Slight improvement, able to go down for meals. Vardy is back at work after his projectile vomiting.

Much argument everywhere about this pay for officers, and the various deductions which Command propose to make and then expect us to sign for a much larger sum of cash.

25 September

16th Note, one page

Feeling very much better so back to work as usual, with a pretty busy day to open with.

Eric Smith came in for a gossip and I gave him a note asking for information. He promises it a safe passage.

News today seems of a brighter note than usual, also contains the fact that 11,000 letters have been forwarded to London and we all wonder if they are ours.

Our news seems to be fairly regular these days and of BBC origin since KGE1 [USA radio station] has apparently been closed down.

Maj Sullivan was also in; he's had no information so far of his wife, promises to visit me again soon.

Played Mah-jong again, and was up a good number, after a 'NEWS' hand.

26 September

Nips out on practice warfare again using our playing fields for a mortar range – the b........ – and blowing holes all over the pitches which have been so carefully levelled after months. Also probably want to spoil our afternoon siesta by the explosions.

27 September

Signed another form today to do with the drawing of 'Pay'; it was headed in Japanese so we couldn't understand it, but we think it was for the receipt of $30 only.

30 September

Awoke very early and started to put out my worldly belongings for the IJA inspection. All my ragged old shirts were piled up, everyone wearing their new ones and best footwear, some had on two pairs of shorts or longs. Much stuff is out of the way, buried, on the roof or on the beams under the Mess hut where it keeps dropping off. Mine up in the mortuary.

Nips came at 1.30 pm, only two of them, and just walked through our room and looked at the stuff laid out[; some] fellows had huge wardrobes, Pitt had out 2000 condoms on his bed. They finished by 4.00 pm. and went off, leaving us guessing as to the purpose of this hut inspection.

Some medical Red Cross supplies have begun to arrive in the camp. Their cigarettes are always being sold on the black market.

1 October

Seventeenth Note, one page

In the nature of a farewell and also some advice for the future in my absence. Information also asked.

Visited Maj Scullion to deliver the goods [note for Elizabeth] in the morning; much saluting and eyes righting to the Sikhs and their guardroom in the dividing strip of about 150 yards between us and SA.

'Peep eye' has published Changi news again after closing down for a few days; quite good reading too, Nip planes not doing so well in New Guinea.

At kit inspection by IJA Maj S was almost had up because he had a large packet of 'Radio' malt and the Nip thought it was something to do with a radio set.

Buried and hidden articles recovered from all over the grounds. I got my case back from the mortuary. Somebody else dug Painter's glasses before him.

2 October

Batman has gone and lost my nice light Whitney fawn blanket over the balcony and he wouldn't even tell me that it had gone – that's that!

Both parties who came from Java during the last fortnight medically inspected today as they are being shipped on elsewhere.

Much air activity during the day.

Visited *I killed the Count* by 18th Div players in their smart theatre. Foyer now has adverts painted on the wall and up the stairway. Also a bar and ticket box. Stage itself is first class and the 'flat' scenery complete with electric fire etc true to life. Really good acting and the females were better than before; 'Miss Lovelorn' was smashing in her silk dressing gown, lovely pyjamas and long cigarette holder. Good orchestra too.

3 October

Blood pressure 115/65

Saw S. this morning and he said that 17th note passed yesterday quite safely.

Took a walk over to Selarang in the evening, quite pleasant bit of exercise.

300 patients suddenly came in from KL Gaol, awful state of malnutrition, many with obvious beriberi, pellagra and corneal troubles, all very pale. Filthy and stinking like animals as they crowded around the reception room, all suffering from scabies and a variety of sores, clutching dirty sacking and bits of rag as their worldly belongings. Some living skeletons on the stretchers.

Java lecture by Sq Leader RAF up in our mess, most interesting, we seem to have done best so far as POW, more liberty and somewhat better food here. Seems Java will be difficult to retake; he spoke well of the Dutch soldiers and people in Java.

4 October

Sikh sentry en route to SA very officious this morning, picking out men from every group going by, making them run back and forth and salute many times – the bastard. He's giving the flag officer a hell of a time making him double march.

Took a stroll over to Selarang, didn't see anyone whom I knew, caught the last flag back again.

Some patients have been admitted from town camps and they have had a liberal issue of Red Cross supplies. Milk eight tins, 3½lbs sugar, two tins Bully.

Lots of Red Cross medical supplies arriving, much useful, but the mass of flatus tubes, catheters, Gooch splinting is not wanted. No Lab stuff has arrived so far.

5 October

Spent the afternoon going around KL patients picking out possible cases of malaria, several found anaemic, spleen +, afebrile but with parasites present.

One patient (L2) new local infection found. ST.g. 5000. BT. all forms 10, −14000/cu [illegible] he is relatively well.

Considerable ill feeling brewing amongst the company because of poor food and general lack of any interest in their affairs by the CO and others. Their meals have been really bad and today it's been worse − just rice. Meat issue of 2oz for two days.

6 October

Wrote officially to CO asking about correspondence with relatives in the prison and also if MC has asked after E. at all as a Military Nurse.

Austin B. and Franks we hear have had parcels from SA. Both of them have parents in the Cape, who have been able to get their £1/1 to the Red Cross folk. We all feel a little tinge of jealousy.

7 October

Best and Franks got their parcels. No food sent, only clothes, soap, razor blades. All very useful things at the present time. Major Feinhols has received one from his wife containing many bottles of vitamins of various sorts − the most useful yet.

8 October

An awful lot of ill feeling in the camp over the distribution of Red Cross stores, [as] more and more fellows arriving from Singapore with huge shares actually distributed. The men here are angry because it looks as though:

i. All the stuff will go to the stores.
ii. The leakage from stores is bad and only too obvious, even in the hospital steward's store.
iii. The company would rather eat and see the items as far as possible.

Col C. has already gone around smoking 'V' cigarettes, and we have had no issue as yet. Very good cartoon by 'Akki' outside the Lab door: 'Give all to the patient'.

Nip food ration for us is down too, I suppose because of the Red Cross stores.

9 October

Note to Jack D.

One RAMC went over to the Sikh guards today (Hereford) and has pushed on to their camp.

News says that Sir R. Craigie and 1100 British repatrees have arrived at Liverpool from the Far East, probably Japan and Shanghai.

Also strong rumour that a Nip vessel the *Lisbon Maru* has been torpedoed in the South China seas with 1400 British prisoners on board, ?? 200 were rescued.

Still no news as to when the Nips are going to give us pay and we are getting rather dry.

Canteen orders are not as big as they used to be, only eggs and peanuts asked for; and the former are more often bad these days – but are eaten.

10 October

Saw Roberts of the Red Cross; he mentioned that he might be allowed to see Ethel Mulvaney at the prison in a few days.

The RAMC orderly who went over to the Nips was seen on duty outside our area during the day.

Our Red Cross stores are now being issued, much of it goes into the Mess. We have been issued: cocoa, sugar, milk, bully beef, vegetables, biscuits, 65 cigarettes and we believe there is more to come.

11 October

Cinema show up in our Mess was going well when the bulb fused in the middle of a lively Harold Lloyd picture; rather a pity – we were all enjoying it.

13 October

More of the Java Party leaves this morning for upcountry. The green straw hats are rather scarce today. The two Dutch doctors have gone away too, nice chaps both of them.

14 October

At last we receive our first payment actually in hand – $10/- only IJA says that Captain's rate of pay is $126/- split up as follows:

$60 food and lodging
$30 payable to individual
$36 banked in Singapore

Of the sum allotted to individual:

$13 retained by MC at source
$7 Mess subscription

So I received $10/- new Japanese note in my hands.

Of course the canteen has very little for sale at the moment as the Singapore camps seem to have bought it up already.

Two soldiers caught masquerading all this time as civilians have been sent out from the gaol.

15 October

Cold delightful rainy morning ending with the most glorious sunset we have seen out here. Streamers of red going out from the red nucleus, and a variety of purples, violets and greens in between.

Some more people have left today for ?? upcountry. Most of them are British party back from the Indies.

We hear that KL Gaol is being emptied too, those who are well going north and the sick coming down here. Non-partisan to be sent away from here.

Saw de M. today, says his wife is living with Dr Cicely Williams in town and being paid $50/- a month out of which everything has to be bought. Dr Blakeman lives there too; he didn't come up today.

16 October

At last got all the articles together to do blood sugars (Folin and Wu) [blood sugar measurement], and the first batch has been quite a success except that the plungers of the coldmeter leak.

Lennon was up from town, they saw a Nip submarine sink in the Roads, survivors were brought in. Not much air activity these days and only an occasional vessel passing to the Naval Base.

Capt Brahan RAMC is undergoing an investigation as to why he sold a bottle of Marmite given him for 'Sore Feet', says a court martial, deserves it too!

Another party from Java arrived in Singapore but were not brought here, [it's] said they have been taken straight upcountry.

17 October

Lennon also said that Mrs Mulvaney is running the canteen and Red Cross section in the gaol, she goes into town about every ten days, hopes to meet M. at Ally's store, also to form an exchange there. Hope it works.

20 October

M.? Tidd QM has a sugar tolerance test done by us, the first in the camp. I did the estimations by Folin and Wu micro method and it worked out all right. Now can look out to do some more of the glycosurias about the place.

Vardy and Lt Col Cotton Harvey called in to town to see Lady Heath who is a query aplastic anaemia. Saw Hugh Wallace and Miss Webster. Latter said that you are keeping well Elizabeth and a verbal message was sent on my behalf to you.

21 October

Lecture by the schoolmaster of the HMAS *Perth*.

22 October

Lecture by L.C. Harwood of USN *Houston*.

'Say boy, did you hear a gate clang behind us?' as the *Houston* came through the Sunda Strait. 'The flowing ass-hole.'

It was a most interesting and amusing account, [which] also showed that we had practically no air power out this way at all, not even for naval protection.

Confirmed the story of our lecture last night.

23 October

I hear that my note to Jack D. was delivered this morning. Now to wait for a reply.

Bill B. also told me that Fridays are rendezvous days from now on.

Sgt Jenkins got a brief note from his wife, only three days old. All seems to be well in there.

Later – I hear that Elizabeth, Mrs M. and Mrs Jenkins have been in town today shopping.

24 October

Pitt received a letter through the Red Cross from his stepmother in SA. Several others have received letters too, all arrived open and censored. Wish I could get one too, even if it was from the gaol here.

Did another sugar tolerance test, an Aussy patient of Lt Col Cotton Harvey; went quite well, and the plungers of the machine don't leak now.

Not feeling so good today, possible prodromata of dengue and I had to go to 18th Div area gun park to take anal smears for the Nips. Party of 1000 was down from 11th Div. They form another overseas party leaving tomorrow morning.

25 October

Still more and more folk coming through from Java, all sizes, shapes and colours. Some look from Malaya, others are blond Dutch, in various degrees of ragged uniform; I like the green colour of some. Those that have packs are lucky because they are very good hiker's pattern. Beards, moustachios and stubbly chins, general health looks good, but they look awfully unkempt – worse than convicts.

Over to 11th Div in the evening after the rain, feeling a little feverish but it was a pleasant walk even so. Only about 450 left there, the rest went off ?? overseas this morning.

Not feeling so well, lay up in the afternoon with T[emp]. 99°, but I don't like bed very much, so took the evening walk.

26 October

Pencil note – Mother wrote Peggy [his pet dog] died today [note added later]

Woke up feeling bad but had to complete the report on the Carrier tests just carried out; gave that to Benson. We have a BF [illegible] in our own kitchen, no others were found.

After lunch went straight to bed, T. 100°, feeling awful. Slept soundly. At 4.00 pm told to go straight down for another 'bum sticking parade' but I refused this time, couldn't make it at all.

Vardy gave me Mist. APC [mixture of Aspirin, phenacetin and caffeine], pretty concentrated I think for I perspired very much, and went to sleep before lights out. Feels more than ever like the dengue.

Parties passing back and forth all day through our camp, all moving off. Dutchmen were 'poked' today, and I hear there was considerable confusion.

27 October

Terrific storm early this morning, it blew my china cup off the ledge, broken after 8 months of care.

After that I tried to sleep but awoke having a terrific rigor, gosh did I feel awful and miserable.

Temperature 100° before breakfast and same general malaise. Blood sample taken by Pte Wharton, negative last evening. I feel this might be the onset of MT malaria.

Had a terrific laugh which I'm sure sent my temperature soaring again – Paddy Doyle pulled a round worm out of …'s anus, latter gave an alarmed cry as he thought it was a lizard trying to get up that way, the tail hanging between his legs!

Big dinner this evening as a farewell to Max and Ben and also to old 'C.'. Lt Col Collins takes over command. I have my food upstairs but too bad, and think it a poor meal.

28 October

Max Pemberton and Benson go off early this morning. I awoke quite early and wished them the best. Max seemed to take away a terrific amount of stuff, don't know how he's going to carry it all.

Collins put on the Red Band first thing. I am beginning to feel a bit sorry for the old man now, in spite of his tricks and discrepancies.

Feel much improved today though still pyrexial [feverish]. No pains or aches.

Campbell and Best both received letters today, latter got five. Hear that Kiwi Gibbs is well and in India.

29 October

18th Note, one page.

Feeling somewhat better this morning. Still feverish and poor appetite. Had a fairly good night.

As I was unable to get up, sent my message down to Bangs in the fish place. Hope he gets it all right.

Have a feeling that Elizabeth may be writing to me soon.

Although we contributed $6 to the Mess this month, the food is such that people have returned from lunch today and opened tins of fish and bully in the Mess.

30 October
Still little fever, but much improved and enjoyed the better part of my meals today.

31 October
Lived in hope of a letter from you all day, but none came. Now Bloom tells me that he too received one last week. Why can't you write to me Elizabeth, surely you can find a way too. Makes me feel pretty miserable.

Went downstairs for lunch, first time for a week, felt quite dizzy and my legs awfully weak. Expect they'll soon recover though.

Lecture [on the] 'Slim River Fiasco' by Lt Col Collins who had his FA up there. It was well told and what a muddle, both Brigades had received warning of a tank attack, only six came through, caused absolute chaos and defeat of our forces. Took Slim Bridge with three old tanks.

31 October
Lecture by the schoolmaster of the HMAS *Perth*.

1 November
10.00 am. Bad tidings that 20 MOs and 400 men are to leave here within the next few days. Caused quite a stir up in the room, the names are coming out slowly – Malcolm, MacFarlane, Vardy, Frankland. So far I'm off.

Took a slow walk to SA and looked over the sea towards Pengerang and mused awhile. Very few people about there now, but in the Java camp, what a motley crowd and babble of tongues.

150 Officers from SA to leave by the weekend with our batch who are to form the nucleus of a hospital.

De Soldenoff is the surgeon to go, may be more peaceful in the Mess now.

2 November
19th Note, one page
Back to work but my knees are feeling pretty shaky. The stairs I find are exhausting.

Maj S. called just before lunch so I gave him another note; he's extremely hopeful of getting it through. I said Bloom was on the party and now he has managed to get off. Freddy will be mighty disturbed until she hears to the contrary.

MacFarlane is still dashing about all over the place like a frightened hen, making efforts to get off this party. All yesterday's list of names have been altered except for a few, as Lt Col Bassett is going and taking his own FA folk as far as possible; there's much squabbling as to who is to go.

Our news system has revived, being read out at a meal everyday, [which] put a stop to some of these wild rumours.

3 November

Maj Sullivan has come to live in our Mess and Squadron Leader Farrell has gone out pending his going away on the 6th.

Patient admitted to Best's ward from the Singapore gaol where he is doing solitary confinement (five years) for attempting to escape from a Bangkok camp. He says conditions up there are quite good, accommodation ok, meat daily and chicken every third day, plenty of fresh vegetables as well. Knows nothing of the health state. Attempted escape with seven to ten others RASC of 18th Div, making for Calcutta, but were only at large for 21 hours before Thais gave them up. This was in July and he was sent down to Singapore for his punishment.

4 November

More furniture has been salvaged from other Messes that have cleared out; we look more than ever like a junk shop and much of the stuff looks bug infested. Dartboard, scoreboard etc has been set up at one end and is already in full use. Singles champion wears the padre's square cap.

Some of 'B' Mess have already moved in to floor with us, we'll be a terrific crowd in a few days.

Blackout tonight and possibly tomorrow as well.

5 November

Vardy is still packing and repacking, one can hardly lift his kit bag as it is. Soldenoff walks up and down in a confused state. Lt Col MacFarlane still not sure if he is going or not, or what is the best policy to adopt. Later – the rumour that all Lt Col left behind are to get ready for Japan has cheered him up, [as] he thinks he would rather go north to Bangkok than to Japan.

A limited amount of medical stores has been allowed by the Nips, viz two trunkfuls only. Our chaps are taking as much kit as possible but the Nips have been leaving stuff behind in the gun park!

6 November

Up quite early and walked to 18th Div gun park to see Vardy, Soldenoff and others off. Away by 9.00 am packed like sardines on the trucks, no room to move even one's hands, control ones [those in charge of order] on the trucks had to stand. Many a tearful eye as the trucks went off, though it was like a school party going off and there was much laughing and joking. Malcolm had his usual self-confident swear, and Mac' was querulous even to the last, eventually glad to get away, I think, because of the new rumour that Lt Cols may be going off to Formosa shortly and we shall all be breaking up over here.

I decide that I must make or acquire a 'pack' from somewhere in case we are given short marching notice. We draw lots for the bed Vardy left, [and] I have it to sleep on tonight!!

?? News that the 8th Army has had a big victory in Egypt and is advancing.

7 November

Hear that 19th note went through this morning, hope it's successful.

Saw Sgt Blackhurst of the Sanitary Squad looking very perplexed with his fatigue squad of Dutch and Javanese who don't understand his English; seemed to be several high officers in the party.

Had a somewhat uncomfortable night on a camp cot after eight months. Spent the afternoon cutting out and doing the preliminary stitching of a rucksack, fear it is a little small to my dimensions. Dutch packs are more serviceable than our army pattern, [I must] try and procure one of them! MacGregor has already got hold of one.

?? Libyan news is still good. Advance continues there.

8 November

Secured a flag for the afternoon, took Pitt, Best, Cooper, Houghton and much cocoa in thermos and water bottles. Visited Lord de Romsey's pig farm, 65 pigs of all sizes in quite decently arranged pens. Pitt took a few snaps. Then on down the Telok Palin road but we arrived at the wrong part of the coast through a *kampong*; beat it back before the Nip sentries at the point had time to follow up, picked up a few coconuts, [then] back to 18th Div. Ate the coconuts and then out again, to a lovely weekend bungalow along a pretty mangrove avenue full of mosquitoes that were pitifully hungry and fed voraciously off everybody, dozens at a time on bare backs and backsides as Pitt and Austin visited the latrines! Delightful place to spend a quiet day, solitude, quiet and jungle closing in.

10 November

As/Surgeon Perrera has been posted to the Lab. My staff is quite large now and includes:

>   A/S George
>   Perrera
>   S/Sgt Cooper
>   Sgt Houghton
>   Pte Wharton

Work is continuing lighter these days so I find more time to do a little reading and take an interest in special things.

Doing two lots of Kahns this week.

12 November

Blackout tonight again.

Woken up at 6.30 am by a Nip officer in the room looking for the CO re blackout as from this morning. The conversation between the Nip, the old and new CO was extremely humorous – each sentence ending with 'Now!' 'Farts' and noises off butting in the while.

13 November

Blackout again tonight, and late breakfast as kitchen fires cannot be lighted early enough to get the rice cooked.

Some Nips came up to the officers' ward and put on the lights after 9.00 pm. There was much shouting of 'Lights out!' etc. We were enjoying a delightful gramophone recital – excellent records for a POW camp.

Later – we discover that it's no longer a blackout but our Command, to make sure of being right, had the local order, same mistake as last time!

?? News is increasingly good, big advance in Africa; New Guinea and Solomons slow but doing all right.

14 November

We were all up early for our first local roll call at 8.15 am. Anyway couldn't have slept much because of nine fighter planes which flew out over us at 7.30 am. Nips are a bit more active in the air these days than they have been for months.

The Dutchmen are wandering all over the place and ride on the ferry services; these are being discontinued and limitation of movement is brought into force again.

Best, Gawn and I visit SA, [and] we inspect the old Battle Rooms where the Brig used to work during bombing protected by yards of concrete, also the Fire Control Station on Temple Hill. One of the finest views in Changi, now occupied by three boreholes upon which B. sat and admired the view while he did his business.

15 November

Austin B. has got a flag and we can go for a swim after lunch, although our MC has imposed a lot of restrictions on moving from area to area.

Gorgeous afternoon, walked by cemetery outside 11th Div, lost between there and the sea, back round the creek to Duncan Roberts' house, quite high water so we had a good swim, good to feel the sea water around one again; couldn't swim much, easily tired but played about for about two hours. Then out and drank cocoa. B. broke my thermos too. Lazed on the verandah while ... swam amongst a mass of jellyfish that suddenly appeared, [and] he was eventually stung on his glans penis well and truly. We all laughed but pretty painful for him.

16 November

Used some of the washing 'Blue' that I found in SA on Saturday for my sheet, of course it came out all patchy – but clean, and has a lovely light blue colour now. The boiling of articles on the Lab hot plate is a boon, and it does more work in that line than for the Lab.

18 November

We received our $20 pay this evening from the IJA. Mess took $9.0 and as MC had loaned us all $5.0 before, that was also deducted, so it comes down to $6.0.

Heard earlier that the possibility of hearing from you E. is extremely remote, that M.? Shepherd has been arrested for note carrying, he fumbled a matchbox, and a few others have also been given solitary confinement for a period including a Mrs McMoran found with notes or something. So I still have to hope that you will be got out of this soon.

19 November

Making progress with my Entomology revision and note making. Work a little less though there have been more Kahns to do owing to the Yanks and Dutch coming in in such numbers.

20 November

Meeting of the Medical Society.

Cruickshank and Maj Hunt read papers on the March–April epidemic of encephalitis which we had here of 37 and 12 (Aussy) cases quoted, possibly more in hospital even now. One of the best papers yet; a suggestion was put forward of a relation to dengue fever.

Cinema hall staged first show of the season. SA concert party. Full to capacity and a good show – band, vocalist, good compere, short acts and three Javanese Dutch. Latter were awfully good as harmonists and one could sing soprano like a bell. One Yank musician was good too.

?? News is still good – African events moving fast.

21 November

We hear that Maj Gen Beckwith Smith of 18th Div has died in Formosa of diphtheria and cardiac failure. Nips had it in the *Syonan Times*.

They sent the hospital 1.3×10^6 units of antitoxin in a bottle yesterday.

Apparently the fact that we had a concert in our hall last night has rather riled the 18th Div and they don't want to entertain our Area any more – blaming the ban on the hospital. It came from MC and had been in force a long time before their show was closed down last week – and their theatre is the most ill-ventilated in the place.

IJA came and removed the flags from the cinema hall, Union Jack, Stars and Stripes, Dutch tricolour.

22 November

New notice out about the diagnosis of malaria, but the delay in treatment is between time patient moves in and time the MO sees him. Two cases in at 3.30 pm diagnosed BT malaria, but not seen until 7.00 pm and later by their MO.

Had a long talk with Lt Col Strachan on the subject of malaria and treatment; he's 'agin' intravenous injection of quinine and I'm all for it, used properly. So far been used twice and each time wrongly and the man has died. I feel that the malaria wards are run by the wrong people, [with] no experience (even yet) of the disease and its manifestations, all GP or newly qualified men.

Other medical depts are also pretty slack, mainly due to MOs.

23 November

Canteen got a lot of cigarettes in yesterday, all sold by mid-day. So far the IJA has been most unsuccessful in running the canteens, no food for at least a month now – so our money is not much use at the present.

Morning and evening roll call parades are still on; so far the Nips have not been along to inspect us at all, though the areas are being regularly visited.

Hardly any shipping in and out of the Naval Base, [and] very little air activity either.

Syonan Times – beriberi bad in Penang. Dr N.K. Menon says that he picked out over 60 cases in a walk down one street alone.

24 November

Strachan was in today, discussed malaria in this camp, said that of our 60,000 in here only 412 new cases in the area to date, but over 2000 cases altogether.

Talked of a course of lectures on malaria; I am doing the Pathology and Lab. Techniques side of it.

Syonan Times of Sat 21st says Eden said in House of Commons that reports say that the POW camps in Bangkok are now being run well, and no epidemics of sickness etc.

News still continues good, no mention of real events in the local rag which says great new Axis gains, never a loss to them on any front, nothing of Allied advances. Darlan [who ordered French troops to cooperate with the Allies after Operation *Torch*] they denounce as a traitor.

25 November

Another 'bum sticking parade' today of Gen Heath and others who are to go off to Formosa (Taiwan) shortly; party 1000 altogether.

Nips in the *Syonan Times* now claiming destruction of 42 American cruisers since outbreak of this war! They have scored a victory in each naval battle in the Solomons according to their reports, but say nothing of affairs in New Guinea.

Dacca has at last come over to Free French side, also the battleship *Richelieu*, some cruisers and other vessels.

'Gona' in New Guinea is taken, but we can't quite place it.

26 November

We are getting rain almost daily now, good heavy downpours.

Watched the 197 FA beat the Selarang Dutch by 5–0 in soccer. Game spoilt by the watery slippery surface and the nippy little Dutchmen couldn't keep their feet, [but] their goalkeeper was superb.

We all signed our names for next month's pay already, probably won't get it until the middle of December, [and] still absolutely nothing in the canteen to purchase – no food and our Red Cross stocks in the Mess are steadily going down. Mess secretary says there's only enough for about two weeks and then we go on to basic rations once more and I am hungrier than ever these days.

27 November

More cigarettes and cheroots came into the canteen, it's all the IJA seem to be giving it. Some of this new lot are pretty powerful too; Tom Smiley required resuscitation after 20 puffs at one cigarette and a man was admitted to hospital after smoking another elsewhere.

Hospital is almost international these days; a walk through the wards and we see all colours and faces, Yanks, Javanese, Dutch-Malay, Dutch and all manner of uniforms. The Americans seem awfully nice fellows, much pleasanter and certainly more knowledgeable than the average British 'Tommy'.

28 November

Hospital area vs. 18th Div Dutch at 5.00 pm. We all went down to see the match but alas, the Dutch didn't arrive, most disappointing.

29 November

This morning went and had a tooth $+_5$ filled by Forbes Finlayson; he was good and skilful, caused little pain in spite of boring and chiselling. Won't have to pick out nuts from a cavity anymore now.

30 November

Strachan delivered his first lecture, many charts and specimens accompanying it. It opened with the biggest attendance yet for any group of medical lectures so far given.

Elizabeth, we should be celebrating tonight [St Andrew's Day], perhaps next year it will be so – let us live, love and hope for it – what a longing to see you once again, all these long blank months.

2 December
Maj B. came in today, says no possibility of news at present to E. Starvation in Singapore is increasing and becoming more evident than before.

Four Nip vessels, all big transports, 8000–20,000 tons, went out this a.m. from Naval Base, one was a NYK passenger boat of peacetime, it looked fine. Two were loaded with troops; wonder if they're off to New Guinea.

3 December
Lecture [on] Pathology of Malaria by Capt. J.E. himself, S. followed for a few minutes on Immunity. I had out four good slides, the cerebral cortex smear was most favourably commented on – class was still extremely well attended, including Dutch and Americans. I felt a bit nervous at the beginning, but warmed to it later, even though J.T. and ADMS were present.

More Nip vessels passing in and out of Naval Base; a heavy cruiser left this morning. They must be preparing for something – ? air attack on India to counter the North African affair.

Strong rumours of the Red Cross vessel arriving in a few days and may be with some letters for us as well.

4 December
How we look forward to our Bulletins these days, told after the style of a church service by Padre W. [Wearne]; he adds his bit and makes things dramatic enough. It does us all much good and I must say our morale is not in the least down – although the Nips seem to think that the war as far as Malaya is concerned is over; sometimes they even suggest that as the end ?? is near we shall all be sent out of their territory soon.

Changi Medical Society Clinical Meeting. I showed more malarial slides and one fatal case. Others were awfully good too, two Bantis, peculiar TB, two hearts, two not yet diagnosed, two painful feet E. hypertensia and J.T.'s hand injuries. Well attended and too many cases again. Discussion not long enough; we all thought of our meals.

5 December
Canteen has got in yet more tobacco. I managed to buy some bananas, oranges, peanuts and four eggs so I live well for the next few days.

6 December
Blackout.
Rain, rain, rain – all day. During afternoon patient from Naval Base came in. L.A.C. White with malaria ST f 31% of red blood cells infected; has been ill for 10 days but the Japs would not let him come up for treatment.
Nips at roll call again, the little B........, and later they rushed up on cycles to put out all our lights. Prison and town were out as well this night.

7 December
Blackout.
Yet more rain and it blew and blew, into the Lab and flooded the cinema where Strachan was trying to lecture, awful din on the roof, 6in of water down at the front – lecture ultimately abandoned.
L.A.C. White ST malaria of yesterday died this evening.
Nips were at roll call again this evening and also gave the order that we were to maintain a blackout again – but fishing lights were on, so were the prison and those of Singapore. The *Syonan Times* said 'The Great World' was reopening tonight.
Still reading *Memoirs of a British Agent* [by] Bruce Lockhart – very good.
News not so cheerful, hear the full Pearl Harbor losses.

8 December
Blackout.
Rain and more of it, off and on all day, everything getting awfully damp and smelly.
IJA are celebrating the beginning of the Great Asia War today; we think that they have imposed 'no lights' for us for four days as a minor irritation, and to lower our morale. We don't like it, especially as the gaol and Singapore are a blaze of lights in the inky dull nights we are having. Don't think they could have had much of their outdoor celebrations with this awful weather.
Received $10/- of pay for last month. Canteen has some stores but very expensive, eg. Fish is up to 90 cents/tin from original 55–60 cents.

But tobacco is down and folk who can afford it are smoking as much as ever before.

9 December
   Blackout.
   Thank goodness it's last night of blackness. Rain, rain all day blowing from all sides. We had a musical gramophone recital up in our Mess.
   We hear Churchill's 'optimistic' message to all internees out here, it's all very well but how many years more of this! These Nips are past masters at causing minor irritations and pinpricks.

10 December
   Rain for yet another day, plenty of it. Minor floods all over the place out here. This is the fifth day of continuous downpour.
   Dewar was in from town, [and] took some Fields stain away, said that the blackout was a real alarm and the Nips in town were really scared, the locals too were expecting some sort of a sign by the Allies on this anniversary so were not a little disappointed but there was a rumour that planes came over KL. More Nip casualties came to Singapore from ??, mostly head injuries and were taken to a hospital in Seletar. The General and Alexandra I hear are full, malaria is pretty rife amongst them.
   It's grand to have lights once again at night.

11 December
   20th Note, half a page.
   The sun is out after days so all the bins are full of washing out drying, but the evening threatens rain.
   Strong rumours that letters from England have arrived in and are being sorted tomorrow; an excited voice yelled it at the window of the Lab as I sat writing greetings to Elizabeth – hoping that Cordiner will be returned to the gaol in a day or so.

12 December
   Tidd went up to the supervisor's office early this morning to sort letters. Returned late and tells us that there's only about 40 for our whole area, all from home; about six officers are lucky recipients. I am certainly not one of the fortunate ones. The letters seem to have come through Tokyo Red Cross or Vatican City, and were written end of July.

Went up to M2 and wished Cordiner goodbye and good luck, with plenty of advice and warnings.

13 December

Went to Evensong to hear Douglas G. deliver the sermon. He was short and sweet, I liked the service. To my astonishment Cordiner turned up at it, says he has to go for good and all tomorrow morning. The Nips seem to be most careful about reclassifying anyone a civilian; three other civilian patients we have at the moment, they are not inclined to take over.

14 December

Rain again.

Had a very quiet comfortable night but the bugs are everywhere in this new block, all lean and hungry, so we'll have to disinfect more frequently.

Hear that Mr Cordiner got to the Prison and in quite safely. Pte Bates took his luggage in and had a long talk with many of the women; they look well, shabbily dressed, babies carried on mothers' backs, several appeared to be wearing QA badges but all in civilian dress; thinks he saw Beth Murray of 20 CGH at some distance but wasn't able to talk to her.

Didn't see Elizabeth at all; apparently they are allowed out periodically and men and women to mix at certain times, he saw them together this morning. Also the women pushing a 'Changi Truck'.

?? Flash – Rommel's army retreating again from El Agheila.

15 December

Find eggs [of] helminthes [worms] in old Tidd's stool; he now has a carbuncle, glycosuria, and we still query his TB.

Went up to the Office and arranged that Bloom and I be sent up to the prison when more of the civilian patients are being interned, [so] there might be a chance to see you Elizabeth – this only for Christmas.

16 December

Bloom came up with a rumour that the Nips wanted a list of those with relatives in the gaol – our hopes soar again – but our office hasn't had it yet. Meanwhile patients and men are making dolls and other toys for the children in there, and I hear that 11th Div want to run a Fun Fair on their *padang* for the kiddies – if the IJA allow it.

?? Flash – at last we hear that Burma has fallen.

17 December

Letters, long letters from home for lots of folk; how is it they get theirs and I do not, surely Mother and all know that a letter has been allowed – and the little yellow apes won't allow any from prison either.

New IJA GOC for our POW camp did an 'inspection' this morning, came about an hour late, drove to the office, walked through M^2 and drove away. Big, surly looking Jap, mass of decorations including an MC and other Great War decorations.

Fixed our reading light by the washbasins; it works now.

Strachan gave a good lecture today.

Maj Maynard [gave] Bacteriology lecture in Aussy Mess – on theories of bacterial metabolism.

?? Flash – Burma taken, but fighting still goes on there.

18 December

Ledingham's wife said it was the third letter she had written and was very brief. Some received letters addressed to 'Changi Hospital' direct, others to POW Tokyo. Saw Matheson and Sgt Jenkins up from town; latter has had more letters, now through Ally's store. M. has established a regular correspondence for himself.

J. told me the story of the Nip sentry watching a game of poker; awkward, one said 'Couldn't play with the little yellow B……. standing by' – pause, then the Nip replies in Yank 'Cut out the little yellow B……., I'm waiting to be offered a hand.'

We think the Red Cross vessel has gone on to Bangkok.

Changi Medical Society meeting; we had a lecture by a Dutch officer on 'Volcanoes in Java', very original and interesting.

19 December

My depression is about at its worst. No visiting to be allowed to see relatives in the gaol, no personal money can be sent, no Christmas party, maybe the Nips will allow a message!! I feel our Command is not trying all they might in this matter; none of them have any personal interest in the matter. Irritates (and rather humiliates) me when I have to tell folk that I last knew E. was well in June last; others know about their wives, what could be wrong? Even my interest in a wife begins to flag under the conditions.

McGarrity's letter says his pay is still being credited at home, so I hope that mine is too, and Mother's getting some of it.

We have to move again out of R Block; certainly looks as though Command has spite against the doctors, always have in this camp.

20 December

Feel that our MOs have never had a square deal. Now we are 24 in the billiard room of the NAAFI 18th Div area, as crowded as when we first arrived out in Changi. We'd not have been so if our OC was a bit stronger and if MC had a medical representation at the space re-allocating conference. We have a good kitchen but lighting and privacy is out of it altogether. The morning spent moving in, carried two lockers with MacGregor; the lighting circuits have all been interfered with so at present we have to be content with just four lights – cut holes in the concrete walls to fit up hanging lines etc. I have a pleasant airy place.

Official – No more meat issue from the IJA, all the cold storage stocks have given out.

21 December

Air Raid warning in Singapore.

Feeling awfully depressed and fed up, [as] we hear that there is to be no visiting of relations and maybe no letters either to the gaol. Elizabeth I have not heard from you since end of June. What's wrong?

Opening Night of Pavilion Theatre

Seats by pre-booking only, I get one for this momentous first night through Wearne. Queues, hall packed, lovely lighting. The two large murals at the back are excellent, fill the wall space, also fitting frescoes by the box office done by [space] of *Lilliput* magazine fame. Top lights fade out then the stage lights display to advantage.

23 December

Up early and over to 11th Div by 9.00 am. Collected toys and cash and walked to the prison. Saw the huge garden we are cultivating in the valley below Selarang. Rubber charred at the bend. Curran camp manned by Sikhs of 21 Mtn Batty and also RIASC [Royal Indian Army Service Corps] people. Much waiting about, emptied out the toys at the Counsel House, made a list out of the things, left the books as the IJA would not pass them, put the presents back on the trucks, then <u>you</u> passed, darling (? 11.30 am) dressed in white uniform. I was talking to a Nip Officer and wonder if you saw me at all, to pass me so close and not know!! I was the only one with a Red Cross on. Made me feel deeply how much I miss you and just want to crush you to me – and be just ourselves again. Went all 'blank', the Nip giving me your list of presents must have thought I was mad – and away you went bound for Singapore via Tampines Road. We went up to the outer gate at Nip NCO then to the inner and deposited the toys and handed over $11,000. Talked to Johns and ?Rendle, [and] sent a message to you Elizabeth. Returned slowly. I hung about expecting you to return but never did – it was too much to expect. Jack Draper, I hear, was in camp in Singapore.

24 December
   Air Raid warning [in] Singapore last night.
   All excitement today of the intended visit to the prison tomorrow; time is passing slowly for a change. All over the camp last choir practices are going on. I don't know quite what to do with myself. Saw Maj Bevan who gave me $10/- for you Elizabeth. I shaved off my little moustache after supper and feel quite naked without it. Feel awfully weary and to bed early. Time is now to be 11.00 am tomorrow and not 5.00 pm as originally ordered. Much carolling tonight.

25 December
   <u>Shortest half hour of my life</u>
   Woke very early, much singing all over of carols, we even heard a band on the hill above us. Light drizzle continues after the storm of last night. We assemble at Office at 10.00 am for the ambulance [–] it fetched civilians looking very ill [–] then the journey down. Mul', Bloom and I, Jenkins and others, turned up from Singapore in time, including one chap with a duck. We hung about for 1½ hours, 26 in all; we checked and re-checked then marched to south wall of 'H.M. Prison 1936' where we met again MY OWN DARLING – what a sensation and you promise me a present of a child when we get out, isn't that wonderful to live for. 12.30 pm–1.00 pm. and it's all over and finished until when??
   Night; a green light just shows where you are now. Sleep well.

26 December
   Hear that Darlan has been assassinated.
   All day anorexia, funny feeling in my stomach as though I had just left E. at the beginning of this internment. Can't keep my mind off thinking of

her and her lovely promise of a present to me at a later date – must wait, wait, wait, be patient, it'll be all the sweeter then. Oh darling. Spent much of the day recounting the story of the visit, and had to tell all our friends about you; had an endless stream of visitors.

Went swimming after lunch until 4.00 pm, back for tea and England v Scotland soccer match. Scots XI was piped on to the pitch. We won 3–0. Tell E.

Good night my sweet.

27 December

Still thinking of a promise of a child, what joy has suddenly awakened in this POW camp. Off my food and feel rather depressed all day.

Really couldn't concentrate on any work during the morning. Still answering enquiries about the Gaol. Read Lockhart's *Retreat from Glory* all the afternoon, then visited Rogers of the RASC. His wife Kathleen must have plenty of cash, he reckons ? > $1000. I wonder how you are managing, Elizabeth.

No meat issue now, instead get 4oz of bony fish for four days; it's not very much, so that all meals except two a week should be pure rice.

28 December

A very busy morning, [with] all the accumulated work of holidays coming in. More units from town have come in; in a few days there will be no more troops (British) outside of Changi.

Prepared my share of the lecture 'Diagnosis of Malaria' this afternoon and it went down quite well. Always seems to rain at the time of these lectures.

Still no further sign of a Red Cross vessel; our stocks of bully beef are now dwindling rapidly, though we only eat about ⅙ oz per head daily.

Had a bit of 'Durian' this morning, it has a most extraordinary taste.

Tone of news remains good.

Buna has not fallen yet!

What's going on in Burma?

Celebrity Concert at cinema hall.

29 December

Yet more camps have come in from Singapore but the areas are still by no means crowded. Gawn and I took a pleasant walk by the swamps in 18th Div, brought back some sugar cane and chewed it after supper.

Poverty and famine is increasing in town, rice ration is 15 katties a month (usually [one per] day) and is 20–24 cents/katty (usually 4 cents). Beriberi must be increasing, if even Malay and Tamil doctors comment on it in the *Syonan Times*.

George I. (mortuary department) has an excellent razor blade sharpener so I should be able to last well with my present blades.

These fellows from Singapore have slipped badly, very dirty, unkempt, uncared for appearance, ringworm all over – due to the conditions they've been living under.

30 December

IJA seem to be doing roll calls more carefully these evenings, though since we have been through the wire they have never counted us; others are counted daily almost and a strict parade too.

Yet more rain today, weather is remaining pleasant and cool though.

Interesting lecture in the Mosque at Indian Lines [of] 18 Div 'Why France went to war'; speaker Lt Col Aubrey RA painted a pretty correct pathetic picture of the French nation.

Hear of death of Sir N. Henderson.

Wonder why all the prison lights were on at 0030 hours this morning; ask Elizabeth later!

31 December

IJA have made us all an issue of 2oz spirits and ²⁄₇ tin of pineapple to celebrate the New Year. Had our 'firewater' at supper, really raised the roof off my mouth, tasted like liqueur brandy gone bad. Several people who had three to four portions were definitely tight; MacGregor had a still going in the mortuary and several MO imbibed there. Our meals were not very bright, just as bad as Christmas Day.

Thinking of what's happening in the prison, are you drinking to our future happiness Elizabeth. We see your lights burning until 11.00 pm.

Much shouting and singing all over our camp and at 12 midnight, bells ringing and imitation hooters all over the camp, terrific noise. Party from 'C' Mess paid us a visit and sang us 'good cheer' in the early hours.

Good bye '42.

Nip Gestapo plain-clothes men came in and escorted away Lt Col Simmons AG [Acting General] HQ MC, Maj Wyatt 'G.' Aussy, Roberts of Red Cross service. Went through their kit and papers and removed diaries etc. We are all wondering what it's about.

Last Statement of Accounts from FCMA Poona for month of Dec. 1941:

Nat Credit Rs 566/3.

Later (1944) [note added to diary over a year later]

Simmons was returned in a few days, Wyatt and Roberts are to spend some time in Outram Rd Gaol for some offence?? [For] intriguing with Chinese and [an] attempt to escape.

Chapter 5

Jack's diary – 1943

1 January

No further news of those taken away yesterday. All their belongings were thoroughly searched. Mattresses and pillows torn open etc. Rumours are flying about, some say they've been getting out information, others that it's a connection with black market sale of Red Cross goods – however Capt James, Interpreter, has been sent back to this camp after long residence up at IJA HQ near the gaol; he has always seemed very pro Nip.

England v Scotland soccer at SA and again we win 5–0 before a huge crowd there. Holiday everywhere.

2 January

Watched a League rugger match on our ground; British team is improving at the game. Visited SA to see Diver, more folk in from Java including Brig Blackburn (AIF) [Australian Imperial Force] and a General Sitwell and other 'red bands'. I felt I was visiting a foreign town to hear the variety of tongues there; Yanks all seemed very jovial and jocular. Called in at the SSVF [Straits Settlement Volunteer Force] camp at RA Mess Temple Hill but didn't see Len Marsh. They live very poorly now, lie only on boards and cover with rags. Nips took away Lt Col Glyn White (Aussy DDMS) and also 'Black Jack' Galleghan (OC Troops AIF).

3 January

All abuzz this morning, wondering about the new Nip arrests; they took a radio set in SA too last night. No Sikh guards to be seen anywhere today, [but] occasionally Nips patrol the roads instead.

Visited Selarang after lunch, then 11th Div, got the 'Borehole', found that much of what we heard this morning is rumour. De Moubray didn't see his wife after all on Christmas Day, but hopes to get permission as yet. Also saw Len Marsh today, he looks well, bit thinner, says he's been working in QM stores and put on weight there. Had many stories to tell; the local population is decidedly pro British now, even those who were pro Nip before have turned.

Evening – dined with Diver at Malay Regt Mess, vegetarian meal but quite decent. After it, Yanks and Dutch gathered for bridge and a gossip. Officer from the 'Film Unit' arrived and told some of his experiences with the Nips. He too says feeling is pro British everywhere.

10,000 men arriving from Java. Several leading Dutch are here including Dutch NEI [Netherlands East Indies] Governor General. Air Vice-Marshal Maltby, General Sitwell are already in SA waiting to move overseas.

5 January

Simmons has been released after a short uncomfortable stay in a dirty cell with little to eat. He was not the right man apparently. Other two are still in there.

Went out and collected some more sugar cane to suck at. Our food is steadily getting worse, all carbohydrates these days, about four prawns for four days as fish issue.

6 January

Went with Wallace gathering durians, found the Nip sentries already at our tree having a huge feed; they laughed at us, but we found three at the lower group of trees, [and] ate them in the Lab.

'Great Cortini' show at 8.30 pm. Glendinning over for supper but would not stay and see it. First class performance with 12 [in] orchestra, made bodies hang in the air, disappear, card tricks, Chinese rings and everything.

7 January

About 3000 more Dutch and a few Yanks have arrived from Java, and some 1500 have gone away today, it's said overseas.

8 January

About seven officers and men went up to the Supervisor's Office and were given wireless messages from their relations in India, South Africa and England and they were allowed to reply to these. Wonder if you got one, Elizabeth. Of course I am unlucky again.

Meeting of Changi Medical Society at which our diphtheria outbreak was talked on, rather poorly I thought. No discussion followed for lack of time.

9 January

Excellent lecture tonight by Maj Wild on 'Japan and its history'; estimated that this war would last at least five years, and Japan would fail by revolution. Stories from River Valley camp – the civilian with a radio set when tobacco was being looked for, 'the elastic bomb crater' near a rich godown [warehouse] at the docks and the Nip sentry's talk on stealing to Aussies. Man with pistol and 20 rounds found on tobacco search at Thompson Road camp, [but] nothing happened to him.

10 January

Pte Crustyen (Dutch Army) 'Cortini' has gone with the 2000 batch this morning after a most successful week of showing to a full house every night. Destroyed much of his outfit, but took the 'rings' with him. I learned the secret of some of his tricks today.

Finlayson filled another tooth +^{4}

11 January

I hear that Yanks and Aussies are eating dogs now, several including Sgt Barrowman's fat black pup have disappeared. Purvis was offered $3.0 for his big black dog as well. I am not surprised as the food is entirely carbohydrate now, no protein to mention, a trace (1oz) of fish twice a week.

12 January

Wish old Wearne wouldn't go into a trance when he is giving out the 'weather report' [war news] which he modifies and comments on as the mood fits him instead of giving it neat to us.

13 January

Short time after the 'weather report' two Nips suddenly appeared round our mess, just snooping about?? We are getting a trifle tired of being prisoners now and wonder when our forces are really going to do something in the way of attack; so far all the efforts seem small. The weather is lovely and cool; in fact shower water is really cold these days.

Now that a nice lot of Dutch forces have come in, we hear that they will be leaving again at 650 a day for four days.

14 January
   Wrote [to] Mother and Olwen.

15 January
   Did another blood sugar curve today and had to repair the plunger. Roll call today was tedious, stood about a long time then Nip soldier came to do the check, first dressed us by pushing us back and forth; I was pushed into line back to front. Then one NCO stood in front and we had to 'look' at him on the command and Bull saluted. The apes were looking about to slap somebody.

16 January
   A West African from NEI now does the German classes; good teacher, and is not afraid of expression. Also teaching Phonetics, Spanish, French and is attached as interpreter to the hospital.

17 January
   'More About London's Old Pubs' by Sgt Newman last night. There is an awful lot I want to see when I get home again.
   Am reading *London Diary* by Quentin Reynold; he ought to be in here to write a story for the *Express*. Got it out of the Aussy Library, which I joined by handing in *The Last of the Mohicans*.
   Several thousand Dutch have just arrived and some left this morning.

18 January
   We were able to buy much from the canteen today; Chiltern got us bananas, peanuts and *gula malacca* [cane sugar]. I seemed to get quite a store of food for $1.50. It would be awfully difficult if one couldn't supplement the diet these days. I take about one ounce of rice polishings extra as well as that mixed in with the food.
   Shortly deficiency diseases will be appearing again; that Red Cross boat is long overdue.
   Hope you all are doing a little better in the gaol, my love.

19 January
   More and more Dutch have been arriving all the afternoon; believe about 4000 in the last few days. They are disagreeable dissatisfied patients and many suffer from 'plumbi pendulosa' but one of them has today

swallowed some mercuric chloride tablets in a suicide attempt, [and] last fellow slashed his wrists but the surgeons thwarted his attempts.

British have only had one death (a bacillary dysentery) so far in the New Year, and the Aussies two, one an accident case.

20 January

Cruiser still at the end of Layang Pier, it's been there about a week now, having a rest? Rumour has it that there are a few cases of typhus fever aboard.

Syonan Sinbun reports a case from Penang of a youth convicted of stealing and selling dogs for food; a note adds 'of course there is no shortage of meat on the island now'! Says who! The anti-malarial coolies are hardly even getting their rice ration of 15 katties a month, and the black market is thriving in town.

21 January

A London school has been bombed, 40 children and six teachers killed; hope Olwen isn't there!

The IJA have turned down all the requests recently put up for more and better food; permits to the swamps for morning work, permission for those who missed seeing their wives at Christmas to see them now. The food question is really bad – no protein for weeks now, 'Changi balls' is appearing again, and sore mouths too. Nobody is allowed to town either to do local purchases as Roberts (Red Cross) abused his privilege in some way, so they will not open it again; he is said to be [doing] nine months solitary in Singapore.

Maj Wyatt is still here after his appendectomy but no-one talks about him and he has a Nip guard the whole time, [with] only one MO to visit him.

22 January

A busy full day. I find this German is getting difficult again. Rushed off to Changi Medical Society meeting on 'Amoebiasis', [where] Maj Hunt, Hutchison, Capt Young spoke. Useful points were – give a full diet, cases can have very acute onset, plenty of water in the beginning of treatment, diagnosis by faeces sigmoidoscopy, and therapeutic test. Hutch tried to say pH of an old stool was useful. Meeting ended in heated argument.

De Moubray lecture – rather pessimistic, reckons that Hitler must be finished first before Allies will attempt any real comeback out here, [so] looks like years for us out here.

23 January

A 'high person' is visiting us today; roads cleared from 1000–1300 hours, not a soul to be seen. Sentries (Nips) patrolling the roads preventing patients looking over the balconies. Queer 'inspection'. Just about 1.00 pm the retinue appear, nine cars, all sorts of flags.

Visited the coconut grove, and Austin and Steve decided to bring down some; we were successful and got five, small and rather green.

'Weather report' improving, Tripoli should soon fall.

24 January

I am getting awfully flabby and fat, so decided to play soccer; almost the whole Mess turned out at 4.00 pm – rather hot and bright. One was out with a torn abductor longus muscle during the preliminary warm-up. I was right-half, quite early I twisted my left ankle, played on, and, in the second half, went down heavily on it; agonising pain and felt nauseated. Had to limp off and lay on the grass. It was good fun and nobody else got hurt. Austin played a good game; we certainly have the makings of a good team.

25 January

At last we hear that Tripoli has fallen, but the Tunis affair seems so slow, and as for out here, we feel that we have been forgotten altogether by the Empire. Although we must see that we must wait for Hitler to be finished off first – long time. Meanwhile E., civilians, nurses and children have to spend years of their lives in prisons (literally). Is the Red Cross so impotent that they cannot influence the Nips at all? And we think there will be no more Red Cross ships allowed into the East.

Ankle swollen and blue but can get about with a stick.

26 January

The canteen has a new staff; people talked much of the acquired wealth of Cpl Garrett (Bushy) and it was said that [he] is now cashing sterling cheques. He's certainly never without cigarettes. Big stocks have come into the canteen.

Saw *Jack and the Beanstalk* at our theatre. It was good fun, especially to see the beanstalk grow and take the bucket up with it, quite like a pantomime at home.

27 January
Canteen has lots of eggs today, at 8 cents, after a couple of months, so we are all buying them like mad. Pitt, McGarrity and I had supper in the lower lavatory because of the second light; smell of urine was bad, however the fried vegetables, onions, eggs and snails dominated and we enjoyed it immensely until about 12 midnight. All water was off; we had nothing to drink until remembered some coconuts so we had their milk to wash down the meal – and did I sleep well! But I missed the usual nocturnal shower.
?? Tripoli fallen and our troops well beyond it, behind Rommel.

28 January
Up early for a bath as the water comes on early this morning. Dutch parties are still pushing off daily.

30 January
Hospital XI beat a good Dutch team from SA 5–0 in soccer. Started out well but after a goal, the Dutchmen were very demoralised and later our side was making circles round them. A good revenge for the British defeat I saw in 18th Div last evening.
After supper went over to the Cherub *padang*, 18th Div, to see some 'Horse Racing'. Well organised affair, floodlit track, bamboo spacers, numbered horses, tote etc. I laid a bet of 5 cents and looked like winning 'til the end, [but] lost by one place. Tote betting was in 5 cent units, no 'lock-ins' allowed. Provided us with a new form of entertainment.

31 January
Raining all night and pretty well all day today.

1 February
TAB ½cc today – material made by the Nips.

2 February
The whole Mess is taking quite an interest in the Atlas Moths that we hatched out of some cocoons off a tree nearby. One female is dropping

unfertilised eggs but the other has got herself a mate last night after much clatter and flapping of wings early this morning. They are firmly wed all day; the copulation is attracting many sight see-ers to our verandah. She has a wingspan of 8½ inches, and the male is smaller and ventrally attached. Wonder how he knew how to find her, how the information gets to him?

3 February

Played Mah-jong until 1.00 am up at Col Collins room, quite an enjoyable evening, and then had to wait before the showers came on downstairs. Sat in the next room reading. They have screened light there and stay up until all hours, particularly Bell and Cruickshank, but are no longer as talkative at this time as they used to be.

Our room is probably the noisiest after 'lights out', and McGarrity usually lets off some choice 'farts' as a goodnight salvo.

4 February

Strong rumours everywhere about us moving off somewhere. Today about 2000 of 18th Div have had their rectal cultures done (Bum Sticking Parade) – it seems we are all going to be done.

Then again the 'weather report' has not been so good. Nips claim a huge naval success off the Solomons so one way and another, our spirits are rather low.

Captivity seems interminable and the Allies [appear] to make no headway out here, and are slow enough against the Germans; only the Russians are doing well.

5 February

18th Div were 'bum stuck' today. More Dutch going away. There are still 20,000 British in the POW camp and about 7000 Dutch forces left.

Played soccer again today at 4.00 pm; terrifically hot sun and the glare was awful. I must say I was not very energetic – thought of Noel Coward and 'Mad dogs and Englishmen' etc. We lost 2–0.

'Weather report' is indifferent. There must be a big naval battle in the Solomons and US Navy are getting it!

8 February

TAB (Nip stuff) 1.0cc today. Gave me little general reaction but not too bad.

Interesting post mortem – old case of bronchitis, died with a couple of awful abscesses and a lung abscess, duration of 12 years since diagnosed.

Been raining more or less all day, [but] cleared a little in the evening.

9 February

RAIN, RAIN. There was to have been a big parade of 15,000 on our big *padang* this morning, not quite sure what the Nips wanted it for, however the rain has stopped it all – possibly in connection with this film work they are doing. They have almost finished filming the Malayan campaign now; doing landing scenes and fighting at Pangar Pangay (Indonesia?) now.

10 February

Still raining like mad, [but] cleared sufficiently to allow *Badger's Green*, a Sherriff play at our Palladium theatre. It was produced and acted well, but what a poor play. Our theatre is improving more and more each time I go to it. Now have a lovely curtain, superb lighting, fading of auditorium lights etc. But the whole show is run by an incompetent committee. Padre Wearne gave me a seat as though it was a great personal favour although I had booked. There is much confusion over this booking business.

11 February

RAIN, RAIN and more. Are you thinking of this day a year ago too, Elizabeth [when they were married]? Wasn't it eventful – girls with less guts than you would have turned back.

12 February

Dickie Dawson comes from SA every afternoon, collects Pitt here and they return to mortuary to do some dissecting. Just finishing an arm at the moment, and are going on to hand and neck. Parts removed from corpses and left in formalin. They managed to replace a head and neck on a corpse by a pumpkin on a stick, well sewn up in a shroud. The part is lying in formalin but insufficient, I fear, for I saw it bubbling gently today. They have several bones, bits and pieces. Other MOs go down and practice surgery every now and again. It is a good opportunity – although corpses are fewer these days.

15 February

Pitt opened a 'Fish Oval'. Have to record this now as he seems to think that he is being done down. Frankland and I form the rest of this fish combine.

?? Rostov falls to the Russians again.

17 February

Did another blood sugar tolerance curve; things worked well.

Cooked some whitebait on the lab hot plate in the afternoon and gosh, did it smell and attracted all the flies from all the latrines and kitchens to our place! This is in the nature of an experiment; Pitt fries it after the boiling process.

?? Kharkov has been retaken.

19 February

Rumour about special pay for RAMC personnel, but the Nips are first inspecting all their army forms A050's up at the hospital office.

20 February

Our syndicate has managed to buy another 12 ducklings, [and] now have 22 in the mortuary fowl run of our own. MacGregor is looking after them as his own. He is already feeding them carefully on Nutrino and some 'Bully'; where it comes from, I don't know.

21 February

England v Wales in SA rugger – very poor match indeed, Welsh won by a try. Our hospital side could turn out a better team than either.

We have another issue of postcards to send home, wonder if the first got there, and no reply as yet.

Syonan Times says negotiations are in hand for the exchange of internees, particularly women and children – raises my hopes about you again, darling.

Dance in the Aussy Hall this evening – incredible show, good dance band, floor and what 'women' turned out. They looked so real and pretty. The scene caused me quite a heartache, thought of old times, freedom – and my own darling Elizabeth.

22 February

To see Chopping and borrow his Samson Wright *Physiology*; must read some of it again.

Fancy, have a short wave receiver set which would go in a water bottle – tiny wee valves only there, but sufficient with earphones to get London.

There are plenty of bananas and eggs in at the canteen again, very high percentage of the latter are bad, about 20%, and are at 14 cents each. Pitt has brought 10lb of whitebait for our table.

23 February

Second postcard home: 'Still in good health. Saw wife Christmas Day, also well. Am interestingly occupied. Longing for news. Cheer up. Much love, J.'

No date allowed on postcard, but hope Mother infers much from this news – time, place and about E. Everybody has discussed the best wording to put in – just like sending out a very special Christmas card.

24 February

Weight is 11 stone. Am awfully flabby and lack energy – could sleep all day. My abdomen is rather large too – resolve to cut down the rice. Our table has an extra dish, our own fried whitebait for supper, and it seems to make all the difference to the meal. Sometimes fry an egg or two as well. The stove is an old Primus. Pitt is chief cook and we sit over it in the verandah; much smoke before the stove gets going properly. Everybody passes by and says 'Ah... Bisto!'

It does smell good, attracts an awful lot of bluebottles though.

25 February

Was 'bum stabbed' today; Capt Franks did me, most politely. Rods thick today and had broken off ends. Most of the hospital staff were done today, and for the first time, an Aussy officer did some of the stabbing.

In evening it was high tide, so, passing the big drain in 18th Div, took off my clothes and swam up and down it; water was quite clean too. Only trouble was one had to watch the edges all the time, about six inches in parts.

Then after supper saw *The Admirable Dyeton* by Command Players, fair, pathetic satire as they think it's funny, particularly as the same is going on now. Orchestra and production was good. Pity nobody said 'All the characters of this play are fictitious and do not refer etc'.

26 February

Bevan just been in to say that he has 20 more ducks for us, sent Griffs to SA to collect them. Quite a good lot – and, after one night, none has died.

Met de Moubray; he received a verbal from his wife on Tuesday, an Australian saltwater party met the women at the beach??

1 March

A friend of D.? Wallace has just sold a Nip a camera for $100. They celebrated the deal with a huge meal and SA gin to finish it off.

This is the first deal in cameras, normally it's in watches of good make like Rolex and Omega; these fetch $50 for a wrist model. Lighters too are on sale all over, quite cheap at $1–$2, and good makes at that.

2 March

Definite news of letters having arrived at 'The Control Offices', said to be 40 mailbags.

3 March

More in the *Syonan Times* about repatriation; they speak of second and third batches being exchanged in the near future.

4 March

Report that there has been a riot in a New Zealand internment camp, and about 40 Nips have been killed as the result of it.

RAF MS Sq Ldr Cummings, Fl/Lt Willy [and] Fl/Lt Simpson have arrived here from Java with three Dutch MOs. Came by themselves and Nips want them for special malarial work somewhere.

5 March

Changi Medical Society meeting: we saw some of the many 'Skin Conditions' of Changi including the usual scrotal dermatitis and pellagra. Followed by a talk on 'Skin Treatment' by Capt Sefton.

6 March

The 'Tables' order of pork at 14/- per lb has come in – very fatty, salted but looks awfully good. All rest of Mess is rather jealous about it.

7 March

At last the entire stocks of X-ray film are about to give out, and they can only do a little screening. This puts Beck out of a job.

We had fried pork this morning, cooked on Pitt's stove with Diesoline, very fatty but succulent with rice, gave out an awful lot of fat.

9 March

Set out for the garden area with M' and Marsden at 10.30 am, got there and hung about by the crossroads until 3.30 pm. Saw a party from the gaol of men cutting bamboo, none I knew, but wished them [good day]. Pleasant spot, and our fellows appear to be doing very little work.

If the women pass that way to the sea it would be very easy to see them and talk.

Had fish, sausages and rice for our lunch.

The 'Visiting Party' is on tomorrow so I wrote a quick note and also typed out a letter for the FCMA allotting you Rs 350/- and cancelling any previous one.

Hope you are well, darling.

10 March

Lt Barber (QM) RAMC was allowed to see his 'fiancée' with the party today. They were allowed 60 minutes today and Mrs M.' was prominent organiser. Steve C. took in my message and allotment letter, hope it gets there all right. De Moubray saw his wife and brought out much information for Bloom. Pte Bates was told by Cicely Williams 'that E. was in hospital and has ? been rather ill'. What's this all about? So much I should like to know, funny I feel quite miserable about it, hope it's nothing serious, [but] worrying me no end.

Later saw As/Surgeon James and he gave a message from his sister of Elizabeth, but I am still unhappy about her – wish she had sent a note instead.

This is Japanese Army Day.

11 March

The order about yesterday's visit was not broadcast enough so several folk have not yet seen their relations. Austin B.' is to go as my cousin-in-law. There is promise of another visit at the end of next month.

Had an awful night thinking about Elizabeth, and still no letters from home for me, according to Welch who is sorting them and brings us back a list of recipients daily. All the letters are dated back to July–August 1942, very old.

Johnny Falk got a card, [which] says he has a son.

Funny message that Bates got yesterday! Would like to have a chat with Cicely Williams.

Started on the 2800 blood slides today of the party going upcountry; all must be free of malaria.

12 March

Playing Mah-jong with the Colonel when M.' told me that he was due to visit the gaol again tomorrow. Neither B.' nor I are down to go but several who have already been once are going again, including many from SA who visited at Christmas.

<u>Next morning</u>: gave Mulvaney a message for E. and also $10/- for her, hope she gets it alright. Mrs M. wants to discourage note writing; all very well for her, she sees her Denis again and gets more frequent verbal messages.

<u>Later</u>: M. is back and E. is well and out of hospital. Talked with B.', wish he could see you.

Rumours of repatriation for them, but I am still miserable. No letters from home as yet.

At last, a letter. Olwen is the first, wonder what it is going to say – and she probably doesn't know I'm married.

Have I made a big mistake? Can't say until I'm with E. again. What a dilemma. If only our letters had gone to each other regularly during 1941.

14 March

What a mix-up this war has caused; still thinking about Olwen's letter and also E.'s health.

Hurrah! A letter from Mother. 'Mexico Pete' Eastwood only married five days before he left home, got a card to say he has a lovely baby daughter – what a man!

Take note of this, darling.

15 March

Paddy Doyle has a letter from Gwen Dowling (17 CGH) to say that only nine QA of the '13th Batch' got through to India. Ginger Black, Margot Turner and Miss Spedding (20 CGH) are certainly prisoners, perhaps in Pelembang?

Chiltern brought me a Nip Officer's blood to do a Kahn on, 'very urgent' from Command, but I feel I cannot waste antigen for our blood.

16 March

Letters from the Gaol keep trickling in slowly, one by one; the IJA here are censoring them once more and taking their time about it. It seems that they copy out each letter again.

The parties for upcountry are all now tested for malaria, rectal swabbed again, vaccinated and inoculated for plague and cholera.

Syonan Sinbun is advertising for technicians who can identify mrps, and classify mosquitoes and larvae.

17 March

I (we) are informed that our wives in the gaol have been paid today a sum of $10/- each, and this will be done every month in future.

Red Cross tried to buy some stores in town today. Prices are absurd eg [illegible]. HCl gr½ at $2/- [illegible] 1lb at $75/-, pot [illegible] 1lb at $25/-. Sulphur is a little cheaper.

Sale of unpolished rice is now restricted and only on production of a doctor's certificate and controlled rate of 0.15/katty.

19 March

Cigarette paper is so scarce that fellows are now using any thin paper; the thin leaves out of pocket bibles are fashionable.

20 March

Food getting bad again, and I have no cash to purchase with.

Len Marsh (SSVF) goes with the upcountry batch tomorrow; hearsay that they are bound for a camp at Bangkok.

By Wednesday 5000 will have gone, 2800 British and 2200 Aussies, leaving 25,000 in this camp including the Dutch.

21 March

Read and reread letter from Mother. Olwen still visiting! Stanley married. This letter is only eight months old but it is good to see that all is well at home. No cards have reached there yet. Now I have an Army number.

Went down to 18th Div Gun Park and saw Pitt off this morning. Felt quite sorry at his going; must see him again in later life and visit his sister in Kenya if I do get that way sightseeing. Feel I must see Africa and the States.

Visited Free Church to hear Padre J. Foster Haigh preach; he is really good and seems sincere.

22 March

Syonan Times says quinine is now controlled by IJA and obtainable at 0.30 for a day's quinine on a doctor's signature. There must be more malaria about.

Petrovsky left for upcountry this morning.

Churchill's latest speech is rather depressing for us out here; we have a prospect of another three and a half years of internment.

23 March

Awfully hot and glary these days.

We hear of the offensive in Tunis as having commenced at last.

24 March

Another blood sugar curve on an AIF fellow.

Think the women go out to swim today.

26 March

Letters, letters; more of them coming every evening. Some are just a side and brief (like mine) others both sides and typewritten full of news. Douglas G. has a nice long one from his wife; he's in seventh heaven. Wish Mona and Stanley had written too. Some folk have had 11–14 each. How fortune ill-treats us!

27 March

The IJA are allowing us $40.0 a month now since Col Harris had a talk with the General, but Command want all of it to spend for the general fund. We hold a meeting after lunch and, by a majority, voted the whole sum to be used as Command think fit – not without some feeling from several parties. However I felt that too much tobacco is brought into this camp, and more of that money should be spent on food by the individuals themselves. Then again we wonder if all the extra foodstuffs which this further $10 can buy will be obtainable or not. There is already difficulty in keeping the canteen stocked with *towgay* [bean sprouts], soya beans and whitebait etc, all the major accessory items of diet.

28 March

A party of 1000 AIF and British have gone overseas at short notice; Charlie Campbell RAMC went with them. He said that they are bound for Kuching to build the airfields there as they have not been able to get sufficient local labour.

30 March

MacGregor brought me up early morning tea with milk and sugar. It was lovely except that it was so early, 7.00 am. Lawson, Gawn and I relished it. We can have it daily if I take down the containers.

There's a queer story about that IMS, IMD [Indian Medical Department] and IHO are all to be amalgamated into one corps called the IAMC [Indian Army Medical Corps] and all British 'cadre' IMD are to be commissioned. Wonder how this will affect our service, terms, salaries and pension – would like to know more about it but it's reported to have come over the radio.

31 March

Hardly slept last night for mental worry and abdominal pain that would not be eased – due to soya beans and *towgay?* But of Olwen and Mother – if only Olwen had written so before, this date two years ago it would all have been different – she loves me and I, well, cannot say until I'm with E. again.

Later: the abdominal pain and mental worry are getting worse – looks like little sleep tonight!

1 April

Felt rotten all day, no fever or diarrhoea, abdomen all blown out but couldn't pass anything. Looked at my stool carefully but found nothing, not even any ova!

Still thinking much of Mother, Olwen, Home. Hoping Mona has married too. If only I could get some more news – and Elizabeth – when are we going to be together again? What a mix-up this war has caused in my life.

Went to SA to see their concert. Bevan had reserved us (Sullivan and I) some seats. Not very good, after the excellent polished show on in our area. Band is good, three or four players from the Tanglin Club and they still have the same old rhythm and expressions on their faces. What 'women' are appearing all over the place, blondes, brunettes etc!

2 April

Still haven't got over Olwen's letter – why didn't she write it before, one year or two years ago? All different now. How shall I find her at the end of all this, what has Mother to say too!

Have just had to start wearing my pair of new shorts and two 'new' shirts. The three army shirts and my three old pairs of shorts have served well for the last two years, and have to be discarded as they are so fragile now and tear very easily.

3 April

We are all getting rather tired of this, tempers rise easily, irritable, complain of everything, feel like doing nothing but sleep and eat.

The news is not helpful, all long speeches of post-war proposals etc but not for us at present – nothing. We all say what are the Yanks and British doing? Look at the Russians, although even they seem to be temporarily held up. How many more years of internment – at least three, we say. Why don't we try to get the women and children repatriated! Affairs on the Burma Front seem so swell, the Nips will take a lot more yet to beat them in war, and our folk still do not seem to realise that.

4 April

The Nips have started dismantling the huge gridiron framework buildings just by the hospital area and taking away the iron. A party of British supposed to be on the job but as usual they stand by while the little Nips get on with the job.

Food is just a mass of carbohydrate, our fish portion of prawns (200lb) for the hospital had to be thrown away again – it was so bad. This happens at least every other time so that we get about ¼oz a week of fish excluding bones. Eggs at 8 cents in the canteen; I took six out on credit.

Doug Gawn gave quite a nice sermon this morning in the Palladium.

5 April

Our ducklings are not progressing very well at the 'Mortuary Farm'. Out of 42 we have 29 left – rats killed off four – and these have stopped growing through lack of greenery. Have taken ten down to 'Pop' Farwell's run behind the cinema; plenty of good feeding ground down there and his younger ducks are four times as big as ours.

Pitt is an extraordinary chap; at breakfast he mixes his porridge with more rice polishings and Red Palm oil into a thick cement-like mixture and eats a whole plate of this. I eat *gula malacca* and salt. What does he do all day? Always late for his meals and vanishes at night, to come in about 12 midnight, breathing heavily, snorting and throwing dirty clothes about.

6 April

The Nips have started dismantling the sheds in the gun park. They number each beam and note it on a plan – most methodically, and really do work hard.

Went for a swim this morning with the Party in 18th Div. Nip guard counts out and back again, about one hour allowed. High tide, but the large numbers of jellyfish spoilt any good swimming. My first time since Christmas.

7 April

Padre Daniels is awfully upset about the canteen 'racket'. They sold him and others underweight and were rude when he complained. Lt (QM) Barber is in charge and he must be making a packet on illegitimate profits. Eg. 3g less tobacco on 1oz, and 200lb sold per week works out pretty high and that's only one item. Usually the tobacco is short by 5–8g. Very rarely does it weigh correct! Others are *gula malacca*, peanuts, bananas. People being served short do not like to make a scene when there is a huge queue standing behind.

8 April

We get paid today $25/- instead of the usual $20/-. The IJA are actually now giving us $40/- and Command taking $15/- for the Common Fund, then we pay $10/- straight to the Mess.

Whilst at Mah-jong with the OC after supper, heard about the new moves in the near future of 7000 British and Australian to go upcountry, and a hospital staff of 20. Of course, back in the dormitory there was much arguing and speculation as to who is in the party.

9 April

Commence the blood examinations of the 3000 Dutch party for upcountry, to be finished in four days. We see several packs and baggage going up to L3 'Grand Hotel', the officers' ward.

Later walked over to the Dutch café for a mug of coffee; it's awfully good, with sugar and milk. The crowd was terrific and the room full of smoke, rattle of mugs leant the place a low saloon atmosphere. Couldn't get in at all, the Dutch were in force, having been paid today. Even the canteen is cleared out of anything useful!

10 April

More and more malaria slides, and still no positives, even though they are Dutch and Javanese.

Tonight visited Selarang and saw the Aussy concert of *Pass the Baby*, quite a good farce written by one of their MOs. The young wife was very attractive and feminine; cook and maid were good too. It provided plenty of laughs. The orchestra was rather better than ours at the Palladium, 14 pieces, and the overture was a fine classical potpourri of popular pieces. They have an enormous hall and gallery, [with a] huge capacity.

News continues to be good from North Africa. Montgomery is still advancing, Sousse fallen. But Burma news is not so good.

11 April

Went to the Free Church to hear Padre Foster Haigh for possibly the last time as he is down on the upcountry party. Preached well 'Tis easier for a camel to pass through the eye of a needle'.

Thinking much of home, how is Mother, how will she take the news of the marriage, and Olwen. If only E. could get home soon, clear things up a bit.

12 April

The Dutch party have started to leave, odd hour (4.00 am) for them to have to set out to travel upcountry.

Ref 7/4 [7 April] Daniels complaint has fallen through. Collins refuses to go against the word of Lt (QM) Barber in spite of the absolute proof. And apparently Cpl Wilson's evidence of being served underweight was completely disregarded – 'Barber being a man of 21 years service etc.' But everybody thinks he is crooked but difficult to prove so. They sold $3600 of tobacco last month; I reckon a minimum 'rake-off' of $360 on that item alone. It is openly suggested by men and officers that Lt Col Waters, Collins are in the racket! Of course Kingston, Neale and Barber eat little with us.

13 April

The canteen, through the 'legal' sale and mart department has purchased 4 gross pencils for the Lab. Quite a lot of items are up for sale, chiefly articles of clothing including mosquito nets. The Nips working on the demolition of the gun park sheds have established contacts with our personnel for the sale of cameras and good watches. Rolex at $80–$120 cash, and anything up to $800/- for a good make camera. No crooked business either.

Rumour that another 20 bags of mail have arrived at the gaol offices for sorting out.

News: Things are moving in North Africa; Sousse has fallen and Montgomery is pressing on.

14 April

Walsh went up for sorting letters today and I saw my name on the list, one from Mother again – cheers. Olwen – is there one?

The Hospital soccer XI played 18th Div today and still maintain their unbeaten reputation by a win of 4–1 after a good game.

15 April

We hear that our second postcards home have not yet left the gaol offices as yet. Rose has had a letter from India dated Nov. '42 and they have not received the first postcard up to that time.

Played Mah-jong at Gawn's hut and won 5 cents at it.

My letter of yesterday's sorting was delivered there, from Mother dated 22.6.42. Still has no news of me or of the marriage. It was a lovely letter, all about home, gave me such a heartache for it – and Olwen, once again it made me think deeply about her. Olwen, forgive me.

16 April

Poor Sullivan's letter from his wife just gave no news at all, he's absolutely fed up – read it, crumpled it up saying 'I'll slit her throat for this'; this is the second one like that he's received.

Later – Sully' has received yet another dated 2.3.42 full of nothing, not even commenting that he is a prisoner. Others have received letters saying 'Write soon', 'What do you want sent in a parcel?', 'It's time you wrote home', 'Enjoy yourself as much as possible'. People seem to have no idea what it means to be a POW.

Went down to see *I killed the Count* but the lights failed so the show was put off; visited the Dutch café instead and managed to find a seat and have two cups of quite decent coffee. Place absolutely crowded, gossip, eating, smoking.

Must tell E. that when she writes to put in as much useful news as possible, finances, home, journey etc. Type[-]written large page!

18 April

Visited the Free Church and heard Padre Haigh preach another stirring sermon. The service is very simple.

19 April

A high tide this morning so joined the swimming party and found it very pleasant. Plenty of jellyfish about but I felt more confident after I saw Barber catching big fellows and lugging them out onto the beach. I tried to grasp smaller ones but they're awfully slippery.

Came back and visited the Dutch café and ate delicious doughnuts with a few cups of morning coffee, 3 cents, and doughnuts 3 cents. This café is a wondrous affair in a POW camp. One can have a lunch or supper there if the order is placed in the morning and number of places required.

20 April

18th Div upcountry party are taking a piano and their electric light plant up with them, also an ambulance is following by road; what next. After this 7000 party, another of 1500, mainly Dutch, must be ready to go to Japan.

All the men are 'bum stabbed', examined for malaria, vaccinated and inoculated with cholera and plague vaccines. They are supposed to be given quinine 10gr. for five days prior to leaving but we are not giving this out!

21 April

Heavy rain again this evening and no electric lights because of a break between here and the gaol, and it takes a long time before the IJA decide to let our folk repair it. Also means that the water will be off as the pumps will not be working.

Last big rugger match in this camp, Hospital v the Rest – quite a good game, we won 15–13, began to get rather rough. After that watched the AIF start their athletic meeting. 100yds – 11 ⅚ [sec], 880[yds] – 2 [min] 24 [sec], 220[yds] – 24 [sec]. Quite interesting, but rain, very heavy rain, came on and flooded us back to shelter. It felt just like home, cold, blowing and soaked through.

Found two malaria cases in the survey of the upcountry batch today, our first success in about 8000.

22 April

Lights are still off, and we still economise in water because of breakdown in the power supply.

23 April

Letter from Olwen, dated 25.7.42, has arrived. Awfully nice, she has lost her heart, and I think I still feel more than just friendly to her. Gosh she will feel it when the news is broken to her. My fault entirely. If it weren't for the acute state out here, I too would have waited for her.

24 April

Did some slides for malaria carriers in the upcountry batch and found one case of BT.

With Bloom and O'Neale knocked a hockey ball about, quite a pleasant bit of exercise, not too energetic. Our Mess 'The Pukhas' won their game of soccer in the league; quite good play.

A lot of services today, including a choral one at 11.30 pm in the church just by the Mess.

We were woken up early by 18th Div party leaving, took a huge amount of luggage, cupboards, tables, tents, piano, huge boxes etc., and the Nips sent some back as excess so they returned the medical equipment and rations in preference – fools.

25 April

Easter Sunday. Went to Holy Communion in the Church adjacent. Much noise from early morning because of the parties going away, and services one after another. The additional 1500 party for overseas also left today for, we think, Kuching or Tokyo.

28 April

The last of the 7000 party have just left (4.00 am) and now there are only some 6500 left in the whole camp, including Java parties. All moving over to Selarang and G&W [Garden and Woods] area (British 11th Indian Div). More and more Officers are flocking around Command Area and they are giving themselves, through Lt Col Taylor, Area Commander, plenty of room but we are still sleep[ing] 19 in our room alone and more are being tacked in to our Mess which is ponderous enough, about 60 now.

Still expecting news of an intended visit to see E. tomorrow!!

29 April

A day of depression and disappointment. Bloom, I think, is even more fed up than I am – but in the morning both he and Cornelius received letters and I (as usual) none at all. E. doesn't realise how it hurts when so many others get news and I don't get any at all.

Tenno Hirohito [emperor of Japan] birthday so we were hoping that a visit to the Gaol would be allowed; so far we have had 30 minutes at

Christmas and no communication allowed by the IJA although letters come from home.

30 April
Our food these days compared to 12 months ago is vastly improved. Breakfast is porridge (rice) and fried whitebait, rice and tea; lunch – soup (soya bean), rice, sweet potato and a rissole of something, tea and sweet biscuit; supper of rice, fried potatoes, pasty and a little fish and some kind of rice sweet, tea.

In addition we can buy more bananas, *gula malacca*, tin of fish ($1.05), tin of chicken curry at $1.25 and sauces. Eggs at 16 cents occasionally but we can't afford this luxury very much. Green vegetables we get from our gardens and are chiefly potato leaves, tapioca and spinach.

1 May
Our lab batman Rivers of 125 Anti-tank who developed pulmonary TB was doing quite well but suddenly (24 hours) got acute dysentery and died early this afternoon; he was almost pulseless this morning – query shigella infection.

The party of 3000 is now being got ready. Austin Best is down to go as the physician for the hospital, Snell who was court-martialled recently in SA also going. We took our last walk in SA, it was delightful, so pleasant; the beautiful views over the Straits, towards the Naval Base etc., made me feel awfully homesick.

3 May
SA is closing except for a few RE working in the Nip workshop repairing cars and trucks, and 18th Div is closing too, except what is also Command Area near our present quarters.

There is now a great deal of selfishness being displayed by senior officers at Command, carefully choosing their rooms, getting a host of their friends around them too in comfort and crowding out others; a few more oddments have been added on to us. Our OC seems too weak to oppose Holmes in anything.

All of us, with one or two exceptions, dislike 'Command' as an incompetent, muddling, selfish crowd of pseudo officers.

4 May
We are told SA is closing tomorrow so I went with a small party this afternoon to scrounge all I could. There was plenty; first we found a

Changi truck, then filled it up with chairs, tables etc., a school desk for myself, size 4, and other oddments. Rest of the party cut a lot of eggfruit, raw bananas, and chillies. Strange how empty and deserted the place is. In one quarter I found a dog waiting for its master to return – when! It was sleeping inside and came out to greet me.

5 May

Had a good game of hockey yesterday. Our wire at 18th Div is being taken in now and we can no longer get at the coconut grove of an evening.

Visited SA again this morning with one trailer, chiefly to get more cooking utensils for Austin's party. Hot, hard work pushing a trailer up hills. I collected an air raid siren (hand model) and another *parang* [machete], screws etc. McGarrity took the siren for his show tonight; it's well out of the Lab because Cooper and Houghton were making such an infernal din with it. I also acquired a bed in SA, army pattern, to replace my present sagging hospital bed; debug it first.

6 May

Mac's Revels produced by McGarrity, saw it last night and roared with laughter. Few items dragged a little, but it's a bumper show for a POW camp, grand settings, lighting and orchestra. I think it's the best show we've had yet, and packed full of clean humour compared to the Aussy shows which are lewd throughout.

10 May

My bet with Dawson that Tunisia will not be finished by this date ends – and it looks as though I'm going to win by a few hours or a day at most. The bet was made a month ago so my reckoning was not bad. Twenty cents and ten cents from Farwell.

The officers and staff of hospital have to do fatigues twice weekly now, owing, it is said, to a shortage of men.

12 May

We hear that Tunisia campaign is now most definitely over and we have taken ¼ million prisoners. Rommel is away.

Went up to Selarang this morning to see Austin Best away and his party 'H'. He leaves for upcountry early tomorrow morning. They are told only to take what they can carry and no more; he has a pack, suitcase, bedding roll and oddments, wonder how he'll get on at all. John Diver and Maj Thyer IMD are also going up. Pereira went up two days ago.

14 May

At last we are doing blood ureas by the Urex method; trouble is the continuous suction used a Potains aspirator for the first effort but it's hard work; must borrow the Aussy foot suction pump next time or the theatre electrical one. Houghton was just about browned off getting the apparatus together because his first attempt I turned down, it leaked at all the bungs, but it seems alright now with proper rubber bungs.

15 May

Capt Nancy (SA) has gone this morning, Party 'J' said to be bound for Formosa and Japan.

Later – we hear that officers have very comfortable cabin accommodation. All the parts of their radio set were collected after a hut inspection and returned to this camp. As each party goes off, a set is sent with them, being distributed amongst several members for safety, but the Nips are now getting wise to it.

Absolutely no mention of our successes in Tunisia by the local rag *Syonan Sinbun*; that part of the war is just left out, only say that Rommel is sick in Germany, but the local guards who call at the Lab know that it's all washed up now.

16 May

Did a post mortem today, after a long time, on a Dutchman. Very little pathological present, he just seemed to have resolved to die, and ate very little. Many of the Dutch forces seem to be fatalists.

Afternoon, another case to do. Surgical ward, had a gastrojejunostomy. Done without gloves and now he comes to me with general peritonitis. I couldn't see any adequate reason for the big operation under our present circumstances and facilities yet the surgeons persist in heroic efforts.

About 9.30 pm a Nip private, must be a shopkeeper, came up to our room and sat down to bargain for items. As usual wanted cameras, pens. Told us that Rolex and Parkers were No.1, others 'No OK'. Bought Bloom's watch for $40.00, Sydney's pen for $80. Then dropped the gold watch. He seemed to know all about gold values.

Next up came two Nip guards, put their rifles in a corner of the room and asked for a doctor; one had pains and fever (query dengue?)

and wanted advice and treatment, said 'Japanese doctor no good, slap face.' Was dealt with after using their Nip-English dictionary, [and he] thanked us very much. Meantime Steve C. kept demonstrating to the other fellow that he would dig up a good camera to sell him next night – an extremely funny performance and much 'OK, OK' etc. They know that we bury our cameras and also take them upcountry in water bottles like Pitts. Next the 'shopkeeper' turned out to have a chance when we found that he had palpable supra-trochlear glands; this seemed to astonish him and we turned him on to Chiltern as 'No. 1 Cock Doctor' who he proceeded to consult at length as to treatment. Wouldn't buy a cine-projector or give good prices for some other pens. Only left us at lights out; the other two went straight off when we had finished seeing the sick one.

18 May

The officer party 'K' left this morning, no one from our Mess.

Did another post mortem today, a (query) chronic nephritis with a small granular kidney; very fine specimen.

The blood ureas are doing well. I wish I had thought of this earlier.

The Nip, we call him 'Nancy Ming', was in again tonight and bought Dougie Gawn's Zeiss Ikon for $100/- although there was fungus on the lens and the shutter stuck on all the lower speeds. He spotted all this but took it in the end and left $200/- with Steve to buy him more cameras – he wants a Leica! The two bottles of beer, very weak stuff, were soon disposed of.

19 May

The Nip was back in again for his bargains, but S. only had a Retina to sell. It looked well used but was in excellent condition; must say I coveted it somewhat! Get one later on as a not so expensive camera, and they take good pictures.

The Nip wanted to return Nardell's pen, says he can only get $5/- for it in Singapore but we won't return the cash. Went off after S. returned him the remainder of his deposit of $200/- long after lights out. He's getting to be a nuisance now.

20 May

Work is going down these days; are told that there is only 5300 left altogether in this POW [camp].

[At] 5.00 pm we get on parade for a check roll call by the IJA. Most wearisome procedure and I have no book to read. They arrived late (as usual) and then counted everyone, staff and patients up in the wards, apparently all correct so we dismissed by 6.45 pm. Not so long this time. The other areas were counted too.

The hospital received 800lb of pork from our piggery. I inspected the carcass, looked awfully good; of course old Wolfe DADH [Deputy Assistant Director of Hygiene] was awfully annoyed that I should be called in and not him in the first place.

What beautiful sunsets these days.

Last night of *Mac's Revels*; I would have been bored but the show was brightened up considerably by us catapulting pellets full of rice at the actors.

21 May

MacGregor put aside some pork from his cookhouse, [and] most surreptitiously brought us some to eat in the Lab, which I sampled like a thief at night feeling awfully guilty about it. At night went to Mac's cave and had a huge dinner of lovely soup, roast pork and potatoes, fruit salad and cream. It was a terrific meal, [for] Cooke, Julian, Cuthbert and I. Afterwards I had many dreams, chiefly of Elizabeth, she was allowed to visit the camp – it was wonderful but just a dream.

How much longer is this to be! Our life arrested like this, years being wasted, poor E., cooped up in a criminal gaol, under the eyes of Asiatics, living from day to day, food monotonous, no privacy, wondering what they're going to do next, the lack of work and insufficient facilities and drugs, rotten fish. E. so near yet so far, poor girl.

No communication with home, no Red Cross vessels. And very little hope of relief being held out to us by Churchill for years yet, [with] nothing active being done out this way. We seem to have been forgotten after being dishonoured and made fools of at the Fall of Singapore – poor fish who had to stay behind here.

26 May

Apparently a Colonel and five other officers have been taken up on the Burma front and brought down here. They are housed in Changi school, old SA, and no-one allowed to see them or go anywhere near them, not even anti-malarial squad – curious this isolation! Also said that a lot of Nip casualties have arrived in Singapore, presumably from Burma.

We think there is little activity going on there, chiefly defensive and bombing judging by our news bulletin.

IJA has cleared everybody out of the G&W area so there are only Selarang and hospital areas left now. Nip guards have replaced our sentries just outside the exits of the wire SA gate, 18th Div gate and Changi village gate; road to Selarang is open, likewise the big *padang*.

27 May

I distilled some of Middleton's brew down in the Lab, the first fraction was absolute firewater, pure alcohol in fact; it was fermented honey and raisins, only about a litre, and got a yield of 8 [illegible]. Others are doing it on a big scale and a bottle of proof spirits sell at $3/-, cost with *gula malacca* etc. is 80 cents. McGarrity suggests we start doing this in a big way ourselves for a profit at under price.

28 May

We live fairly comfortably, good bed, net, mattress etc. Have had sheets since the beginning and pretty clean too as I can boil all my things in the Lab! Most other folk do not sleep so comfortably, naked, beds, ground sheet and a blanket suffice. What a luxury our showers are; have two or three a day.

Diet is getting poor again as there is insufficient in the canteens to purchase, of tinned food, only chicken curry at $1.25/tin of about [illegible]. No other good protein. No meat since last year.

How are they doing in the gaol, and E. darling, hope you are keeping well.

Repatriation – is the British Government trying to do anything about it!

We feel forgotten, and given up.

29 May

Changi Medical Society Clinical Meeting yesterday showing 6 cardiac valvular lesions, a carcinoma of lung, and poliomyelitis in several in this camp and a queer VII, VIII cranial nerves, said to be due to deficiency disease.

30 May

'A' Mess v 'C' Mess in a vigorous game of hockey. Score 0–0. Steve C. played our goal keeper awfully well. I was Right Inside and almost scored. Our new players began to improve in the second half and some dirty play began – but it was most enjoyable; bit tired and hungry later, and oh for a shandy or a cold beer!

I find I can play two games a week now and enjoy them, but do not exert overmuch as a forward.

1 June

News coming in regularly, also the *Syonan Sinbun* (Soya bean Times) to compare items with. For the most part it's rather dull for us out here; we have been lost sight of it seems, except by our families. The taking of Atta in the Aleutians has cheered us up a little, but there's so much talking and threats with very little action so far, except for bombing, out this way.

The Nips in Singapore do not seem to be at all bothered about the situation except that there's more air activity.

2 June

Am plodding along revising Bacteriology and Tropical Diseases slowly; there ought to be a good synopsis of the latter, as neither Manson nor Megan's book are any good. Think I ought to write one as soon as I get out from here, using my notes if they are still with me.

Dawson, Smiley and Falk are busy dissecting 'parts' in the mortuary every afternoon; they all want to get their FRCS [Fellow of the Royal College of Surgeons]. I plan to go first for MD (Trop. Med.), do DTM and H [Diploma in Tropical Medicine and Health] at the same time, then do a study visit to the States – what a lovely dream, of course it doesn't include what E. thinks about things and the post-war situation.

When is it all going to end!

3 June

Up early and volunteered to join the wood fatigue party to fetch a load of wood from along Tampines Road; about 3½ miles there, 24 in the party including Mulvaney and old Cornelius. Latter did his fair share of loading and pushing while M. did the steering. Went through Selarang onto Loyston Road and thence to Tampines Road guardroom, numbers checked and picked up our two Nips. Two to each trailer, quite sociable fellows. Passed a civilian men's party pulling up their trailer, saw no one whom I knew. They had Sikh guards, malicious looking swines too, watching like cats to see if there was any communication.

We loaded 1¼ tons, very hot, sweaty work too. Drank coffee after at the new Selarang café called 'Smokey Joe's'; it'll be a better place than the old Dutch one of 18th Div area.

4 June

Did some tailoring today, a job I heartily dislike. Cut down a pair of long drill trousers to shorts for general wear and playing hockey. Very tedious work but finished it eventually all in one day – if only I could have sent them along to Elizabeth.

5 June

We have not been troubled by Nips much at night lately, but 'Ming' turned up again to try and get back $8/- from Sydney N. for the dud pen which he was sold a week or two ago. They are still keen on Parker pens but not so much on watches, [so] prices of latter are now falling.

8 June

Went over to G&W area with a trailer to fetch lockers for the hospital but I pulled up several papaya plants and have put them down behind our Mess (seven) where there is to be a garden, and, I hope, they will bring forth some fruit if we are to be here so long.

Dickie Dawson, Nardell, and Markby have 'volunteered' to work in the cemetery and were at it today under strict direction, pulling up blades of grass; have to turn out three afternoons a week for this job.

9 June

Food in the canteen is getting less and less, bananas are insufficient to fill our needs, only tinned food is curry chicken at $1.50/-. Bananas come in about twice a week and are sold out in a few hours. Yesterday 1000lb was sold from 3.00 pm to 4.30 pm at 12 cents a lb.

Unfortunately our canteen is still the most expensive and never has enough for all who want to buy. The Aussy side control affairs and get first choice of goods as their office collects and distributes them, consequently they have a greater variety of goods too.

Another Nip came up to the Mess wanting Parker pens and Rolex watches; Blue Spot are their chief want.

10 June

Went on the trailer party to Tampines Road again. Saw civilian men and they all looked awfully fit. I didn't feel at all fatigued after the work today and went and cut grass on the hockey pitch in the afternoon.

For supper Sydney N. and I had a great meal with a tin of curried chicken; [we] shared $1.50.

11 June

At 10.30 pm tonight we heard that Pantelleria [between Tunisia and Sicily] has fallen to us after more shelling and bombing. Our time is nine hours in advance of GMT so our news service is pretty good.

Last night sold George Sullivan's CYMA watch, of which the winder had jammed in its socket for lack of use and oil for a sum of $50/-, of which he gave me $5/- commission so I've purchased another tin of chicken curry.

Changi Medical Society Meeting – lecture by Maj Denaro on 'Malta'.

13 June

We hear that Lampedusa [south of Pantelleria] has also fallen; story that at first signified its capitulation to an RAF Flight Sgt who made a forced landing. We received the news about 4.30 pm whilst having tea.

14 June

The Lab has started a garden in the triangle of ground adjacent, [which] probably means we shall be moving shortly – I've never been lucky with gardens.

Went over to Selarang to see the Aussy concert; fair. Their pranks were as usual awfully good, but a poor show. This party is getting browned off as they have been putting on performances for the last 15 months in Selarang and now have to do general duties as well. So far all actors have been more or less exempt from all except the lightest duties. In our areas they are kept in wards as patients or find a job in the cookhouse and so forth.

15 June

Our lighting has been suddenly reduced and the IJA say we must be ready to 'brownout' at any time.

'Ming' came in to see us after a long spell. He ate 21 of Frankland's ripening bananas and then paid him 70 cents for them. Said their food was very poor, only rice and rice and three bananas with it, but if they could shoot a monkey it made a good meal. He's living by Changi village so they must be killing the troop down there. Also said that it was common gossip amongst them that we (Hospital) were going to be moved into Selarang area as well. He had most distorted news to give us, awful lies told to them it seems, in an army news sheet which is handed out daily for their consumption.

Went over to Selarang in the afternoon to play for the hockey XI of our area, in place of Glancy who is in the new show. Easy game and we won 4–0. Awfully hot so we (Frankland and I) had coffee over in 'Smokey Joe's'. Shared two tins of chicken curry today so feel awfully bloated, but could still do with a nice cold drink of fresh lime squash.

17 June

Joined the wood fatigue again today; brought back 32½ cwt, a record for us. The civilian men were on both sides of the track and close, but many Sikh guards about. I yelled a message over for you, Elizabeth. If only I could get one too, it's such a long time since we heard.

Coming up the 'Cresta' run, a digger on the front trailer had stamped on a young cobra; it was still alive so I picked it up and brought it back for demonstration. Swallowed three cups of coffee before coming home. It was hard hot work today but we enjoy it as a weekly outing. I'm a volunteer. Others on this party are awful slackers.

Finished the day with Padre Wearne's *Midsummer Follies* which turned out most entertaining – all these shows are wonderful for a POW camp.

18 June

We hear that Wavell has been appointed Viceroy of India as from October 1st.

Bit of a surprise as another party has to go away upcountry including 18 MOs and 150 ORs from this area. A lot going from our Mess but I'm still off it.

Unfortunately MacGregor of the post mortem room is down to go. He is up against Caldbeck and MacDonald over their ducks so off he goes upcountry, and they have a big say with the OC. It's been the same all along; as soon as one is a little uncooperative with office staff, they are down on the next list.

Lighting has been suddenly reduced and we must be prepared to brownout at any time – since bombing in the Celebes [in Indonesia].

19 June

IJA inform us that news of all prisoners has arrived in London – at last.

Disaster – I lost three handkerchiefs by brewing on the hot plate as the water had all evaporated while I was down collecting manure for the Lab garden. Houghton put the first bean seeds in a new bed – we have great plans for the garden if we are here long enough to reap the profits!

20 June

News that IJA officially inform us that our last postcards (second) have now been censored and are awaiting transmission from the Offices at the Gaol, written on 23rd Feb.

The 'wire' has been brought to our side of the Changi Road and the Base Supply Depot is moving up to Selarang in a few days.

21 June

We hear that a lot of Nips have arrived in old SA from the Burma Front and that they are in disgrace ([according to] Nip interpreter) because they cracked under the steady RAF bombing up there. They are said to be on half rations and are not allowed in to town at all. We see their lorry loads of food passing through.

About six 'Specialist' officers (i.e. Ordnance, Signals etc) have to go into Gillman everyday to examine and explain to Nip officers the use of a lot of material which they have taken from ? Java; much of it, Bevan tells me, is in excellent condition or brand new – a radio detector set, secret telephone set, field radios, guns etc.

22 June

The Nips came around today and checked up all the good tyres on Changi trucks or trailers, so we can no longer take off the tyres for making footwear and re-soling of boots. Some efficient sandals have suddenly appeared all over the place, since a lot of tyres have been pinched and cut up. Previously the tyres were only being used for soling of boots and shoes.

The AIF seem to have got hold of most of it

23 June

A surprise – Lt Col Benson is off the party and Wallace IMS is in his place. Benson has had his stool looked at six times, all negative, but says he is suffering from abdominal pains, wind etc. Later heard that he is off because he told Evans that 'cysts had been found', quite untrue of course, but the CO does not know this.

Maj Crawford is now OC party, others are Henderson, Garrard (ADC) [Aide-de-camp], old Marshall, Durrell, Pete Eastwood, Dickie Dawson, Bob Brown, Clarkson (ADC), Wallace (IMS), Gibson (C Mess), Franks, Tomlinson, Davis – 19 British, six AIF (including Maj Davis, pathologist) five Dutch MOs. One Aussy dropped out and was replaced by one of our fellows.

1913 Peshawar, British India. A young Jack Ennis, seated, with his brother Stanley and sister Mona.

1914 Edinburgh, Scotland. David Petrie, his wife Marion holding May and Betty (Elizabeth) standing on the chair.

In 1939, having completed his medical training in London, Jack returned to British India. Posted to Malaya, his duties allowed him plenty of time to explore his surroundings. He delighted in walks through the dense rain forest, listening to the sounds of birds and insects, identifying butterflies and snakes, tracking and observing animals.

1939 The newly opened Princess Elizabeth Ward, Deaconess Hospital, Edinburgh. Betty Petrie can be seen leaning over a baby in a cot. *Copyright of The Scotsman Publications and used with their kind permission.*

1940 Mrs Rosamond Scott with Susan aged 5 years and Douglas aged 3 years sailing to Hong Kong on P&O SS *Narkunda*.

Colonial life. From the right, Elizabeth with Susan at her knee, Rosamond Scott with Douglas, and family friends.

1941 Singapore. A postcard sent back to her mother in Edinburgh. Little did Elizabeth know that only two years later, with other women and children, she would be held a POW in a bungalow in Katong.

1941 Singapore. When Elizabeth's nursing duties allowed, she would often attend services here. During the Japanese invasion, the nave of the Cathedral was used as a hospital, as was Singapore Cricket Club on the other side of the padang.

With an abiding interest in horticulture, Elizabeth enjoyed many visits to Singapore Botanic Gardens

10 July 1941. Now fully recovered Captain Jain left Kuala Lipis. Pictured from the left to right, Captain Jain, Nurse Elizabeth Petrie, Captain Jack Ennis, Nurse Court

1941 On a drive through the Malay rain forest, Jack with his car 'Marion'

1941 In happy times, Jack and Elizabeth, a boat excursion on the Lipis River.

In late September 1941 Elizabeth transferred to Queen Alexandra's Imperial Military Nursing Sisters.

BOAT QUAY, SINGAPORE

Singapore quayside: In 1942 Jack and Elizabeth were hastily married in Fullerton Building. At the time the building housed Government offices, the GPO, various administrative offices and the Singapore Club. As the Japanese invaded Singapore, the Governor and his wife took refuge here and a temporary hospital was also set up. After capitulation, it became the Japanese headquarters.

Jack's small 'pocket diaries'. Kept throughout internment, these were often hidden in his laboratory in prison camp. *Ivan Young*.

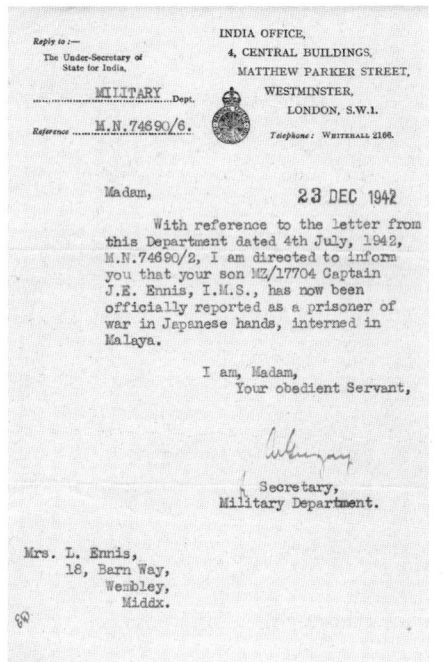

The letter no mother ever wished to receive. *Ivan Young*.

Where possible, POW often used crafts to fill some of the long hours of captivity. Cut out of aluminium scrap from a crashed aircraft, this paper knife features the emblem of the Indian Medical Service. It was gifted to Jack by two Dutch POW in 1943, just before they were sent away as part of a work party. *Ivan Young*.

Barn Owl by Dr B D Molesworth. While interned in Changi Gaol, medical officer Dr Molesworth continued his studies of bird watching and art. His greatest achievements were the water colour illustrations for the first edition of "Introduction to the Birds of Malaya' by Guy Madoc. (The first edition of the book was completed and bound into hardback while in Changi Gaol.) He also found time to sketch some British birds. Two sketches were given to Jack, both in pastels on photograph album paper.

A section of the patchwork quilt presented to Elizabeth by the Girl Guides in Changi. The complete quilt measures 185mm x 980mm. *IWM*.

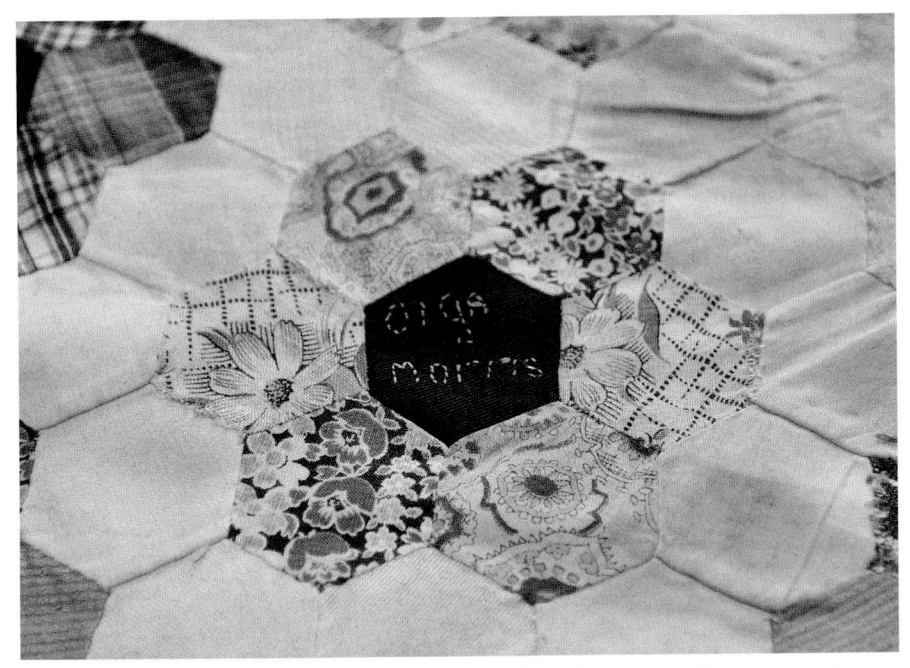

This 'patch' was embroidered by Girl Guide Olga Morris (now Henderson). Many years later Olga and the quilt would be the inspiration for a children's book. *IWM*.

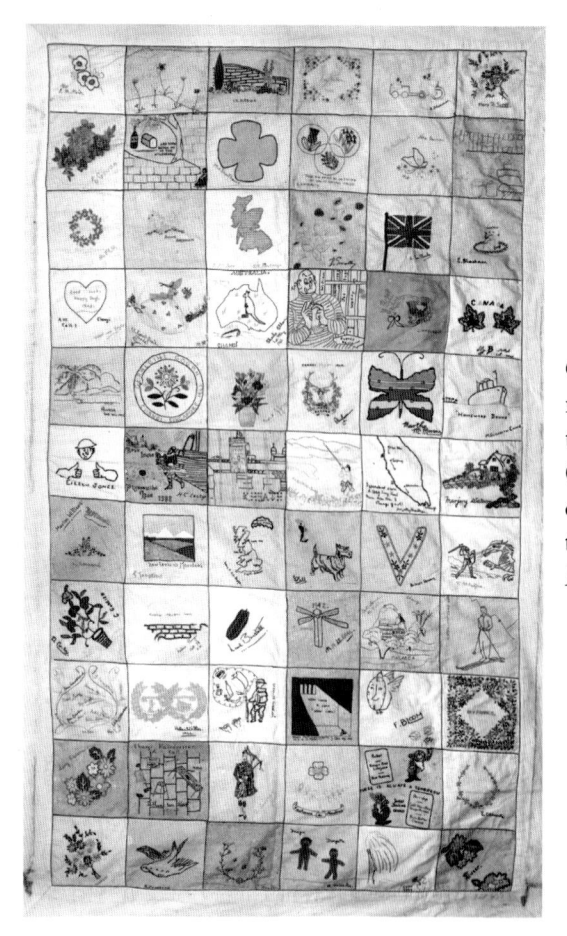

One of the 'Changi quilts' now carefully conserved at the Australian War Memorial, Canberra. Elizabeth's patch can be seen halfway down on the right hand side. *Laurie Richards.*

Elizabeth's patch was a strong message of freedom from internment and hope for the future.

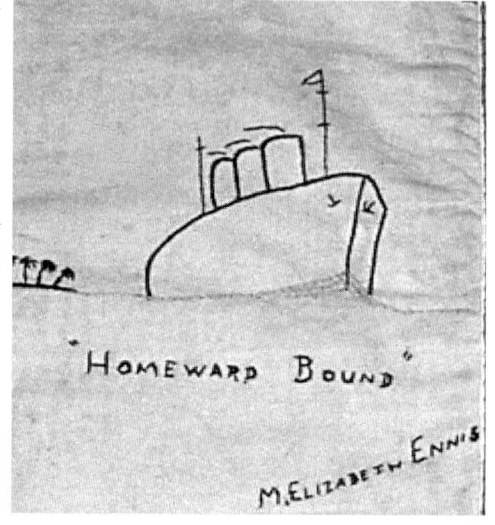

1944 This sketch, chalks on thin brown card, was drawn after a hockey match. The artist, 'Willie' (Francis John) White, was a Sherwood Forester (Notts and Derby Regiment). Sadly he died a few months later and is buried in Kranji CWGC.

In 1944, Christmas in the lab at Kranji was celebrated in style. Sixteen medical staff gathered to share a meal; each guest received a copy of the menu drawn on a playing card. The main ingredient of the ragout [stew] was one dog. *Ivan Young*.

September 1945. Still too ill to travel back to the UK but finally fit enough to walk very short distances, Rob Scott left Syme Road POW camp to convalesce in a British hospital in India.

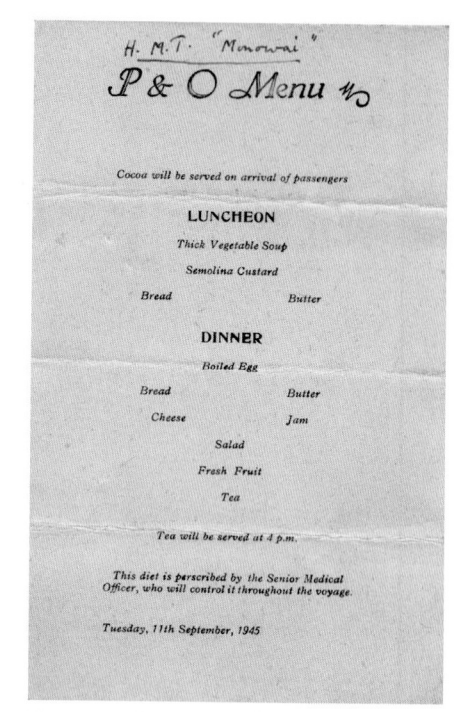

Concerned that newly released POW would not be able to cope with too much food at once (Re-feeding syndrome) initially meals on board ship were very light, to the dismay of the FEPOW. *Ivan Young.*

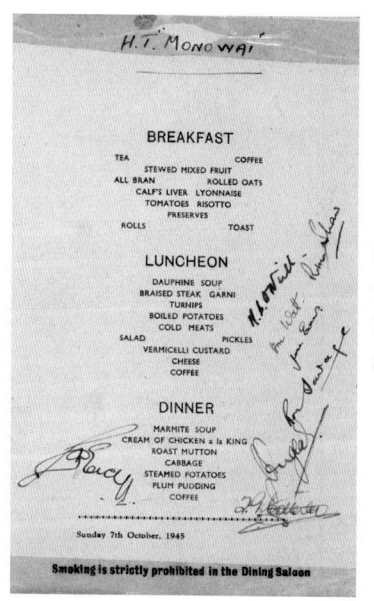

On the 7th October 1945, the *Monowai* stood off the Mersey. This much-treasured menu, signed by fellow FEPOW, was cellotaped safely in an album on return home. *Ivan Young.*

Jack's kindness to some of his guards was never forgotten. Some years after the war Hayashita, a former Korean guard, wrote 'How can I ask you to forgive me …?' *Ivan Young*.

After the war, Jack continued as a pathologist with the IMS, here in his bacteriology lab in No. 3 Indian General Hospital, Poona.

Certificate of Merit

Name   Mrs. Ennis
Rank   -   Singapore
For   Gallantry under Enemy Occupation.
Date   1942-1945.

Chief Commissioner   Chief Guide

Very proud of Elizabeth's courage and resilience during captivity, after the war Jack always displayed this framed certificate in his study at their home. *Ivan Young*.

Early adventures staying with the Scotts after Rob and Rosamond moved to Peeblesshire. Camping at 'Ennis's End', at the end of the former railway track, Lyne Station near Peebles.

After the family settled in Durham, Elizabeth ran a Girl Guide company; the quilt was often on display at fundraising activities. Later, as County Commissioner, Elizabeth was instrumental in raising funds to establish a permanent camp in the beautiful wooded grounds of Whitworth Park near Spennymoor, County Durham. Opened in 1965, the Camp House, with capacity for 30 people, is a lasting legacy of Elizabeth's wish to provide opportunities for young people.

April 1973. Jack and Elizabeth at the wedding of their eldest daughter Jacqueline in Edinburgh. *Jack Fisher*.

April 1973. Sir Robert and Lady Rosamond Scott. *Jack Fisher*.

Sir Robert Heatlie Scott
Lord Lieutenant Peeblesshire 1968–1975
Lord Lieutenant Tweeddale 1975–1980.

Remembrance Day 1989. The proud holders of the Burma Star, survivors of the war in the Far East, march past the City Chambers, Edinburgh (Elizabeth can be seen extreme left, Jack second gentleman from the left). *Copyright of The Scotsman Publications and used with their kind permission.*

MacGregor has to go, too much 'opposition' in this office to his staying behind. McDonald and Hutchins hate him.

24 June

Last night had a big supper at the mortuary in honour of Mac's departure – bread, chicken curry soup, haggis, fried egg, potatoes, pineapple cubes and artificial cream. I just staggered back to bed feeling very heavy in the stomach.

25 June

Just back; a sad parting up at Selarang square when the big medical party left at 9.30 pm in a slight drizzle, 25 MOs and 200 ORs for upcountry.

Some had stacks of kit but others good packs. Loaded 26–28 per truck with personal kit and a Nip guard each. Didn't take off with any trouble in spite of a recheck when their NCO said we had four extra.

In the Mess find George the friendly Nip, [who] gave us the details about the Thai camps – much malaria all camps and cholera very bad in the Dutch ones, less in the British ? 300–400 deaths. Water supply poor, only tracks leading out to each camp along which their truck is driven. Said to be building a railway but are still quite near Bangkok.

We find this out now too late to be of use for the medical party; no hint given as to what they might have to deal with up there.

Willie Chapman came back as reserve officer and the Nip seemed genuinely pleased that he hadn't gone, patted him on the back saying 'OK, OK you stay' (*Khing khai*).

P.S. He had brought us packets of toffees as presents.

26 June

Opinion is very much against Benson's behaviour and his telling a deliberate lie; all sorts of rude remarks are being passed in front of him.

The Lab has now had a cat for the last three weeks and she is pregnant. Everybody admires her Siamese colouring and is asking for kittens as she is pregnant. Diet is several pounds of rotten fish every other day; there is plenty of it as it is not fit for consumption by the time we get it.

We have had no fish for three or four weeks now.

27 June

Went over to Selarang this evening to Padre Jones' church, the senior AIF chaplain. He is much nicer than any of the British chaplains we have left.

Saw Frank Wright and went to hear the open-air orchestral concert at the YMCA pavilion behind old Gordons' Mess; it was quite pleasant.

Amazing the things we have in this POW camp.

30 June

More stories about conditions up at the Bangkok camps – they do sound pretty poor conditions there.

No more wood trailer parties for us, all the wood is going to be delivered to the areas by truck – end of quite a pleasant weekly outing for us; most of us enjoyed it.

1 July

We have to move our ducks and fowls from the mortuary area as it is all to be pulled down. McDonald, Wolfe, Hutchins have been whispering in the CO's ear, all because they didn't get MacGregor's big drake and two ducks and blamed him for stealing their three ducks as well.

2 July

Changi Medical Society Meeting. Maj Orr read a paper on the 'Eye Deficiency Diseases seen in this POW camp so far'. It was quite good, but the Aussies always take sides and they get at one another if one of them starts the original discussion and they cannot help getting personal.

Glyn White, their ADMS [Assistant Director of Medical Services], has an awful accent.

3 July

A gorgeously cold night after a drizzling day. I used a blanket to cover with, first time in the last year I should think.

MacGarrity said 'Who would have believe that in a POW camp we eat tins of curried chicken, smoke big fat cigars and sit bargaining over the sale of Rolex watches and fountain pens to Nip guards until lights out, while they put their rifles on one side, with bayonets off, and hand out cigarettes.'

Canteen is all right for bananas, papayas and cucumber these days; one can afford these and share a tin at least every other day.

4 July

The Americans have launched an offensive in S.W. Pacific and seem to be doing well; lost 19 planes to 120 Nip ones.

Our burning question is where we are starting a second front in Europe; hot debate takes place nightly about it, or to where and when. I'm inclined to think it'll be Greece, others say Sicily and Italy.

Provides a good subject for whiling away long hours.

5 July

News says that Tojo [Japanese Prime Minister and Minister of War] is in Singapore; maybe that was his big passenger plane with fighter escort which flew over yesterday afternoon?

There is much air activity again these days.

Syonan Sinbun has had much in it lately about air raids and a large scale practice, but the date is being constantly altered.

Had coffee and cakes at 'Smokey Joe's' and stayed awake until about 3.00 am; had to get up twice. This canteen coffee seems to contain a great deal of caffeine in it, [and] has the same potent effect on everybody.

No more of it at night for me.

6 July

The Germans have launched a new offensive on Russian Front [Battle of Kursk]. Made no progress so far.

8 July

Inspected by a Nip officer who went around the hospital; he seemed incredibly ignorant, more like a coolie than an officer.

9 July

At 1600 hours we hear that our troops have made a landing in Sicily and are doing pretty well.

The 'Slums', i.e. our 14-bed room, has invested in an electric lighter that consists of a motorcycle dynamo turned by a handle, the spark igniting a petrol wick. It's very efficient, cost $3.50/-. Frankland and I didn't subscribe, being non-smokers, so others say we mustn't touch it at all. I offered to fix it for them on the table but even that was disallowed – McGarrity and four others put in the two screws. So there it sits now ready for use.

10 July

Feeling bit depressed and impatient these days; Mother must be very lonely at home, where is Stanley and Mona, what doing – and Elizabeth so nearby – how much longer are we going to be here?

Watched two AIF fishing in the creek drain below the hospital at high tide; it seemed such good fun that I've decided to do some too, but have no tackle or hooks as yet – set about making the hooks out of bits of Kirschner wire [steel pins used in surgery].

12 July

The Nips brought in body of an Aussy today, [who] died in the gaol, Singapore; awful condition of starvation, he was 6ft2in and only weighed 70lb. Gross pellagroid changes of skin but [no signs] of maltreatment.

A Dutchman from Singapore prison says that O'Neill IMS is no longer there, maybe moved upcountry. Also said that Nips were not going to send in to us any more sick prisoners. Roberts (Red Cross) is said to be in a bad way now.

Rumour from a Nip sentry that another medical party is to go up to Thailand, maybe 300 plus four to six MOs because this cholera outbreak is so bad.

News – Sicilian affair is going all right. German offensive only local gains in Russia, Yanks working slowly in New Georgia [in the Solomon Islands]. Syracuse has fallen to Eisenhower's forces in Sicily.

15 July

The Aussies have been outside the wire again at night, digging sweet potatoes in the 18th Div gardens in Chinese Valley.

Nip guards caught them and brought them back for our own punishment, but our guard is being altered for nights and Sgt Houghton has been taken away from the Lab as he is considered the only suitable Sgt for this job – I had a squabble up at the office about it, and McDonald doesn't like me.

16 July

Julian Taylor was allowed to go up to the gaol today to talk to Munro and Mackie. I gave him $10/- and a message but he couldn't deliver either. He went up to the Supervisor's office and the conversation was conducted across a table with three Nips present, and not allowed to talk of people or affairs at the prison, their health or the progress of the war – there was little to talk about except our statistics.

J.T. got the impression too that the civilians are very cowed and being hard treated.

Went swimming this morning; it was a delightful high tide and we thoroughly enjoyed it, [with] very few jellyfish about today.

17 July

Wolfe brought in another two snakes from the creek today, both the same ?Acrochodidae. Awfully tame. We let them swim about in the Lab sink, [and] one vomited up quite a large fish. The other I took up to the Mess and let it swim around in the big white bath. All sorts of conjectures as to where it had come from – many seemed to think it had come through the tap. I eventually returned both into the large drain at the bottom of the valley.

Flash – air support is being withdrawn by the Axis from Sicily and our forces are steadily advancing towards Catania!!

18 July

Officers v the Rest in hockey; we won 5–1 after an awfully bitter game, [with] much dirty play on both sides, so that I feel I am not going to play on Ass/Surgeons side again. The result was in no doubt but they say that we started the dirty work. Regret I was short of temper with Staff Sgt Garry. Play less of this game henceforth.

Must read up post-war how much fighting is actually going on in New Georgia, what scale of operations, are we really putting anything into it.

19 July

Six prisoners brought in from Outram Rd Gaol, Singapore. Awful state of malnutrition. Scabies, dysentery. They have sentences from five to fifteen years 'solitary' for attempting to escape up in Thailand. Some were at large for 27 days and they think they would have made it but for the shortage of food.

The Nip who took Steve C.'s Rolex valued at $300/- leaving a deposit of $150/- has not shown up again since the night he said it stopped on his wrist after he got drunk. He said he had given it for repairs in Singapore. Anyway he brought me two tiny fishing hooks as a present.

20 July

Weight is now 11st 2lb, almost up to my normal weight for this country; somewhat flabby but feel fit enough.

11th Div (G&W) Area is full of Tamils and Chinese who it seems are impressed labour and are being gathered prior to moving upcountry. *Syonan Sinbun* advertised for 'labour' but none was forthcoming and this is the result. Said to be 1000 at least over there and are being smacked about quite liberally by the Nip sentries.

We hear that Rome has been most successfully bombed. Makassar also raided and the Nips were taken by surprise.

21 July

Mother's birthday. Wonder how she is, or is it Elizabeth's? I seem to be a day ahead. No chance of a letter to either this year.

BBC says that our first postcards have arrived in England from Malaya; hope mine is in the batch so that Mother and Olwen shall get the news of my marriage at last.

The second postcards are still up at the Commandant's office here.

Syonan Sinbun has a paragraph that Tokyo is making arrangements for some repatriation in the 'near future'. It's time the women and children left this awful prison.

The tide had turned at 5.30 pm when I tried a little fishing, [using] snail bait; unsuccessful, [and] my keenness has had the edge taken off it a little.

22 July

Today is a red-letter day and Mother's birthday for I caught a fish *ikan embilang* down in the tidal drain by fishing over the wire.

About 1lb+, measured 18.4[in], used a bit of *chicha* [lizard] as bait and the tide was on the turn at 5.40 pm. Great excitement in the Mess about it and now several want to join me in angling. I filleted the fish and put it in the hospital refrigerator for the night.

Two pretty little sunbirds flew around the 'Slums' this morning, picking insects off the many cobwebs. Maybe they're going to build one of their delicate nests on one of our 'mosquito strings'.

24 July

Fishing again, no big bites, [but] caught six small garfish (*toda*), which I presented to Cruikshank for his ducks. Later I'm informed they are very edible.

Late flash – Yanks have bombed Surabaya [in Indonesia], round trip of 2400 miles.

25 July

I am 32 years old and have not shaped much out of life yet. Wish this internment were soon over.

At last the Lab cat has twins; we thought they were overdue, born at 1.30 pm today.

The OC gave out at lunch that the Hospital is to move shortly to ? G&W area. What a business again, and we are so comfortable where we are. I sleep well and have a good room to work in, nice airy dining room too. Very few huts there, 30–60, for the 2000 of this area, limited water and no electric light. The area will require much cleaning up, and half the huts have been taken down by looting Chinese, Malays and Tamils.

Fished after supper; no good. Three *embilang*.

26 July

Now 2000 odd coolies in G&W area, all being 'bum stabbed' and inoculated, hear they are going to Thailand. Several large convoys of trucks have been around here lately.

More preparations for our big move, all furniture is having Nip labels stuck on it today. The solitary prisoners from SA have been allowed to join us (six officers).

Our news says Mussolini has resigned and King Victor Emmanuel is in again with Marshal Badoglio as Chief Adviser. What was it!

27 July

Our main topic of conversation is the News, what next, how long is Italy going to stay in, what about Germans in Italy, and Italians elsewhere. We get at least two bulletins daily, but things seem to happen so slowly. We are thankful for the News though and such a thing as radio.

Officers trailer party went up to Selarang for canteen goods; told we would have to wait for ½ hour so we parked the trailer and went to Smokey Joe's for 1½ hours as we meet the Yank airmen who had been shot down in Burma. Ball proceeded to draw the news.

28 July

There was an air raid practice this evening, of sorts. We had Nips all over the area and they didn't seem to know the signals at all. Also two officers appeared separately and gave different instructions so there were lights going on and off all the time, wrong time, or not at all. 'Command' erred on the safe side, as usual, and seemed to spend the night in darkness and wanted us to do the same.

Capt James, interpreter, was issuing his own instructions.

29 July

It was near high tide so joined the swimming party. It was grand. [...] misbehaved on the beach, as of course we all bathe nude, and he lost his temper when teased about it in the evening up in the 'Slums' room. I always seem to be causing trouble by practical jokes and wise cracks – better stop.

D'Abrey takes the party out to the beach; we are counted out and on the return again by a 'coolie-looking' Nip sentry at the wire exit. There is not much formality about it; we give him a salute too.

30 July

Rumour has it that we have to evacuate this area because IJA are going to lay down two fighter strips across 18th Div and the hospital *padang*, and those quarters to be occupied by their air force units, a Nip even said the particular unit. In corroboration, a bulldozer/leveller has arrived in Changi this morning and a number of wind flags are hanging about the place showing wind direction.

We don't know how many are to go to G&W but it will certainly be a greatly reduced hospital – who's going to be sent away?

1 August

Goods are a terrific price in Singapore. Rice >50 cents a katty, shoes are $10/—$20/- a pair, shaving soap in one canteen at $4/- a stick. Cake of toilet soap $5/-, tinned fish at $2.35 each. Even the *Sinbun* had a 'leader' about the rising price of articles and that it's time the Nips did something about it. Of course they are importing no goods here for lack of shipping.

2 August

Bank Holiday. We tried to celebrate it by having a half-day cricket match 'Slums' team v The Gentlemen (Officers) Players who think themselves good. Great fun, had a pavilion rigged up, tea and cakes served at 4.00 pm. Much barracking from our side and supporters.

We batted first and were all out for 69. I made four and was bowled. Then we went in to field and had seven wickets down for 49, but bad strategy in bowling lost us the game by two wickets. Think I broke Collin's finger with a hard drive into him.

Later went to Smokey Joe's for coffee and came back to find a drunken party going on in our Mess. Doyle and Campbell were very sick on the spirit later on.

3 August

The Nips have started clearing the aerodrome site by us, pushing over the big palm trees with a tractor in the former 18th Div area. Really looks as though they mean to do things now, and quickly. Also knocking down the wooden buildings by Changi Road and on the site.

Meantime AIF and British Commands are wrangling as to which of them is going to get into G&W area with the hospital instead of moving with the Selarang crowds. It seems Lt Col Holmes has forced himself upon us with several satellites for 'administrative' reasons. It's amazing how many folks have sheltered under the Red Cross out here, combatant officers and padres.

4 August

We all had to 'fall in' at 2.00 pm for a check roll call by IJA but it turned out to be a surprise search of all our kit. Radio sets were just hidden away in time although a pair of earphones was picked up in the hospital, but the set, wrapped in paper and a foot away, was missed. Similarly cameras, compasses and binoculars were missed though a few were picked up. My boxes were ransacked because I've an electric heater and wires hanging up in my locker. Locked boxes had to be opened or forced.

Some people had been tipped off but most didn't know, and I didn't hide my diary or a few maps that lay right on top of my locker, as did Markby's camera that was missed. They only collected old torch batteries, bits of wire, and a few accumulators.

5 August

Played hockey over at Selarang; we lost 3–0 in the League match.

For the evening, our 'combine' had two ducks, our first dividend since we bought them at the beginning of the year. Great treat for seven, there was quite a lot on each. Our Mess cook did them beautifully and I ate a practically rice-less meal for a change, and really felt comfortable – delightful taste of roast duck.

After supper heard a lecture by Sq Ldr Matheson (Aus RAF) a Blenheim pilot who has recently come into the camp from Burma. Very pessimistic talk, he thinks Burma will take two seasons to retake it. Our hopeless failure to take Akyab and lack of jungle warfare experience told again.

When are the British going to wake up!

6 August

The letters in the gaol are old ones of last July batch, and included a number of first postcards sent from this camp a year ago. Sorting proper begins today.

Went fishing this afternoon and caught a lovely *ikan sembiling*, about 3lb, had it cooked for supper, flesh is not unlike sole. My catch is encouraging others to have a go as well. Awfully sunburnt.

Went on wood fatigue to Tampines Road early this morning. A lovely walk out and not too hard a push back. Saw many civilian men and D. Molesworth. Wish I could get some news of Elizabeth; it's so long ago since we heard.

Some letters have started arriving, all date to last July–August. I have had no luck so far.

<u>Later:</u> Nip sentry came in and said there might be another surprise search.

7 August

News is getting good; Orel and Catania finished and rumour has it Sicily today. Am glad the radio sets still function though bulletins are not so frequent since the raid and one station has closed for a few days.

A Nip guard came into the dormitory last night and said we had the search because there have been transmitting sets detected in this area of Selarang though none have been found. He warned us of another possible search.

Fishing today but caught little, several *toda*, nothing big.

Sicilian news is all 'Borehole', and rather premature.

8 August

Command v Hospital Area in cricket on our *padang*. Our team was much too strong and easily won on the portion of an innings. M. ? Shaw IMD was star batsman for our side and a good bowler too.

Very hot afternoon but I tried more fishing and had no luck at all, not a single bite. It was most disappointing, such a good tide too.

Letters are still being sorted, no luck so far but there's lots to be done yet.

Eden reported to have said that negotiations are going on to transfer 'long term prisoners' to neutral countries; we are hopeful that we might come into that category at best.

Lt Campbell-Paterson of Wingate's guerrilla force (Burma) gave a lecture on his experience before being taken, very poor. Did say that the forces defending Singapore were thought very poorly of at home when it fell, 'but people are beginning to forget about it' – the bitterness of it for us out here.

9 August

Nardell and I went over to Selarang to hear Capt Roberts of the 'King's' talk about Brig Wingate's Burma Force. Very good talk and most informative, but he tells us that Burma is held by four Nip Divisions and one Burmese so it looks as though it's going to take a much longer time before we can retake Burma.

Nips arrived today to take away the stacked water carts near our Mess. Unfortunately somebody kept his radio set hidden in one and they have taken it away – what luck.

10 August

Chopping has come to live with us because of his special technical knowledge and has been made OC 'canarsis' (ducks). He will be bringing in his own in a few days.

Letter sorting goes on, Welch says about six for me in this day's lot. Cheers.

I am now a regular trailer pusher and join the officer party twice a week.

Cholera in Singapore, story is that it came off the *Asama Maru* that was in a few days ago and maybe had several cases aboard. No fishing or swimming allowed around the island until further orders. What are the natives going to live on as fish is a great part of their diet?

13 August

At last, cheers – seven letters from home. Four from Mother, one Stanley, two Olwen. Last dated 14th October 1942 and still no news of me got home, no card arrived there. How homesick they all make me, and dear Olwen, she doesn't know yet of Elizabeth; she has written such lovely letters too, to think that I thought she didn't care even after almost five years ago. My brain is in awful turmoil, if only I could see E. some more – out of all this. Mother – how will she take it, wonder if my first postcard will be an awful shock too.

Can't take my mind off Olwen now. How many years hence shall we meet again, perhaps I'll be forgiven by then, but I cannot forget.

If only I could get more news home. Oh for Home – and Mother.

14 August

We are told that the hospital has to move, by next Saturday, over to Selarang Square now. Also rumours of a party for upcountry, only medicals.

16 August

Preparations for the move to Selarang. Lab is packing up, RE are busy everywhere taking down sinks, electric fittings etc. I find they have a 1000-gallon Diesoline buried behind the theatre block. About four diesel engines and dynamos besides. I have managed to get a stock of five gallons of oil, may be useful for cooking and lighting.

17 August

Nips are progressing on the airfield by us. Today we saw materials for hangar building going in, also a couple of new looking aero radial motors went in.

AIF have started moving already. They always get off the mark pretty soon, but the buildings have already been allotted in Selarang.

18 August

Hospital started moving today properly. Trailer going back and forth; we are providing six MO parties daily. I did two runs this afternoon. Awful hard work but the ambulance meets us at the bottom of the hill and tows the loaded trailer up. We do the rest of the way. Good fun on the way back because of the element of risk at the steep hill – one trailer crashed this morning and three are in hospital – one a fractured skull, others not so bad.

CO, Julian Taylor are doing their share, but I'm afraid Lt Col Walter, Nardell are dodging it, to say nothing of all the padres and Stuart of the Red Cross. Latter won't do a stroke of work involving any effort. I'm becoming quite an expert trailer man now with plenty of experience.

?? Messina taken.

19 August

Busy day of movement again. Dougie Gawn et al are busy packing up for their move upcountry. Lt Col Benson is still on it; he's sent three stools already to the dysentery Lab but all negatives, as they were last time.

Apparently the Nip Commandant and other IJA round here are not keen on this camp breaking up as they would lose a comfortable job looking after us and good bungalows too. Also they have established a number of illicit sidelines – selling food (rice), cigarettes, medicines that should come to this camp, to Chinese in town. One 'racket' has just been caught, doing nicely for last six months between Chinese contractor and several Nips. Case is being reported in the *Syonan Sinbun*.

21 August

0.5cc of cholera vaccine today. Commonwealth material of 4000 units per cc; no reaction. Big drive in Singapore to get everybody 'protected' and it's reported that several cholera deaths have occurred already at Loyang. The party going upcountry get cholera and plague vaccines.

24 August

The medical party with Benson as OC left early this morning, 'Soda' the bitch was left with Craven. Dougie Gawn and Syd Nardell were the only despondent ones about going. Left about 12.30 am. Dawe also went, a Nip said not to worry about his wife as she would soon be repatriated.

I worked all day in our Mess garden. Felt damn tired. Soil is very poor, and by mistake, planted 'C' Mess brinjal plants in our plot. Had a fracas with Caldbeck over it.

27 August

Seem to be having persistent cold rainy weather. Still rather tired after yesterday's final effort back and forth in the rain.

Combined with 'C' Mess, we are rather crowded in this NAAFI block, sixty in the block, twelve in our small room.

The Lab room is not too bad now that it has been cleaned up and our things are in it.

Bought 2lb of sugar at $1.80 this morning, bananas are 15 cents/lb. An advantage is that we have three canteens within 100 yards of each other now.

Our fowls have settled in all right; we collected two eggs today and they haven't strayed like others have.

28 August

Col Middleton went in for chicken farming. Bought six about two weeks ago. One died, two strayed away so he thought best to sell the [other] three. Whilst exhibiting them he stood on another, [which] left two. When walking out of the run he trampled another chick of somebody else's – so finally gave away his remaining two in disgust.

Front of our Mess is a mass of chicken runs and ducks; nearly everybody has a share in a farm and it pays too.

Frankland, Ledingham and I are getting about an egg a day from our four hens. I believe they are laying out in the grass somewhere – we can't keep them in all the time.

29 August

An awful day of rain and wind.

Went up on the officers' ward roof; had a wonderful view of the gaol. Unfortunately the entrance is blocked out by trees. Can see the windows quite clearly but didn't see any figures or heads at them. Wondered what E. is doing at the moment, how she is. Over eight months since we last talked and now so close.

There are rumours of a possible visit but that's all, also of some repatriation for the women and children.

30 August

Cholera prophylaxis completed, 1.00cc in left breast, quite a good site I find. The scare about cholera in town seems to be dying down.

No 'weather report' today.

Thank goodness the 'move' is about over as we were getting awfully fed up, tired, hungry. New quarters seem to be awfully crowded. We have an excess of furniture in the room, and others come and play cribbage on our table. Two padres in our room and four next door, with the Ch/G [Chaplain General] sleeping below. We seem to be accumulating more and more of these folk. Also a 'B' Mess sleeping below of a number of combatant officers who are attached to the hospital too. Very mixed crowd indeed.

New Georgia finished.

31 August

Four page 'weather reports' now, very good with this improved service. Nothing stirring our side. Russians have taken Tanganvrod/Tanganrod? [Taganrog, near Rostov-on-Don]

Padre Young (Maj) always wears a big Red Cross although no MOs do now. Some Nips picked him up today in a car and asked if he was with the hospital; said 'Yes' whereupon one Nip demonstrated his penile chancre [ulcer] to the Padre – latter shrank from it. Nip as usual wanted treatment. Young tried to explain he was no doctor whereupon the Nips kicked him out of the car in disgust, saying 'Ah you English man'. Brian Lewis the ACG [Assistant Chaplain General] is the only other who still wears a Red Cross armlet and he has managed to get into this hospital area too.

3 September

We hear that the British and American forces have landed early today on the Italian mainland. At last a semblance of another front has opened and it's not the Russians who are still doing all the groundwork.

What of out here; the Nips are still being underestimated by our Government.

5 September
We still have in hospital the various prisoners who have come in from time to time from Outram Road Gaol where they are doing 'solitary'. Most are well now but of course cannot be sent out as then they go back to their cells. Lt Marriot (A&SH) is getting so fat and ungrateful he may find himself shot out one of these days. The prison representatives come along at odd periods to see them and our fellows have to be smart and get them into bed and make them look ill. Only once have Nip MOs been along to see them, and after a casual look, said they were still unfit to send back. However their Gestapo [Kempetai] paid a surprise visit and thought some were fit; said that all this time in hospital was not going to be counted, that they would still have to serve the 5–10 year terms, mostly for attempts to escape on upcountry parties.

7 September
We hear that another batch of letters has arrived at the gaol. How old are they this time?

Command have agreed to send a further $10/- to our wives in the gaol as from this month. Wonder if she is getting it all right. The price of everything has gone up so much since last year.

> Rice > 50 cents a catty.
> Sugar 80 cents/lb.
> Fish > $2/- a catty.
> Tin chicken curry $2.90 each.
> Tin fish $2/- each.
> Bananas 17 cents/lb.
> Coconuts 25 cents each.
> Pork $2.50 a catty.

8 September
'Weather report' – Russians continue to do well and in S. Pacific we seem to have launched a big attack on Lae [in New Guinea]. Let's see how long it is before it falls.

Interesting post mortem today on an RAF lad. I found a small and contracted kidney and urinaria as a cause of death – clinically he had been diagnosed as acute bacillary dys [dysentery]. Of course the physicians are trying hard to twist things around to fit their case. Second autopsy in a tent up here at Selarang. It was a cool rainy morning, but the smell, flies, lack of running water made things difficult. The odd OR passing by also stops to have a look; I hurry him on his way. CO keeps promising us a decent mortuary.

9 September
At the Lab this morning. Very hot rumours that Italy is out [of the war]. General but suppressed excitement all over. I am very sceptical.

Late – cheers, cheers – unconditional surrender by Italy in our 'weather report'. This is terrific and Winston says there will be more news tomorrow perhaps of sensational nature. Hope it affects us out here, [as] we still feel forgotten.

The attack on Nip base of Lae is progressing too. Wish things there were on a bigger scale.

After supper I paid Steve Campbell $2/- as his winnings for the bet we had on about fall of Italy. I'm only 24 hours out again.

10 September
Went on the wood fatigue this morning. Drizzly but cool and it is a pleasant outing. I did little work, mostly walked behind the trailer. On the return journey as we passed the civilian woodcutters, they all came down to the roadside carrying logs, very conveniently. Looked quite cheerful so they must have the Italian news too. Didn't see anyone whom I knew amongst them. They seem to have a tremendous number of b****** Sikh guards to watch over them.

Played some hockey at 4.00 pm; rather hot.

Some letters for me from home in the sorting.

11 September
197 FA soccer XI remains unbeatable again. It was a good match, v The Rest. Huge crowd of spectators and feelings ran high. What a scene in a POW camp, it would be unbelievable at home. Wish the civilians could see some of this, but they're kept cooped up so.

Followed at dusk by an excellent brass band concert in the centre of our square. Band on a raised platform of green lockers and tables, even with floods and music lights. Conductor was the Yank, Porter, he did well.

Three letters, all from Mother, dear Mother. Last dated 16.12.42, and still they have no news of us.

12 September
Forbes Finlayson had another go at my teeth today $^4 + {}^4$ and only had two fillings to do. Used Cu amalgam, it's the best available and I hope will do. The Right Upper was a huge hole with only the outer wall standing. Forbes says I must get it seen to as soon as we get out [of] here.

Nothing else wrong with my teeth, no more grinding and chiselling.

Wonderful that we can have dental treatment here and quite good too.

13 September
'Weather report' continues to be good. Russians forging ahead, Italy front doing well, good additions to our fleet and S. Pacific front increasing – well, well.

We are expecting a party of 500 POW from Java today. IJA sent instructions about meeting them. None have arrived by nightfall.

14 September
Party of British and Dutch have arrived from Java, about 400. Only one MO from here is allowed to contact them; they've very little illness. Have been fed well down there, plenty of meat and eggs and fruit, complaining of the poor diet up here.

Nobody I know amongst this crowd. Apparently another 3000 are to come up shortly.

15 September
The ban on fishing and swimming around Singapore has been lifted so we are hoping to get something in the way of fish. So far it's been ridiculous, we even get served with a small transparent angel fish per day as our ration of 2½oz. Pity I cannot do any decent fishing in this area as I caught things worth eating and threw them back at that time.

Our fowls (four hens and one cock) are not laying so well these days. We are going to increase the farm by putting eggs under a broody hen, one of ours, but she won't make up her mind to sit or not, and our methods of persuasion have so far been rather unsuccessful.

Damn her and such a nice nest too.

16 September
The Nips have issued a new and rather curious order restricting smoking to 'Smoking Rooms' and areas. No smoking allowed on beds, in bedrooms,

wards, departments etc. Two fellows had their faces smacked for smoking on the roads. Further all private stocks of petrol have to be handed in to QM's store for safekeeping; what a hope! With so many electric lighters and Ronsons about the place.

These days seem awfully short; I can find plenty to do but these quarters are so noisy. I sit in the verandah, [at] my school desk, and try to work here. Inside the area they've gone cribbage-mad and downstairs the RE are knocking the stage together for the new hospital theatre.

18 September

Curious that the *Syonan Sinbun* (English edition) is not sent to the camp now, stopped since the one which should have given the news of Italy's capitulation. The IJA have given no reason for it, and our Commander has asked that it be continued as 'lack of news may cause rumours and unrest in the POW camp!' The paper was so highly amusing and entertaining in its futile attempts to twist the news of the War around, and the Co-Prosperity [Sphere] spoken of Greater East Asia, and the new way of living in Malaya. Maybe the Nips will reply and ask if we need new valves for our radio sets.

19 September

At last we hear that Lae (N.G.) has fallen, but nothing of the numbers of Nips taken prisoner. Russian news remains terrific.

The new Java party were all bum-stabbed yesterday and will be leaving for upcountry or overseas soon. It is said that they were intended as a working party for New Guinea and issued with fishing nets as part of the idea. But things have changed so. Capt James, the pro-Nip interpreter of this camp, is also going – ? on special business with the Nip intelligence to Tokyo.

I have never liked the man and his pro-Nip attitude, even when not with them.

20 September

The Java party have gone off by sea. Six officers were sent back here as it seems that there was insufficient room for them on the vessel. Capt James has gone with a lot of warm clothing given him by the Nip general here.

Visited Lt Col Alford and had a long talk with him about the IMS and our losses through being POWs. Continued the discussion at the officers

Club over coffee and 'eats', such as they provide. We better [all] agree that we shall probably have to put up a fight for our dues. It seems from letters that since 1st August 1942 we have been paid at 'higher furlough rates' and no overseas allowances, also we are still working to full capacity. Let's see.

21 September

Went to the AIF concert, a farce based on some Malayan POW being discharged after the War. Quite good fun – may come true.

LETTERS – more of them, I get five today. Mother and dear Olwen still, if only I'd had faith! Apparently Mother knows that I am now POW, but my card has not arrived, dated last one 23rd January '43. At least she knows I'm alive somewhere.

Score   Mother 14   Stanley 1
             Olwen 6
             Mona 1

22 September

An Aussy who I saw fishing in the big drain leading to the swamp has been taken away by Nip sentries. They must have sat about in the grass waiting for him to go between the layers of wire to get his line that had got stuck there as it often does. Only a further ten yards and there is a lovely fishing pool. Apparently the AIF MO used to buy this fellow's catch off him, so encourages him more.

23 September

The *Syonan Sinbun* has not been seen since the fall of Italy; I do wish it would be allowed in, like to see what they are saying about the War in Italy, Russia, and their defeats by McArthur down in New Guinea. At last things seem to have bucked up down there and the Yanks have the initiative.

Wonder how the Japs are feeling about the impending offensives against them in China and Burma too – how they are explaining things to the 'locals'.

However we are getting a pretty good 'weather report', sometimes as long as 8 sides 4in x 6in and the organisation of it is excellent.

24 September

Our hen has been sitting for three days now and it looks as though she means it this time. Only trouble is that the eggs are somewhat stale, 9 days old when we started her off. 'Tina' who first went broody only sat for a day, this is 'Blondie' and is doing ok. I don't do so badly for eggs these days, about one every other day.

The Mess ducks of 22 are now laying 15–20 a day and the roster goes round in 2–3 days. Ledingham's busy these days putting up a 'duck run' for our 4, using bamboo stakes for the walls.

25 September

Strong rumour that the IJA have interned about 250 Italians off vessels in Singapore. Well they're fighting for us now in Corsica and elsewhere.

Chopping goes down as MO for the airfield working party daily and has been bringing me back various sorts of snakes. Today an AIF party caught a python, and after supper I went out with C.' to trace it. We ended up at their Cen' depot where about 30 men were around a fire and a sizzling frying pan, each waiting for the cooking of his piece of python. They'd tried boiling the meat at first but forgot to de-gut it.

Somebody kept the skin and I rescued the head from a swill bin, in quite good condition except that it has been cut off a bit short.

27 September

We are having several ARP [air raid precaution] exercises these days and blackouts. The latter is far better than ever occurred when we were ruling Singapore. No smoking on balconies etc. It's queer to hear the wail of sirens again in the darkness, but no planes about the place, and no bombs. How eagerly we wait for something from our own planes.

These exercises are a nuisance as one can't read at night, and by day there's such a din downstairs as our Mess is being turned into a theatre. It looks awfully good and neat, but I fear the band we shall have to put up with for a spell of 2 weeks per run. It'll be a case of 'no peace in our time'.

29 September

Awful disaster, the IJA have stopped the Red Cross allowance, amounting to 8 cents per head daily, which the CMF [Central Messing Fund] was spending to improve the diet.

Apparently the item did not look good on the sheet of expenses that goes up to Geneva eventually as it suggests that we are underfed – that's true.

Guest, the Red Cross man, is to see the Nip General, and so is Lt Col Holmes, to have this order rescinded as we all suffer badly. But there is little hope. The Nips say that Red Cross funds must be spent only on patients and drugs – not on extra food.

And things are getting more difficult because of steadily rising prices.

Hen is still sitting alright and two others threaten to go broody now, so may only get one egg a day for the three of us.

1 October

Went on the wood party this morning. Extraordinary sight to see our fellows all over a Chinese house, drinking tea, assisted by the Nip guard, and playing with the ducks and fowls. Even buying some of the ducklings. Last time we tried to buy some Muscovy ducklings through our guard but the Chinese wouldn't part with them even at $10/- for the family. The sentry tried hard to do the deal, but I think life is pretty hard for the poor Chinese.

Clinical Meeting of Changi Medical Society. Bouti's Disease, acholuric jaundice, and Boeck's sarcoridonis and ?? malaria.

2 October

Hear of the fall of Naples and also that an 'exchange vessel' has arrived here with 1500 on board en route to Goa. Lucky people. Wonder when E. and others will go from this gaol.

The new Java party of 2500 have come in with some dysentery. They say that food was plentiful in their previous camps, [with] meat, eggs, sugar etc very cheap. Quite different to this place.

The Nips have refused to allow Red Cross funds to be spent on more rations, so, to make up the loss from this source, officers will only get $12/- a month now; the rest of the money is to be pooled for the Central Messing Fund.

3 October

Beadnell RAMC has arrived with this batch from Java. Tells us the food was excellent down there and very cheap. He ate six eggs daily and plenty of meat. Our state now is worse as there is no fresh fish coming in. We have an issue of stinking dried herrings instead. Julian T. calls them 'the little horrors'.

4 October

Last evening there was a big soccer match, our officers v 197 FA. We had Wilfred Wooller, the famous rugger international, playing for us. What a physique for this camp. He's up from Java too. Huge muscles rippling all over and was he fast; the crowd immediately took to him – leaping about the place like a great panther.

However, we lost 2–0.

Our pay this month is only $12/- in hand, all the rest taken by Command to put into the CMF to make up for the loss of Red Cross money.

6 October

The Lab cat had no food for days now, won't eat dried herrings, so she was given morphia then ether, then buried in front in the Lab garden. She will add a little more to the soil there which has had many snakes and several buckets of urine in it already. Tomatoes, chillies, ginger and mint are all doing well.

The Dutch from G&W area were allowed over to visit us. They've bought everything up in our canteen and are selling our folk latrine paper sheets at 1½ cents each to cut up as cigarette paper. I'm told it serves awfully well. They, on the other hand, have a shortage of tobacco, and, except for the officers, of money.

7 October

No eggs for days now; we have one hen sitting and two broody, one laying away somewhere. The broody ones are spending uncomfortable days in a special wire cage or torture chamber.

Hungry, never been so ever before, one cannot dare to miss a meal, and the amount of rice to eat is insufficient. Led [Ledingham] and I can eat the dish for eight between us, and before each meal I suffer from awful hypoglycaemia.

Instead of fresh fish we are getting almost two small salted 'dry herring' a day. They smell awful, but taste good and help down a lot of rice. Many folk consider them too high.

8 October

Opening of the 'Little Theatre' in our Mess hall with *Outward Bound* by Sutton Vane, produced by Maj Daltrey, with Douglas Rye and F.J. Bradshaw playing. Quite the best show we've had in Singapore, even well enough produced for the West End. The stage is better than we've yet had, any desired lighting, fans in the auditorium and good seating. It went down as any good first night should, and Daltrey made a speech and took a curtain. The play is good too, but what a polished performance.

Usual 'wood fatigue' today. Saw M. ?Johns. Strachan spoke to him and we gather that no women or children have been repatriated as yet. Though there is a strong rumour to that effect of Nip origin.

The mortuary at present is a very ragged rotten tent which blows down in every storm. I am always complaining about it only the CO keeps compromising, [but it's a] pretty dirty affair doing autopsies in the tent. The tin table is sloped so that the liquors pour into a hole about 3ft deep at the foot. The mess is covered up with a layer of mud and the hole is used until it is full up. Site is below the soccer field – rather public.

10 October

Big day on our farm as eight chicks have hatched out by afternoon out of fourteen we put under. 'Blondie' is awfully proud. Five eggs are infertile and one failed to come out. One infertile egg burst under Blondie the other day and made an awful mess; of course the ants came in. We just saved the first two chicks from the ants in the nick of time.

12 October

Information has come down that, during Aug/Sept '43, 216 deaths occurred from the last parties which went away, probably from cholera. Include six officers, one is Capt Nash of 45 AT Company, that's the 3rd or 4th of their officers whom I knew up at Lipis two years ago. The rolls come down here as their pay is still controlled from here.

We are speculating as to whether any Red Cross supplies will be sent from Goa on the return trip of the exchange ship. Most will be very disappointed if nothing arrives.

13 October

Italy has joined the Allies against Germany. Rabaul gets a good packet.

15 October

A rumour that all the civilians have been confined strictly to the prison, none allowed out for any purpose because they've been intriguing with the Sikh guards to get some money into the gaol. Hope this doesn't affect the women and children too.

Plenty of rumours of repatriation of the latter, but I fear none of these are true yet.

Heard a lecture on 'How a USA pilot is trained' by S/Lt Bassett of the US Air Force, who was shot down in his Liberator over Rangoon early this year. Most interesting.

16 October
Deaths to date in this Hospital – British, AIF, Dutch.

Battle casualties	62
Dipth.	64
Bac. Dys.	266
Am. Dys.	17
Encephalitis or 'opathy	30
Malaria	24
Accidents	26
T.B.	18
Deficiency D.	16
Lung inflammation	19
Neoplasm	14
Cardiac disease and failure	13
I.A.T. and osteomyelitis	6
Ac Pancreatitis	2
Ac Appendicitis	7
Pneumonia	7
Liver abscess (Pyogenic)	3
Peptic ulcer	5
Other causes	22
Suicide	2
[Total: 623]	

17 October
Weighed myself today, and allowing for my boots, am 11st 4lb. BP 106/68, bit higher than this time last year, heavier than I've ever been in Malaya.

My razor blades are so blunt that I've started using hot water now and use proper soap and brush once again. Have had the latter lying by all this time as a reserve. What a pleasure it is to shave decently now. Water heated up in a couple of minutes by my electric heater.

18 October
Bulletin today says two vessels will be bringing food etc to the POWs and internees in the Far East. They'll be very welcome here. Little or nothing to buy at the canteen these days, everything is so expensive; worse in town where a small banana is 8 cents and large 12–15 cents. Pork at $3.50 a catty.

Much naval and air activity round here these days, many vessels up in the Naval Base; two aircraft carriers, pretty big ones, have gone up to the Base. Perhaps preparation to defend Burma. They're taking it in the Solomon group.

19 October

Wavell in India to take over from Linlithgow. The exchange of British POWs with the Germans is going well, 5000 now in Sweden to change tomorrow. The exchange with the Nips is going on now in Goa. Hear also that 1500 tons of supplies are being dumped at 'V' monthly for us.

Apparently the civilian internees are still strictly confined to the prison; none had been sent out yet, [and] been in about a week now.

All the latest Java party have gone off from G&W area, over-seas. Nips have said the area to be tidied for a party which is returning from upcountry – we wonder which.

21 October

Our eight little chicks are getting on well. A sparrowhawk keeps flying around here and picks up a bird everyday; so far ours are ok. There are so many runs for it to choose from, and ours is isolated and somewhat hidden. Big drive against fly breeding in farms is going on as flies have been on the increase again and there has been a mild outbreak of dysentery in the hospital area.

An awful lot of air activity around here these days; the pilots in fighter craft practice dogfights all day long. Must say that the Nip planes are very manoeuvrable and can show a burst of speed. They seem to be handled well.

22 October

The first part of Java party, 1300 in all, have returned to G&W area having stayed 2–3 days on a ship in Singapore harbour. They were bound for Japan; their guards were awfully disappointed at the trip being called off, and they were sent back to Java. Ships were awfully dirty but food good on them. Say that a convoy of thirty vessels came in to the Harbour – wonder if these are bound for Burma.

Great bit of work – we had Smuts's [South African Prime Minister Jan Smuts] speech in full, eight pages of it, a very good summary of the past and present, but a little pessimistic for the length of time we have to stay out here.

The news continues as before. I wish we could see how the *Sinbun* interprets it! Difficult to explain things now.

27 October

We are hearing much about a German and British exchange of prisoners going on at present. Lucky people. We are still hopeful of some food supplies coming by the Nip exchange vessel from Goa.

At last there is a decent mortuary and post mortem room again, after weeks of grumbling to the CO about the ragged tent. I intend to use this one for reading at night as it has a ceiling fan and electric light, and is a nice quiet place apart from our Mess.

We took our four ducks away from the Mess run and have a stooge looking after them, giving him a ¼ share. Now we are getting an egg a day from them which is excellent, and our hens are doing about three eggs in two days. The chicks we hatched out are coming on fine; expect four hens in the bunch of eight.

29 October

Reported that some men have been seen coming out of the gaol again, the first time for weeks, and they have not had lights for the last ten days.

We are just finishing a week of ARP with frequent alarms and continuous brownout. The General here thinks our planes will be over Singapore soon and has warned us that we must not show too much pleasure about it.

Apparently Kennedy IMS has died up in Taiwan as his letters from there have been returned as deceased; wonder what of, as it was noted here that he was awfully dirty in habits about himself.

18th Div party is the one returning from upcountry soon.

30 October

Command has issued a brazen order that all reels of cotton in excess of one will be handed in forthwith and 25 cents paid for it. It will be an offence after this to be in possession of two reels. So many of these sort of orders emanate from them now that we have lost all confidence in our present leaders here. A reel of cotton costs about $1.50 if purchasable. I bought mine in Singapore before capitulation thinking of the need. Anyway RAOC [Royal Army Ordnance Corps] should have thought of these things eighteen months ago or more instead of themselves only.

The medical unit brought out all they could for hospital use, instead of their own rations and comfort first, and too readily handed in their food caches to a common dump for use of patients; many units kept their entire rations and lived on them 'til October or later last year.

Also over the money question, we (most officers) feel that there is mis-spending and leakage of common funds. Deductions are made from our Nip allowances without our consent. Tell us that officers will get $15/- this month – how will the rest ($35/-) be spent! $15,000 is being borrowed from our bank account by the Red Cross to replace their lost funds viz last month.

1 November

Ledingham has rather a bad sore throat and is beginning to look ill with it; been on for two days now, he's sick.

Frankland is away in Blakang Mati so I have to do the farm all by myself, not that there is an awful lot to it. The chickens are coming on magnificently.

Later – Ledingham has a membrane and is swabbed positive for KLB so off to hospital he goes, and is given a nice side room to himself. There is some Nip serum available for him, [but] it's awfully weak stuff.

3 November

Ledingham's sore throat is worse: I took a swab and diagnosed KLB so off to Hospital he goes. He gets awfully pulled down by a slight illness, looking rather bad today.

Since the ducks have been given to a caretaker they are doing well. Today there were three eggs, yesterday two and at least one a day – not bad. Twelve eggs from them to date.

Chicks are still doing fine: I shall have to take them over as F. is detailed to go as MO to Blakang Mati camp.

4 November

A Dutch body was brought over last night from G&W area. Had been ill for two days but the Nips would not allow him into hospital across the road. At autopsy I found a pretty severe bacillary lesion of the bowel, query shiga infection.

The IJA have repeatedly bum-stabbed this party and say they have no dysentery – that their sick are due to 'enteritis'.

Not so much aerial activity around here these last 2–3 days, probably since the carriers left the Naval Base. It is reported that a vessel all lit up at night, painted white, has gone north out of Singapore – suggested that it is the exchange vessel returning from Goa.

'Weather report' continues good. No neutral representatives of the Red Cross have yet visited our POW camp.

6 November

The Dutch party in G&W have left today for overseas, leaving a few sick behind here.

Ledingham is awfully bad today, wasted, cyanotic, weak and can hardly whisper. Has had three lots of serum now and has suffered a very bad reaction in three stages. Some glottal oedema, acute generalised lymphadenitis, worst in the cervical group, then a very acute erythema at sites of oedema followed by acute polyarthritis affecting first the hands and next day the feet and ankles.

I shall refuse to do an autopsy on him if it comes to the worst.

7 November

Led' is a little better today, though not quite out of the mire.

Our Mess has to provide a trailer party daily now to fetch firewood from beyond the gaol, as the Nips won't supply a lorry for lack of petrol and they are demanding more men to work on the aerodrome site as it is beginning to take shape a little.

8 November

Two of the Outram Road prisoners, both patients, have vanished out of the camp. It is supposed that they have made an attempt to escape – just left their wards during the night. One is an ex-Borstal lad and is said to be a bit mental.

Of course the IJA have been informed about their absence and we expect that as a result the other Outram Road men will now be taken back again to their solitary confinement, and – unless things improve – a slow death in that gaol.

12 November

The Nips came up today with a Black Maria and took away four British and three Aussy prisoners back to Outram Road gaol, Lt Marriott of the A&SH included. It was a sorry sight; Marriott was the only one who took a small pack. The others had no boots or socks, shorts and a ragged shirt only. Just went off with nothing.

They got a cheer round the Square as the bus drove off.

The ward next door to the Lab was very silent and depressed the rest of today, almost as though one of them had died, even worse. All because of two foolish escapees; we all seem to agree that there is very little chance of getting out of this place to our countries.

22 November

Major Farmer Aussy EN&T [Ear, nose and throat] even painted my tonsils over with Argyrol [antiseptic] to try and get rid of the KLB from them, being a possible carrier. I have to attend every morning for this.

We cultured the 'Slums' and our table for carriers and find Riddell, Marshall, White and myself are carriers. Probably Riddell who works in the diphtheria ward started it all. Spike Sullivan, the latest of our room to go in, has a terrific membrane but does not look particularly toxic.

26 November

Lt Col Harris, OC of this camp, has been up to see the General about the treatment of prisoners in Outram Road prison – he was given a hell of a 'dressing down' for signing himself 'OC Troops Malaya' in his petition and also for daring to say anything about the prisoners; eventually sent away, and as a punishment he has to go and work at the aerodrome for fourteen days.

28 November

Awfully busy looking at the smears for mrps of a 1000 party of POWs just come down from the north. Our Lab is doing all the work but Strachan is taking the credit for it. We are doing 650 smears and Aussies 350; S' just collects the lists and gives them to the Nip when he comes for them. We are using Fields stain and examining 50 fields on each slide. Pretty high percentage of positives today.

29 November

Finished the slides today and find 144 in the bunch. Some of these are pretty severe ST malaria cases too near the borderline. Apart from the lists of names we know nothing about the chaps who have come down. No MOs whom I know are in the party; the only doctor seems to be a Major Morrison of the Volunteers.

The Nip NCO who has collected the slides won't say anything about them either.

4 December

A census of fowls and ducks in the area shows a total of 8000, about 5000 in the camp of which in our area (hospital) there are 1800 to <2000 people.

Much grumbling by the piggery about insufficient swill for the 400 pigs, so Command has ordered that all swill will go to them from hospital area, which means of course that, taken literally, our birds would starve. What a hope.

It's a case of pigs v fowls, and most feel that we get more out of the latter as eggs against 2oz of pork three monthly. And again, the piggery people have an enormous number of chicks which they feed off the ground swill, and have eggs sufficient to sell them through the Base Canteen at 25 cents each.

6 December

Still having my nose and throat argolysed to get rid of any KLB.

We are wondering if there will be a visit to the gaol this year; the request has gone in from our side, no definite answer as yet – told it depends on the Civil Administration of the internees.

7 December

Surprise air raid alarm last night, quite a flop. Nips came round and made everybody come off the top floors of buildings and get to their action stations etc. BUT we heard none of our planes, in fact nothing at all. We think there may have been a raid on Sumatra or Penang.

Some American airmen have come into the camp, were taken over in French Indo-China only in September.

We'll hear more about them later.

8 December

Lots of talks between Stalin, Churchill and Roosevelt – but little action.

The Yanks in this camp have received parcels and letters today. Excellent parcels – soap, blades, vitamin tablets, chewing gum etc. Several of the parcels estimated to be worth $50 (USA) of course, plenty of cigarettes.

11 December

Third postcard: 'Dear Mother, Am fit. Don't worry. Received much appreciated letters you and Olwen. I think Elizabeth is well. Greetings and love to all, Jack.'

It's so difficult to say all that one wants to in such a few words. Limited to twenty four; ours are being typed out.

Prisoners in hospital from Outram Road gaol are not allowed to send a card.

13 December

An AIF body was brought in from Singapore by the Nips for immediate burial, certified as 'cerebral malaria' and died on the journey down from the north.

Another party have now arrived back in town. All sorts of rumours that of 'F' Force of 6000, 2000 dead, and of 'H' Force of 3000, there are 800 dead. Nip NCO is supposed to have said that total of 13,000 deaths have occurred up there, hit the Nips badly too.

Conditions for our POWs have been appalling. I saw a slip of paper with 86 names of Volunteers dead on it.

16 December

Cholera vaccine 1.0cc taken by self and Lab staff today. This is a precaution as 2500 are coming down to G&W area and it's rumoured that they've had much cholera amongst them, causing the high death rate.

Later – 76 Aussies came in to hospital this morning. Very emaciated and pale. Came down from Bangkok by coal vessel; say the railway through to Burma is finished. Treatment upcountry is dreadful, many deaths due to exposure. Poor food, ill treatment, malaria, dysentery, cholera and phagedena (tropical ulcer), for which limbs have to be amputated.

Conditions for treatment are poor; 1000 more or less are unfit for moving and these are the fitter people coming down by boat.

The railway connects Bangkok to Moulmein and they say it cost 10,000 British and 40,000 Tamil and Chinese lives. Bodies of latter lying all over the place and in the skeleton camps which had to be occupied by our men. Only what one could carry oneself was taken in at the railhead, all the rest was dumped, including medical items.

'F' group of 7000 under Lt Col Harris seem to have suffered most with 70% British and 50% AIF casualties. They were in the worst zone and furthest from medical aid. Men had to work as long as they could use their hands, even carried to work. No machinery used at all on the track etc. Nips drove the men like beasts, many committed suicide, escapees died in the jungle, and Nips were keen on burning even dying men.

They looked after themselves, ate our 'M&V' Bully and meat rations. Rain added to the misery, worked from 8 am until dark for seven days with no holidays at all, and only two meals a day. Twenty minute rest periods twice a day. Beatings with bamboo were the order of the day.

18 December
Handed in a Christmas present for E., cake of soap and tin of chocolates. Hope to accompany the trailer up to the gaol.

Took a 60 cent seat at the preview of *Aladdin* in our Little Theatre. Young (John) Willie White of our Mess made up as a wonderful princess, very, very pretty girl. Steve Campbell sent up a bouquet of flowers after. The whole show was good, particularly scenery and lighting effects.

25 December
Lovely present of two pairs knitted socks from Elizabeth; hope she's well – all my love. Home and Mother, how is everyone, thinking of you all.

Day of sport and fun for us in the hospital, though I opened with a post mortem at 10.30 am.

We saw the humorous soccer match, drank lovely milky coffee with biscuits. Lunch was a good 'bully' pie, and supper a pork pie. For tea we had bread and butter in the Lab, and cakes. I had a good game of hockey, [and] this was followed by a big soccer match of N v S. Last of all saw J.T. do a laparotomy and patient who died on the operating table, he's a suspicious acute [illegible] but I doubt it!

26 December
I open the day with a post mortem and we have another 1000 smears for mrps. Any amount of work to be done by us.

Was vaccinated (failed) because of two cases of smallpox in the hospital. Classical confluent rashes both of them. There were several cases at their camp upcountry; Nine? And four of them died.

Our vaccine is a small amount that has come in with a small package of American Red Cross stores. There are plenty of rumours that a Red Cross vessel is discharging stores down in Singapore.

Our presents to the gaol have gone in without trouble, I'm told. Nips gave us our Christmas box of twenty cigarettes each.

31 December

Disaster, I broke a pre-molar [4] + at lunch. It had an apical abscess and was an awful job extracting by Forbes Finlayson. Roots had to be dug for separately; it's been rather sore all the evening but did not prevent me from eating my share of duck at supper.

Steve Campbell been pyrexial all day 100–103°F, maybe down to his vaccination.

We have an extension of lighting until 1.00 am to see the New Year in, but nothing to drink this year.

Chapter 6

Jack's diary – 1944

1 January

We were informed that all our presents got into the gaol quite safely after a careful scrutiny at the Nip offices.

The New Year opens dismally as we're getting more and more news about the heavy sick casualties upcountry; estimated that about 10,000 British and Australian have died building the Bangkok to Moulmein Railway. MOs haven't suffered much but groups were set tasks by Nip MO to see if they knew any medicine, and have been posted to look after native coolie camps without any medical supplies or instruments. There is a big base hospital at Bangkok where there are 1000 very ill unfit to move down here. Food at some camps was lavish but at others very scarce. Accommodation was nothing or crowded huts.

Lights until 0100 hours to see the New Year in, none at the gaol. It was not cheery.

I had an upper pre-molar removed yesterday and it's very sore.

2 January

We have established a custom in the Lab of sweet coffee with coconut milk twice a week, as long as sugar and coconut are obtainable within a reasonable price. The latter we buy from chaps who collect them in the Gardens or on the aerodrome. This pleasure we've had functioning for last two to three months, wish we had thought of it before. One more use to which the electric heater in the Lab has been put. It has certainly proved a big success, don't quite know how I got it out of QM Tidd – he has never given away anything so good again.

6 January

Meeting of Changi Medical Society showing of 'Artificial Limbs' made in this camp. The British ones were very good indeed. I'm afraid the Aussy ones were very poor in comparison and their walking was dreadful. About 20 leg amputees on each side demonstrated.

7 January

It's rumoured from Singapore that a Red Cross vessel and a hospital ship have arrived and are discharging food and medical supplies there. About time we were allowed some things in here!

9 January

In spite of the 'Go Easy Campaign' on the aerodrome work, it's taking shape slowly; most of the work there is done by Chinese and Malay labour of men, women and children. Nip guards are attempting to drive our fellows and incidents are frequent. Snail gathering is the chief idea of each man down there as their value amongst duck owners has gone up from five for 3 cents to 1 cent each or more. A great business has started particularly as duck food is so scarce and most of them are off laying these days – like ours. Our fowls too are off, [with] no eggs for days from them.

14 January

Frankland up from Blakang Mati. Nip inspection for radio sets; looked everywhere including the wood yard where lots were hidden, and in the chicken runs; very superficial and ignorant fellows came around. Looked in the mortuary and wanted Cooper to open a 'ready' coffin.

Lost a white cock this evening.

17 January

Soon we'll have been POWs for two years.

I sleep on a good bed, mattress etc, have electric lighting, even a big ceiling fan in our room, reasonable floor space and plenty of work to help pass the day. Defects – the dirt, lack of freedom, lack of drugs etc, the humiliations we suffer from the IJA, foolishness of our own leaders – utter stupidity it seems at times, our own restrictions. Tired of seeing each other for so long.

News service is good; if only things would get on a bit faster, if only the Nips would repatriate Elizabeth and the others.

19 January

Major Wild, interpreter, gave Changi Medical Society a talk on 'F' force. It was a very vivid first-hand account of the dreadful experience. He looks rather thin now; the figures are 3000 dead and more to die yet out of the initial force of 7000 that went up from here last year.

I have taken an extract of the official report elsewhere which has been sent up to IJA HQ out here for their perusal. No MOs have died yet but many are in a bad way. Few RAMC have died. Gasper RAMC who suffered under the Turks at Kut [British defeat in Mesopotamia during First World War] has finished this affair too and now looks well. Says this has been a much worse experience.

22 January

Opening night of N. Coward's *Hay Fever* produced by O. Daltrey starring John Wood and Bradshaw. I couldn't have enjoyed it more at a London theatre. Awfully well played. Good dresses and the scenery was, as usual at the Little Theatre, very good. Our Mess makes a good theatre. Only thing I missed was a *stengah* [whisky, soda and ice] at intervals and E. for company. I propose to go and see at least two shows a week as soon as I get home, good food first, good seats and then a good supper. Ledingham says he'll join the party when we get on the 'senior course' together.

Some new mail has arrived up at the gaol, including from India and home. Two bags are mail that was sorted last year for 'F' force to send upcountry to them, but they never got it; it's been returned here from Tokyo. The new letters are dated as late as July–August 1943. Some are only cards of 24 words apparently.

Had a look at myself today as to health –

Weight	11st 10lb	
HG	105%	
BP	110/84	– and I feel pretty well.

26 January

Saw *Good Morning, Bill* [by P.G.] Wodehouse at the Phoenix open-air theatre – Ken Morrison, Elliot and Norman Backshall starred; latter was awfully good. I enjoyed the performance.

27 January

3½oz of meat issued today, it tasted good. The last issue of meat was about December '42. Think this meat must have come down from Thailand; it was refrigerated and in good condition.

28 January

Word regarding our treatment in the camps is out at home and in the States. Wonder what Mother and the family is thinking. Do hope they have had some of my cards by this time.

29 January

Saw *Hay Fever* again and enjoyed it just as much as the first night.

Food situation and medical supplies is getting serious. In spite of Lt Toraka promising that certain prices would come down, they have steadily gone up worse in the last few weeks. Many essential items – oil, bananas, fish – are not coming in at all.

The Commandant Major General has refused to see our representatives for the last two to three months to discuss this state of affairs; he and his colleagues of junior officers seem to be just crude liars, promising things right and left which they knew they had no intention of doing for us.

1 February

A 'brownout' is introduced all over Singapore; we only got the order indirectly. Apparently this is for keeps now 'til we get out. At any rate wish the bombers would come to hearten us a bit. Things are beginning to drag rather.

IJA have made us dig slit trenches all over the place and we have a very comprehensive PAD [passive air defences] scheme to carry out. The Little Theatre is beautifully blacked out now so that shows can go on as before. *Hay Fever* is still on here.

2 February

The meat ration has continued since 27.1.44, enough to make the afternoon much pleasanter. But the other rations are reduced.

3 February

Gave a lecture in the post-graduate series on lab work in haematology. Think I dwelt too much with mathematics, but kept them at it for 80 minutes.

Changi Medical Society met after supper, a few cases were shown and discussed but the meeting was awfully dull.

Prices		
	Bananas	20 cents/lb
	Sugar	$1.50/lb
	Eggs	50 cents each
	Coffee	$2.0/-/lb
	Towgay	$1.50/lb
	Coconut	50 cents each
	Football	$90–100

6 February

All members of the camp have had to write their 'Most Exciting Experience during the Malay Campaign', length 150 words. I wrote an incredible story of the bombing of 17 CGH in true newspaper style b***ing the Nip air force. Findlay wrote on the loss of his toothbrush, Ward on 'Retaining his lunch', and even more puerile and ridiculous stories have been sent in. Some of the men have let their imaginations run riot and thought up impossible episodes. Wonder what the IJA will think of it all; probably won't sink in for a long time!

They do think up the queerest things for us to do.

Three more letters in from home, dated 24.12.42 and 11.42. Two [from] Mother and one from dear Olwen. It is this sort of treatment of us that makes us HATE the Japanese more than ever, hate, hate and hate for my life. They're oriental, suspicious, distrustful, cunning and liars of the highest order, absolute masters in the art of hurting us without physical injury.

Elizabeth does not seem to have had any (letters) according to the sorters of the mail.

11 February

Elizabeth darling, I wonder what you are doing, we've been married for two years. Where are you? If only you could be sent out of here soon – it must be awful misery for you. Let's hope for happiness in the years to come.

12 February

Saw the usual AIF variety concert, somewhat better than their previous productions. Called this *Bits and Pieces*.

13 February

Food is getting steadily worse. I am perpetually hungry – we don't seem to be able to get enough rice to eat at our table even though we try and divide it out equally. No cooking oil is available, and once more the slight meat issue is very erratic after a fortnight of supply. Instead they've issued the rottenest of rotten fish and expect us to eat it.

In the canteen there is nothing to buy these days, very few bananas come in and rock sugar is $1.50 a lb.

15 February

Because of the scarcity of all supplies now, the Officers Club has had to close down.

Most people are wondering how to feed their ducks and fowls as there is very little swill left over for them; at least the latter peck about the place, but the former go hungry. I think a general killing of poultry will soon begin. Frankland is to come up and take his share of our farm away to Blakang Mati.

The filthiest tobacco ever is on sale in the canteen, 35 cents per ounce, and it's got a foul odour. Huge queues form as soon as it comes in because of the present shortage of tobacco. The Aussy ADMS think there is opium in it but I tried out qualitation tests and found no trace of it.

17 February

Read my paper on 'Bowel Fauna in Changi' before Changi Medical Society. It turned out quite a success and was fairly well attended. Fair amount of discussion after the paper but Maynard and Hutchins talked some rubbish.

18 February

The tobacco issue is good.

Yesterday Ponaber was attacked and today we hear that Truk [large Japanese naval base in central Pacific] has caught it from the air also. Things are hotting up.

Rumour has it that a third of the population of Singapore to be moved because of the shortage of rice on the island. Singapore is about the only place [that has] not been attacked by our forces yet.

20 February

Enmity against the Hospital seems to be rising again; the CO is getting all sorts of frivolous complaints sent to him from outside areas, chiefly officers. Whenever the camp conditions get bad – food, health, work etc – they seem to try and pick holes in the Hospital which is, of course, not difficult in minor things, particularly what is said by a ward master admitting a case, or if there is somebody at the medical inspection room or not and so on. Gasper refused to sign for some Tabs at the Lab one afternoon as they were addressed to me; this provided a letter from Command headed 'Discipline'. It's awfully petty and makes the staff so fed up, particularly as the CO is so weak and DDMS Neal is quite useless in fighting for us.

We have all kinds of combatant officers foisted on to us to look at the food, an RE, an ARP man, all the Information Bureau staff and various other oddments. I dislike them as a crowd.

23 February

Some 350 American Red Cross parcels have arrived in the camp and it works out at about one small parcel to four men. All the milk is to be extracted and given for hospital use only.

The distribution is being done from Central Sources, but I hear that not all the parcels should have gone to them for dispersal!! However on subsequent issue, I have received 28 cigarettes and a 1in cube of chocolate and about one tin of meat into the Mess as a share. Equivalent tinned shares are coffee, sugar, cheese, salmon tins, a small tin of pork. All this should flavour the food for the next two to three weeks at least.

Our basic diet is so bad these days; rice is 10oz, beans 5oz, some vegetables and occasionally now a scrap of meat. The beans are part soya but mainly little black beans used as a cover crop for young rubber. Even the poultry won't eat the latter. Supplies of vegetables are meagre, few ounces of potato tops come in. The oil shortage has been got over temporarily as some has come in. Canteen food supplies have dried up, even the hospital was only able to buy 300lb of sweet potatoes in the last 14 days.

28 February

Major General Arimura, the present Camp Commandant, is going away in a few days so a number of snaps are to be taken around the camp, only in No.1 area (No. 2 is dirty, skinny 'F' group), and Holmes and Black Jack have ordered that we must look proud, well dressed etc, and the photographer will be taken to special nice places eg. prepared barrack room, the massage and dental departments, a set-up of a tennis match and a set-up of a soccer match – everybody has to look very happy when the photographer appears.

A colonel from one of the Java camps is taking over in his place.

2 March

What a blow! All 'A' mess Red Cross food has been stolen from our store, including some tins Findlay has saved for years. The lock of the door was opened ? with a key, and Sgt Sandy's key fits this lock; it sounds like an 'inside job'! There is no trace of the stuff; about two packfuls of tins are missing. A packet of prunes and ½lb cheese left.

'The Fens' lecture by de Romsey was quite good, it sounds like an interesting part of the country – I must explore it when I get back.

The photographs that were taken around the camp on the 28th were not good so they all have to be staged again – or else!

5 March

The IJA sent in a few pipes and some tins of tobacco for the camp. One pipe and five tins to the hospital area (2000 [medical staff and patients to share]). There was also a big consignment of cigarettes but the Nips refused to allow them in because they say 'Offensive Matter' is printed on the packs. They won't allow in the loose cigarettes for a like reason, and have even refused the loose tobacco.

10 March

The photographs taken for General Arimura were unsatisfactory so the whole lot are staged yet again today. The 'crowds' for hockey, soccer and tennis were marched up from each group, all had to be properly dressed and have footwear on and clean shirts. They lined the *padang* and under CMP [Corps of Military Police] supervision looked bright and cheerful, cheered properly and generally behaved well while the Nip photographer took shots of the crowd and play at various angles. The play was limited to about 10 minutes of each game, then the Nips got into their car and drove off.

Photographs were also taken in the massage and dental departments; both of these should look good in the snaps.

Apparently Arimura wants to be able to produce evidence of the success of his administration before handing over to the new man from Java. He has hardly been near the camp since he arrived and knows nothing about what is going on in it as his underlings stop all complaints from reaching him.

13 March

I have a small septic spot on my left leg with much surrounding oedema and tenderness, glands ++ and I don't feel too good today.

A few special postcards from home, of 24 words, arrived today. Our Mess only got two; they seemed to be from Switzerland.

14 March

I had a frightful night, general toxaemia and signs of a deep phlebitis in the left calf, rigors and everything. Oh – I feel awful and think worse. But sufficiently well to remember to take in my own bed and linen as the bugs are frightful up in the officers ward.

Campbell gave me 8g of sulph' in 8 hours and I spent a better night, but still fell pretty bad and have no appetite at all, just drink and sleep. Using a urinal is awful – after terrific effort was successful then spilt some in the bed. Next time I went and did it outside the urinal in error. And these urinals are filthy! Smelly! If it wasn't for the fact that I've scabies as well I would not be getting bathed in bed at all, but the hot rub down by Farrant is cleaning and the [illegible] is not too bad afterwards.

Weight is down to 10st 9lb.

23 March

The IJA have issued a list of minimum diet and certain items that they are going to issue at intervals. On the diet side there is an increase of rice to 13oz, more meat, sugar and vegetables. The articles list also shows toothbrushes, towels, sarongs, tooth powder, soap, toilet paper, pencils, writing paper etc etc. All looks very impressive but we are so used to Nip promises now that nothing is believed until it is a fact – they are all liars of the worst kind!

Just so – after the above promise of a big diet, it's been further reduced and now rice is 9oz/day and vegetables only when available. Eg. 4lb green bananas for 50 (our Mess) or tapioca tops etc.

31 March

Sudden search for radio sets by our Command. Six Nips raided 'The' house last night at listening time and searched thoroughly for a set – none were found. Sixty minutes notice had come in and was useful. Somebody in the camp must have given away 'news' because of the precision of the raid and the accuracy. IJA have said that if they find a set here we will have no rations.

Tobacco came into the Mess as usual today.

More 'T' in but it's going to be intermittent in future.

Poor Wg has died.

3 April

Canteen has *gula malacca* at 2.05/lb and coconuts at 80 cents each, *towgay* at 3.20/lb and black beans 1.80/-. Our rice ration is down by a fifth, [it] is at 9.5oz per day again because the Nips have delivered about 20% short in weight. Very little vegetables come in now. IJA say they cannot get them now so we have to grow our own.

?? in Malaya.

4 April

My mouth is pretty sore today and it makes me feel rather depressed. So little to eat and it's so painful to swallow, yet one remains hungry.

Today some MO are blaming the 'black bean' as the source of the disease, saying it's toxic cumulatively, but some 'mouths' have occurred in non-bean eaters.

The first mouth case, an AIF patient, died today with gangrene of lung (right upper) [but] no evidence of pellagra about him.

Lt Takahashi told CO 'He regretted but that we would not be getting any more meat issue now, dry fish instead'. So today we received – in addition to the rice – 13oz of dried whitebait and 3½lb of green bananas between 51 people.

Fortunately our garden is producing a little spinach so we get some every other day. Work in the garden is on the roster system but many avoid it even so. It's so hot and dry and tiring working away in the sun just like a coolie.

No rain for last six weeks.

6 April

My mouth is awfully sore today. Can hardly swallow the meals, especially the maize and black beans. I spend about 60 minutes over the meal that could be finished in ten. This mouth lesion is like an epidemic all over the camp, although some groups have been spared so far.

Much argument as to whether it is a deficiency disease (pellagra) or an epidemic infection. So far no treatment has been found definitely curative.

9 April

Last big soccer match in the camp, Dutch v 32 Coy RAMC. It was feeble, the players were weak and apathetic, dreadful play. They all just hadn't the energy to play on the present diet.

10 April

Mouth is still bad. I have been rinsing it with weak $NaCO_3$, and swabbing the patches with glycerine twice daily, also careful dental hygiene.

Because of the low diet and general malnutrition, all games on the *padang* have been stopped for the Hospital area.

13 April

Lt. Col. Dillon, HQ 13th Div, gave us his talk on 'Attempted Escape at Capitulation'. Most illuminating and interesting. Told us again of the lack of discipline in Singapore docks, on the islands and in Sumatra. He was with Gordon of A&SH caught on a junk in the Indian Ocean.

14 April

My mouth is vastly improved, swallowing etc. is no trouble but I still have a lot of grey lining in my mouth.

IJA have ordered that all private typewriters have to be handed in today. Still no tobacco.

Awful rumours all round the camp.

15 April

Mouth is much better.

Gardening for the camp as a whole is going a pace; all available ground is being put under tapioca.

Generally realised now what a black outlook it is.

16 April

Holmes gave all officers an address in the AIF theatre. About 350 officers. Was about the present IJA attitude of discipline, new administration and the 'pipe' difficulties. We are asked to collaborate as our food depends on it.

A new 2nd Lt Nip is Camp Adjutant and wants smartness everywhere. Nip orders and forms of salute, rooms to be made tidy with things neatly folded and put away in lockers and cupboards. Chairs, if any, in the centre of room, laundry to hang neatly. All ramshackle shelters to be pulled down. Everything within sight of roads to be absolutely clean and tidy.

But the Nips have crowded up the accommodation still more and reduced the food – so what! And still want more men on the aerodrome work.

Chickens versus gardens controversy rages, and now gardeners may kill chicks damaging gardens; very tempting law this for illicit killings.

My mouth seems to have relapsed again.

19 April

Saw Command Players in *On the Spot* by E. Wallace. Enjoyed it much – Elizabeth, if only you could enjoy a few of these shows too; they are so good and help to pass the time no end.

We have had no news of internees since last year; I do hope all is well. Oft do I dream of the future and a home, travel, post-graduate study. Shall I afford a car or only a cycle? Latter will be good for me!

20 April

Feel rather despondent at times, time just goes on. The sick won't heal, so many die and the chances of seeing home again are so remote, almost impossible. Death from starvation or the Nip sword seems much more likely. Freedom – what undreamed of luxury it must be – instead working on dry, parched, infertile soil swinging a pick or *chungkol* [heavy hoe] like a coolie, hoping to grow a few tapioca roots in 9–12 months time and stave off that hunger.

What are they doing at home? Seems like Nothing, nothing, nothing – only big talk like Churchill made a few days before this place fell.

What opportunities have I missed – where will my contemporaries be? They'll say he was a POW for years and has forgotten everything!! I suppose we'll get a reduced salary too!!

Now we have to learn and parade to Japanese order and give them to our men too, and their lieutenants are coming round to see we know them and inspect dormitories etc.

23 April

Seven bags of English mail have arrived for sorting.

Collins gave out that estimated dead of 'H' and 'F' force is now 4590. More sick are to be expected shortly.

24 April

The incident of the 'Pig's Blood'. I drew about 2 [illegible] of blood from de Romsey, used the serum and gave the clot to the Mess. Neil (DDMS) told me to collect it, in Led's hearing. Now Collins reprimands me for drawing the blood, saying it's an RASC issue. It never has been accounted for until this time (ask QM Kingston) when old Middleton asked the RASC what has been happening to it!

25 April

A bombshell – Changi camp has to close, all combatants to go to gaol and officers outside apart from men. Hospital to be established separately elsewhere. Internees are going to Syme Road camp and all the vigorous gardening will go to waste – we were laying out a huge area.

26 April

The big gardens and the piggery also to close down. All our fowls and ducks will have to be eaten before the move.

IJA now say that Hospital will only be allowed 1000 beds and a total of 300 staff with no combatants. Our present staff is about 800 including RE, cooks etc. and about 1200 patients plus huge outpatient clinics.

The combatant ORs to be directly administered by the IJA but British officers for working parties.

Mouth still dry and fairly sore.

27 April

IJA have allowed officers to wear badges of rank once more. Up go all the 'Changi ranks'. Some Lt. Cols have their pips up wrong.

The sorting of the letters that arrived on the 23rd continues but none have been released yet. Local administration has to censor them again although they have all come through Tokyo already.

28 April

Tenno Hirohito's birthday [tomorrow]. The IJA were requested to allow a visit to see relatives about two weeks back but no reply yet.

Another party have arrived from Thailand with grim news. MOs dead are Eastwood, (Franks??), Deverill, White (IMS) and Henderson.

1 May

Destroyed 18 of Mother's letters to me since POW, such beautiful letters, if only I could reply. How patient she is. They date from June '42 – 23 January '43.

The MOs detailed to staff the hospital to place 'X' are detailed; I am pathologist. Most are chiefly British (40 in all), 14 AIF. I wish they could be left! 1200 patients and 320 other staff. 'X' at present is thought to be Woodlands Camp.

4 May

Scottie (electrical) had to meet Kent up at the gaol today to see the wiring etc. up there. I just caught him in time and he took a verbal message for me, which should, of a certainty, be delivered to my darling. If only I could hear from her.

Trailers and parties are off to the gaol daily to get the camp ready, put huts up etc. RE are taking all sorts of stuff. Huts going up.

I hear there is much tic-tac signalling to the women today by the trailer party people. Maj Bevan has tipped me off to go up tomorrow.

Later – there is supposed to have been a message for me today, but none has been delivered.

6 May

Went up to the gaol with a trailer at 2.00 pm; it was amazing the way people could communicate with the women. Saw Freddy Bloom and Elizabeth as she came out of the gate sitting at rear of a truck. I was running up the road towards it – did she see me and realise? Her head just turned away. Hope Freddy B. tells her I was up today.

Hope they like their new camp which, I am told, is very nice and open.

Ate a big supper, shared a tin of curry with Steve Campbell to celebrate seeing you, darling. It was a bit hot but went down wonderfully.

8 May

Various tools, which people privately own, have to be handed in to QM although they were brought in by individuals or salvaged personally as areas closed. I have to hand in a file, hammer etc. If they wanted these things before, why didn't they attempt to collect them from old SA for example as it closed down. No, there is no organisation!!

Gave Bevan a note that he later told me got across all right. Enquire after.

Tonight had my first feed of dog stew, a portion given me by Benton. It was very good.

9 May

More mail still has arrived at the IJA HQ. Said to be a total of 37 bags.

LETTERS – received three from Mother and one from Olwen. Last dated May 15th 1943. Time seems to be smoothing out my absence, not so much for dear Olwen. If only I could write.

10 May

About 2000 are now in the gaol, all civilians are out. I went in and looked around. God, how depressing it is, and E. has been in there for two years and two months, what punishment. This is how the Nips treat women and children. Awful cells, barred corridors and great iron gates everywhere. The solid, grey, concrete walls. I saw the tiny exercise patches, the hospital – and perimeter. Came back and felt depressed the whole of the evening and part of the night.

Now about 5000 of our men have to go in there.

11 May

The great trek to the prison continues. Two trailer trips a day – huts, barbed wire, pianos, furniture, tools, basins and much junk all goes past our Mess. What an upheaval. No dogs are being allowed so they are being killed and eaten here. Their flesh is getting increasingly popular. Of course most of the birds too are being steadily killed off and there is a terrific stealing going on every night.

Three Italian officers have been admitted to the hospital today. This is the first we have seen of them; they've been at Syme Road since the last four months and can already speak English quite well. No incidents so far although our officers do not like them.

15 May

A high Allied officer has been brought in by the Nips to the gaol. Being kept separate and isolated, and he even has a Nip batman to look after him. Rumour has it that it is Gen. Stillwell.

Orders that we are to move to Woodlands Camp starting on the 23rd. About 4000 men are now in the gaol and some already beginning to feel bit depressed.

20 May

Our 'Willie' John White of the Sherwood F. died this evening, rather a shock to us all; he only went ill three days ago, rather late. I did the autopsy and feel that he had secondary KLB very severe superimposed on his pellagra lesions. This is an unfortunate affair as 'Willie' should have been forced into the hospital before the last play but Collins was so keen on it.

21 May

Attended the funeral, huge following of MOs and men, many beautiful wreaths. Wearne took the service. So it's true – 'Willie, you'll never get off this island'.

22 May

RE and hygiene squad have gone off to our new camp (Kranji) on Bukit Timah Road. Harper took a whole trailer load of personal luggage and the trucks are being loaded to over-flowing; no question of overloading with the Nips. Said to be a good campsite, recently occupied by an Indian POW hospital and Indian drivers we chatted with liked it and said it was the best POW camp.

About four trucks are coming each day and taking away RE equipment to fit up, two trips daily. Of course officers are getting away hen coups etc., sneaking the stuff in and Collins is insisting on such.

27 May

We are all packed and ready for the big move tomorrow. Still wondering how all is going on one truck, Lab and dispensary.

6.30 pm. We are told suddenly that the move is cancelled indefinitely; a few patients may leave tomorrow.

28 May

Four hundred patients left for new Hospital this morning. We expect to go in two days.

At 1.00 pm told that everybody is to leave at 2.00 pm. Hell of a rush getting packed again, catching the fowls etc. Got a truck for the Lab about 3.00 pm and filed on. It was a grand trip, passed down Adam Road to Bukit Timah Road, passed your camp, Elizabeth. Sat in front with the Indian driver and talked with him all the way. Most noticeable were the silent crowds at corners, the gardens everywhere, cycle rickshaws, cattle and bullock carts. Larger INA [Indian National Army] camps along Adam Road.

At our new camp (Kranji) the convoy was thrown into utter confusion by the Nips, [who] made us leave some of our luggage on the road, [then] made the trucks go in without personnel. In fact, utter chaos.

Got in eventually and found the stuff. Later in the dark we had a roll call and Nip Sgt kept us on parade for 1½ hours, much shouting and yelling by him – neither patients nor us had had any food. Very, very tired and hungry this day. The two chickens are still all right but frightened.

Later impressions, very stuffy, close camp, nice cold nights, the perimeter wire is too close, the mat screens by the road spoil the view, too many inquisitive Korean sentries, Parker pens for $60/- and watches for $300/- and upwards. They want to buy anything, stolen and sold one small lighting plant, offered Lt. Baxter $1000/- for a roll of copper wire.

Electricity only on at night, no heating apart from cookhouse. Difficulty of heating is acute. The Aussies are cooking over little fires all over the place, stolen vegetables from the little gardens left by the Indians. Masses of chilli plants doing well, but the other vegetables not so nice.

Roll calls are dreadful, times vary daily and we stay on parade 1–1½ hours at least and even then the numbers are not correct. Seems we have one patient extra and Changi is five short and say we have them.

2 June

Very homesick when I hear the trains go by and engines whistle. Bukit Timah Road is busy, mostly Nip trucks, also see INA troops marching by and they attempt to give us a jeer but our fellows do not appreciate it.

3 June

Days pass quickly while we get ourselves comfortable once again. Got the hen coup ready today and put in the two – the Crow and Droopy – the remains of our great farm of 13 we had at Selarang. Also made Cooper get patch of garden ready and have put in a lot of chilli plants. I have acquired a liking for these now to flavour the meals. Gosh do I feel hungry.

5 June

The Lab is two bays at end of a hut, awfully dark owing to the rubber branches. Everything is rather damp and misty, nights are delightfully cool. I sleep in the 'Slums', five of us to two bays, the remains of our Selarang room; bit crowded and some of my colleagues are a bit careless about their belongings.

6 June

Bugs; I have so far managed to keep free of these creatures but regret to say I am finding one or two daily in my mosquito net.

The Korean sentries are tending to be rather sociable and fraternising with us trying to buy things and selling tobacco into the camp. The 'Marathon' boy who visits with us brought in seven katties of tobacco at $30/- a katty, whilst certain prices are $1.30 per ounce. Robin Taylor was scared stiff when this large amount appeared after lights out and he hadn't the money [for] it nor could he feel up to it to sell it on the black market, although there is an acute shortage at present. Before the Korean left the room (after lights out) one had to go out and do a recce to see that there were no sentries about to intercept him.

<u>Later.</u> In the afternoon one of the guards threw $130/- worth of tobacco over onto Collins' verandah from the roadside over the wire and matting screen. He said to hide in the drain at one stage when a 'flag' car went past.

No goods into the Canteen yet, although the Sgt in charge of the Camp says he is trying hard to get a contractor.

Last night the guards came back quite drunk whilst we were on parade. They were awfully noisy and rough amongst themselves. One in particular was in fighting mood and later beat up the Sgt. Next morning he was tied to a tree and apparently suitably punished. The Sgt has several bandages on too. They do not like him.

11 June

Had a delightful day doing a larval survey with Nicholas. Walked all round the camp environs and Chinese gardens. Also recovered the legs of my desk that had been left out on the road the day we arrived.

The local population appears to be more sociable now and less 'anti' as they used to be.

The guards come in for a gossip and drop fragments of news – the invasion in Europe is on.

Sentries keep interfering with the Church services. They also stopped an impromptu concert last Saturday. Apparently the Sergeant in charge has to be asked before all such things take place. Has been asked (ordered) that the first big show must be musical, and probably the others as well. Whilst we have a number of 'actors' and 'actresses' over with us for straight plays only – which of course we prefer as the band under J.J. Porter is pretty terrible, [but] we all know the tunes.

16 June

Went out with Nicholas again on survey. Collected maculates just near the camp.

19 June

Sgt says all poultry has to be pooled, even if privately owned and although we have asked Collins, he refuses to interview this man and explain that the birds are our own. We all believe Collins is too weak and afraid, fancy a British Lt Col giving every step of the way like this to a Jap Sgt who won't even see him but through a Korean stooge.

20 June

First exchange has taken place to Selarang Hospital. As usual the AIF are not playing fair, they sent out fewer and received more (200%) so they now occupy British beds and so will gradually infiltrate. Nearly all the Aussy MOs are on Marmite for trivial conditions. C. Harvey has just ordered 1lb for his pet Lt Col Osborne, and so the racket goes on with them.

Our Administration is very bad indeed, both Collins and Caldbeck, and the Company Officer MacDonald are hated by all the men. The black market is doing great business encouraged by senior officers, including the CO.

A sentry returned $10/- to a ward orderly saying 'Give this to No. 1 Officer and say I was unable to buy his things in Singapore today – tobacco' and when the orderly took the money to the CO, he accepted it most sheepishly.

22 June

The Nips made a search for drugs amongst the patients today as there is sale of them going on to them – Atabria and M&B 693 [sulphonamide, antibiotic]. Yet Caldbeck has on two occasions taken his Nip friends into the medical store and given them M&B, today 27 tablets, and returned with a present of four packets of cigars.

The Company is very upset about the 'Pay' business as they get deducted more in proportion than officers do, and feel they are being swindled. It's never been explained to them what is being done with the money, and on many occasions the men have been coerced into signing blank pay rolls – they're fed up so refuse to sign.

Matter went before the Nip Sgt and was misrepresented to him by M' so that he threatened to cut their rations, and it was sometime before this was corrected by their interpreter.

My two birds – Droopy and Crow – handed in yesterday. Had 23 eggs from them this month so far.

26 June

Trouble in the Common Bird Pool already as the hens seem to have a disease amongst them causing drooping heads and death. My two hens have been put in the 'infected area' although they look all right to me; I suppose they feel strange in a common run.

Maj Darwell, Markby and I saw the CO this morning about all the complaints of the men. He was all appeasement and blamed the men and NCO although I pointed out that we (most officers) thought it was his Company officers and Sgt Major to blame for the general dissatisfaction. Too many things to write down, but Collins is just a crude liar and not to be relied upon to stick to anything he gives a ruling on. There is dishonesty going on under his very nose and he refuses to see it.

The Sgt and other Nips are not so interfering these days and evening parade has come down to a gesture only. All the same they have Collins,

Caldbeck and Harper (RE) doing and obeying their every whim or pleasure – what guts!

29 June

Disease is bad amongst the fowls; about six have died. Now we have lost Droopy, even so she was plucked and gave a very nice soup and boiled carcase this evening. So our little farm (that was) has gone down to one bird (The Crow). Collins is having his way about stopping 'private ownership'; 50% of the eggs go to the Hospital now and the rest go to the owners. About $580/- of birds have been confiscated (87). They're being underfed and egg yield has dropped from 18 on the first day to one today.

3 July

Caught a cat for Cooper who killed it and had it stewed. I ate a portion after parade; it was excellent, white meat and very soft, awfully good, in fact I must indulge in this a bit more. Very few cats about the camp now as they are being eaten all over.

Decided to make a spring-door trap using a bit of rubber to close the door; collected the material all over the camp. Made the cage of weld-mesh wire. Rather difficult to keep it hidden under the hut. Now to put it into practice.

What would Mother, Elizabeth or Olwen say if they saw me prospecting my staff to catch cats!

Noted too that several come around our Mess kitchen at night.

Morgan, Markby, Burton and I are also on the lookout for a suitable dog. I don't like dog meat as much as a cat however. There are only four dogs in the camp, and these are all registered so it cannot be one of them. Have to wait for one straying in from the *kampongs*.

6 July

A Korean has fastened on to us to try and sell him a waterproof watch, [and he] plies me with cigarettes that, out of politeness, I must smoke although they are fairly tasteless. I am not making any effort to try and obtain one for him or sell my own Omega watch. The IJA dollar fetches so little now and Chinese pay by handfuls in Singapore.

Went out with the morning squad and the Nip bought us a durian for $5/-; it was delightful and fresh. N' and I also shared a big pineapple which cost $1.20 and a few mangosteen each. It was funny seeing the little

Nip chasing the Chinese woman with the fruit baskets, and she was running away as fast as possible.

10 July

About twenty Punjabis, said to be INA fellows, have been added to our guard and twelve Koreans sent to Sumatra. The perimeter is patrolled by one Korean and two Indians at a time. The latter tell me that they are people who have been coerced into joining the INA movement but [are] only supposed to be guarding dumps and stores for the Nip, and didn't expect to be put in charge of a British POW camp. They seem to be very ashamed of their predicament and want to talk to us whenever the opportunity occurs. They salute our officers properly if there is no Nip in sight.

18 July

<u>Big Day.</u> I received nineteen letters from home, oh lovely ones, Mother, four from Olwen and Stanley one. Mother, of course I shall be with you, it's home I think about most, so often, so mythical, so beautiful.

14/7/43 letter says my first postcard arrived. Mother must have been crying over it while writing for the hand is shaky. I shall make up for it all once we are out of here. Wonder what dear Olwen will say, and I do still care for her. We'll have beautiful drives to the country, seaside, see shows and all the things Mother always wanted to do but been unable to. Surely I am not a prisoner for always, and Elizabeth away from me too. What wonderful things to come.

Bloody Nips – one year to get a letter or card either way, I hate them, hate them all for always.

21 July

Elizabeth's birthday – and the Office say that she has received $25.0 safely. Fancy, she is 32 years [old] today.

22 July

Mother is 67 years [old] today and I do hope quite well; such a long time since I saw her last, dear Mother.

24 July

The small flying lizard (Draco volans) is very common out here in Kranji, and watching them provides one with much amusement. It really glides from tree to tree and does not fly; loss of height is little.

It feigns dead readily and apparently has no method of defence except colouring.

We hear that Lt Col Newey has been made OC at Changi; the Nips have deposed Holmes and Black Jack Galleghan. 'A' and 'D' forces are said to have left Singapore for Sumatra during the last week.

We call Tuesday 'Borehole Day' – latest is that India has Dominion status and Wavell is Governor General.

Cooper trapped another cat last night; this is the fourth since the contrivance was made.

Receipt has arrived from Internees Camp showing that E. has received $25/- sent this month.

I find these days passing away rapidly. Always a busy morning and in the afternoon I sit and read. Trying to keep up my medicine and certainly have in mind the doing of an MD [Doctor of Medicine] or DTM and H; if only we could get more communication with home. Must get that 'study leave'.

Evenings are spent gardening, although these are very disappointing out here and slow.

I am also pickling some berries to help get the evening meal down. After supper, I wander over to parade (roll call) and then watch the sunset, have a cup of tea in the Lab; Sgt Mess tea is better than in our Mess, [then] back to the room for a bit of reading before bedtime, sleep awfully well too.

30 July

Yet another cat has been trapped and eaten by the Lab. We are doing quite well on this – the fifth. What will Mother say – and Elizabeth?

31 July

At last the black market has fallen on itself. It seems Koronoto (Korean), Andrews (Interpreter) and the Yank fellow Quarant run a partnership for buying watches, silver etc and 'Q' takes 10–15% for each sale. But Burton, another [illegible] have been out-selling the former so Koronoto passed orders confining Burton to his room after roll call parade in the evening. CO took the matter up and threatened to expose K' to his senior officers and their Nip Sgt, and asked him to prove his case against Burton. Fortunately Collins (NAAFI Tea) for once stood his ground and the No.1 Korean has backed down. The Sgt doesn't know about this but detected tobacco being brought into the camp, confiscated it all from his Korean guard and came over to see Collins about it. Luckily Collins said he suspected a black market but had no proof and blamed the Koreans for starting it. Now they are not allowed inside the camp or to talk to prisoners over the wire.

3 August

A windfall, Tidd has offered me $50 for a £2.0 cheque; this is very useful as I believe officers pay is being reduced next month for the CMF and I was wondering how to send E. the next $10/- and not just $5/-.

Newey has been talking to Lt Takahashi about various things at the gaol. Asked about Red Cross supplies. T. said that the British were sending none, and in fact refused to send any for POW. Also said that anyway the Allies were now sinking all Red Cross ships and none could get through to us. Said Russia was no good as 'the situation with them was very finely poised at the moment' so they would not act as a neutral country.

All urine in the camp is collected nowadays for putting on to the garden. I have a six-gallon tin for our huts and it's filled overnight. I also visit the rabbit pens and collect some of their faeces for my own little plot. Growth in this place is very slow indeed.

8 August

Received a 24-word letter from Mother dated the 25/1/44. Very recent indeed. Some folk have had March letters. It means I have a lot more to come yet. If only Mother knew we had the 'Pipe'.

Fourth postcard: 'Dear Mother, Fit at 145lb. Usual occupation. Much appreciated letters arriving. Wife's home Edinburgh. Don't worry. Longing for home. Much love to all.'

Trading with the sentries is now legalised but it has to be carried out in the presence of office staff Capt MacDonald and Interpreter. I think this means the Sgt Commandant now gets a 'rake-off' on everything. One OR even turned around and asked MacD what percentage he expected after the sale of a pen – that's what they think of their Company officer.

Been in Malaya for five years now; how much longer???

12 August

At last Collins has found out our Padre Interpreter Andrews and has decided to send him back to Changi. He is no use to the camp in the capacity in which he came, stays in his room as an invalid and the Nips bring him things to eat at all times. He is still doing trading too.

All interpreting work is being done by Cpl Ullman and it's a bad thing to be in this young fellow's hands so much.

Hope Collins tries to get Maj Wild sent out to us from Changi.

15 August

Padre Andrews (interpreter) sent back to Changi as he is a menace here and not doing his job at all. I'm afraid RAChD [Royal Army Chaplains Department] has not got itself a good name in this POW camp, with few exceptions. They all seem hollow, artificial and rogues.

20 August

Up early to gather mushrooms. Beautiful mornings here after rain.

Nic' cooked an excellent curry for lunch with vegetables. So, with our morning coffee, today has been a good day for food. The Lab has established coffee with milk and sugar every Sunday once again. I managed to fire up the Primus stove to work properly with Diesoline.

Prices at present are :-

Coffee	$7.00 per lb
Towgay	$5.00 per lb
Sugar	$10.00 per lb
Coconut	85–90 cents each
Onion	$7.00 per lb
(Poor) peanuts	$6.00 per lb
(Poor) curry powder	$5.00 per lb
Limes	$1.40
Pork	$7.00
Whitebait	c $12.00

All other edibles are unobtainable, no fruit etc. Red Palm oil comes in at intervals as it is used more and more as a lubrication oil by all car owners, as also is coconut oil. Our power plant has the above as lubricant and poor quality diesoline to run on. Plugs have to be cleaned frequently. The Nip who supplies the lubricant insists that it must be changed every three to four days and he collects the sump oil and disposes of it. i.e. takes it into Singapore and sells it to motor dealers. Baxter gets issued one drum of Diesoline with three to four of lubricant; the Nip sells one of the latter right away. Of course much of the lubricant oil (coconut this week) is being used around the camp as hair oil.

25 August

Optimism reigns in the camp and of course there is good reason for it too. I wish things would get on a bit faster for us out here, even to see one of our planes; Singapore is about the only place not visited yet by bombers.

Roll call this evening we were addressed by the CO[:] 'The IJA have said that the camp is not producing enough urine, we must do more for the gardens. Else all gardens in the area will be stopped. The Sgt threatens to deal with Ward Master personally.'

Of course there is nothing to prevent the wards watering the urine up to the required quantity, whatever that is. Of course the output cannot increase as the size of the gardens increases. This really emanates from Nip in charge of the gardening group who thinks he is an expert on gardens.

28 August

There are more people working out in the gardens than ever before, but some like 'Dental Dick' Pearson, AIF, Officers Osborne, Harvey, Stephens and others never do a hands turn still, but lie and read on their beds all day. Not that they are incapable, but they <u>consider</u> themselves above such things.

Our camp is steadily improving but it has a bad reputation over in Changi and patients do not like coming here. Of course as soon as they are fit enough they are put to work on the gardens. Comparison of the food at each place shows that we are getting a trifle more per head than them. Disadvantages are smaller camp, fewer concerts, lectures, no swimming parties or other diversions. But we have our '*Kabar*' [news]. Tuesday is exchange day and of course a day of much gossip, in fact so much that it gets dangerous in the wards through carelessness.

31 August

Life is tending to get a bit monotonous, especially as the diet is only rice, salt, tea, pepper and a little sugar. No vegetables or fish for days and very little even when it is in. Wish our bombers would come over and give us a little moral support if nothing else. Most of us do need a little cheering up; it's such a long time, how much more of it are we to do! We certainly feel forgotten and abandoned by our own country.

2 September

It's most unfortunate that the only interpreter we have is a young man made up to Corporal by Collins. He's a poor interpreter and is well under the thumbs of the Nips, [and] does not interpret properly. Besides for many things there ought to be an officer to do the talking. Ullman is not English either but French and Austrian mixture.

The Sgt Commandant has sent in a lot of new orders about attempting to escape, threatening sentries or even looking depressed at a Nip. Of the punishments, capital and solitary confinement figure largely. Also threats about meeting. A double solitary cage has been erected in front of the guardroom in anticipation of troublesome prisoners.

5 September

The gardens are at last beginning to produce a little, both outside and inside the wire. We are getting a little spinach daily with supper and it certainly tastes good after so long. My little plot is also doing well but the tomatoes here are going to be poor compared to what we cultivated in Changi.

10 September

Koromoto (No.1 Korean) is stirring up trouble. He wants Walsh (the QM) changed as he is not playing ball with him in the various food swindles. Also he gave away the 'sugar racket' which resulted in Caldbeck and MacDonald losing their jobs in the hospital office. K. presented them with 46lb of sugar from our rations.

K. was taken before the Sgt by Collins and has had to apologise and asked that the matter be taken no further. But today K. came and had a go at the interpreter, Ullman, saying he was too honest in all his dealings etc. unlike other interpreters he had to do with. Andrews!

Capt Davey, AIF interpreter, has arrived here for duty, much to the surprise of the local Nips. We are all quite pleased as he has a good reputation though half Nip ([through his] mother) himself and was born in Japan.

22 September

Purchased 40 sheets of paper today at ten cents each. Big buy this as paper is so scarce. I used sheets twice by writing in two directions and sometimes rubbing out the pencil on a sheet. How awful this stinting in everything is; I even think of my pencil lead and pen ink and economise on that the whole time. A little poor quality Jap paper comes in to the hospital office but it won't take ink, and pencil hardly writes on it. Like most Jap produce we have seen, it's very poor quality.

How much longer is this to go? Wonder how Elizabeth is sticking it now?

25 September

I find that though I am keeping up my weight, my muscles are wasting horribly; two inches off my thighs and they feel so flabby. Some 'skeletons' walk around the camp, just a little thin skin covers their poor cords of muscle, especially noticeable on chest and back muscles where it looks like so many strings pulling under the skin. Another few months of this, we will all be in a pretty bad way.

Can't our people buck up just a little bit more? Everybody is so expectant, both inside and outside the camp – yet nothing happens.

Even the Korean and Indian sentries are aware of the progress of events.

Koronato gave the full details the other day and thinks it will all be over early next year. I hope he is right. I feel a bit more pessimistic these days.

28 September

We are getting more bulk to eat these days, but very little protein. Stomach is certainly filled up at meals, [with] much rice and green vegetables.

My own garden is now producing quite well, but oh for some real food once again.

Beriberi, pellagra and scrotitis are bad all over the camp. Hardly anything at the canteen to eat, only this dreadful local tobacco and that's very expensive too.

30 September

Lt Takahashi has given out at Changi that the ship en route to Japan with Group Captain More, an American Brigadier, and 1000 troops was sunk and that survivors were picked up by Allied craft and have got away successfully. If it is true, then news of our conditions will get home.

2 October

Entertainment after supper in the camp consists of either the theatre or attending a lecture. Besides reading or bridge, no Mah-jong since early last year. The lectures are well organised by McCaul of MCS in wards and for the staff in our own Mess room. About three to four lectures per night, quite good ones too. I've given 'Kashmir' five times already and still seem to find an audience. The Aussies lap up any talks but as lecturers they are too full of 'baloney' and tall stories, besides I'm very tired of Australia.

Lt Morris has come over from Changi and is doing a very interesting series of talks on the economies of various parts of the Empire, on education and wealth of countries. He's a Welsh school master but talks well and is interested in his subject as a hobby.

5 October

Faulk, the flautist, practises his instrument in all kinds of queer corners of the camp to try and get a little privacy, even down empty Otway pits, but today he was near the perimeter wire by the fowl runs, and the Korean guard sent him away as he thought he was communicating with the Indians, playing their sort of wild music all by himself – and an appreciative Indian sentry standing way off in the far corner.

Privacy; one who has not been a POW cannot understand how much it means. We have none at all, no place to quietly sit and do as one wishes. Particularly at night do I miss this, and a good light and a comfortable chair to sit in, and perhaps some music or a radio.

9 October

The road is very busy these days as is the railway line. Convoys going up all the time and returning empty. The big rice stores at Kranji are being emptied, and daily. It seems much ammunition is being moved up to the mainland off the island, and we hear that two Divisions have gone north recently from Java and Sumatra.

Our theatre has *The Wind and the Rain* at present. Bradshaw and Mackwood do quite well in it; 'Jill' taken by Hugh Elliot is awful. Even so it does cause such a longing for student days and a sight of Bart's again. Shall visit there as soon as I get out and of course take refresher courses every so often! Wish I had stayed on in London now and maybe joined the LCC [London County Council] or something.

12 October

'Q' camp bitch was run over on the road this morning opposite our camp. The guards allowed the carcase to be brought in. Yank Roster got it, stomach contents brought to me for testing; heart had [illegible] in it, however it was well cooked up. She had recently pupped too.

In the evening I was given a mess tin full of the stew and it was awfully good too, very rich and good flavour, but certainly not as good as cat meat which is nice and white.

Slept well after the food.

14 October

Incident today – a small Aussy attempted to hit the garden's Korean (Kanomitsa), been taken away into custody by us. Then No.1 has said that he will be tried by them and is liable to punishment [of] two years solitary to] capital for this offence. We hope that their Gestapo will not be called in over this.

Later – Lt Tania tried the man and found him 'insane' – award is ten days extra duty in the garden. K' is very angry as he thinks he ought to have been given two years solitary.

16 October

We are having frequent air raid practices now, the Nips seem to be expecting things – but nothing ever seems to come our way. Our rice reserve is being scattered in case of fire.

17 October

Kanomitsa took a rifle and bayonet to the gardens this morning and lunged a few times at the Aussy Williams who is being punished for offence on the 14th. However Davey stopped any dirty business. For about three weeks now ammunition and stores have been going up the road daily but it has all stopped suddenly. We have been having any amount of air raid practices and the Nips take things most seriously, shouting and much doubling. They have 'tin' hats but the Indian sentries just carry on.

The pipe is smoking away, very good [illegible] too these days

19 October

What a day to celebrate! Robin Taylor ALP had a birthday party and produced sweet coffee and milk, coconut rock cakes, a cake – they weighed one down like lard and put me off food for the rest of the day, made me feel quite full inside.

Looks a bit nearer to end of time now!

20 October

First real air raid warning since we've been POWs but nothing seen. I was out on the malaria survey party and had to double back after our Korean escort who was absolutely terrified; he didn't even know the signals.

Nothing happens as usual; wonder when the British are going to buck up and give us a little help out here – two and a half years and not an Allied plane to be seen as yet.

Nip Sgt is having a big drive getting ready for air raids. Rice stores being dispersed and the five wells in the area are all being attended to at last. Being dug deeper and wooden revetment of the walls. Our circular saw has been working from 9.00 am until 7.00 pm cutting up the wood and getting it all ready. Once [Sgt] Yoshikawa thinks of a thing he believes in getting it done well and quickly. Our RE are slow because this internment seems endless and there's always tomorrow for us.

All slit trenches have been cleared of debris, pits dug for the trucks too, and camouflage ready for the guard room people.

We see the big rice store at Kranji being emptied daily, convoy after convoy going out, all sorts of trucks being used. We have a reserve of three months rice for our camp already.

Nip fighter planes are up in the sky most of the day practising, but we do not see many bombers now.

27 October

Korean says that Nips had lost 850 planes to 500 of the USA in a battle off the Philippines and we are expected to believe that. They don't anyway. Their propaganda is beginning to wear thin, and of course the Malays and Chinese laugh it off now.

On wood fatigue to Nee Soon area at 3.00 pm. Lovely drive through Mondai forest and Nee Soon village. Lots of Nip fighter planes at Sembawang. Our Indian OR PO collected cigarettes and then handed them over to Shaw. Saw B.L. Kapar who is running their gardens, talked a little at some distance, [but was] difficult. Malhotra, Chowdry and Chawla. Returned at 6.00 pm, [with] about five tons of wood in two trips.

29 October

Ledingham very worried; had a postcard from his wife today to say that his bank has received five years short service sum as though the

Army was not giving him a permanent commission. It sounds a dirty trick to me as he has no say in the matter.

Wonder if the IMS is doing the same to us.

30 October

Civilian cars in the roads are very few now, mostly taxis and a few buses. Petrol at $40/- per gallon, so ordinary five-seater car will take 14 people up to Johore at a time; this is the usual load we see going past us. Others get lifts on oil trucks, sometimes on Nip transport. Only Nip officers ride singly or in twos in big private cars which glide past and make one's mouth water just to see them.

Seems to be very little passenger transport on the railway, and the trains come down only loaded with wood. Most of the Nip convoys travel upcountry at night, noisy long lines of transport.

Motor tyres must be a problem too; we hear a puncture or tyre burst opposite us almost daily.

3 November

Another 60 bags of mail have arrived at Changi for sorting. I hope they are more recent letters, [as I] want to know whether Mona has made me an uncle or not – hope all is well.

5 November

First Raid

10.30 am. Saw the first B-29 4-engine bomber come over followed by another 51. Wonderful sight, they flew 30° east of north, height ?30,000ft. Nip anti-aircraft was poor and little, and their fighters seemed afraid of the huge planes. Only two fighters seemed to make any effort to dive to an attack but veered off pretty soon. Others seemed to be fighting above the clouds ? [against] a fighter escort. No bombs dropped, although black objects seemed to tumble out of the skies over Johore.

No definite formation of the B-29s, many single and easily visible below the cloud ceiling. Last over at about 11.30 am.

Guard not excited.

Later – said that 'few bombs fell in residential areas in Seletar and Johore B.' [according to] Java radio. Other reports say that bombs fell in Naval Base and Keppel Harbour. Wonder who is right as we heard no explosions.

Planes ? from Indian bases.

7 November
    Second raid
    Only one B-29 seen very high this morning over Naval Base and Johore area – slight ack-ack. People in from Pulau Panging camp say no bombs were dropped in Keppel Harbour on 5th but rumour that some damage was caused in the Naval Base and Seletar areas.
    S. Synbun says that 30 bombers were over on the 5th and were dispersed or chased away by fighters or ack-ack and that ARP services in Singapore functioned perfectly!
    All the locals are very exhilarated and hope that this means bigger and more frequent destructive raids to the Nips in Malaya.

9 November
    Changi exchange as usual. They saw little of the raid but one anti-aircraft shell crashed into one of the dysentery wards. Fortunately it was a dud and failed to explode.

10 November
    1000 days as a POW – how fed up we are getting, and our people at home still talking big, uttering threats, changing 'posts' as they don't like them or going on holidays. We wait and wait.
    At least the Yanks are getting on with the business of re-taking their territory from the Japs!

13 November
    Went out with the 'frond party' this afternoon, over the creek, about 20. It was just a big looting party really, [and] came back with three coconuts and a good bamboo shoot for curry. Met an optimistic talkative Chinese by the match factory, [who] says hundreds dying daily in Singapore of starvation. We looked at many shops but none had anything eatable for sale, and only a few cigars, and those very expensive.

15 November
    Many bags (60+) of mail have arrived at Changi and are being sorted there, but the Nips won't allow ours to be sent on to us – it all has to be censored by their men and then delivered here by them, not by the 'exchange of patients'. They are so very suspicious of everything. Another two months delay of a letter will do no harm, I suppose.

20 November
<u>Third air raid warning.</u>
We saw no planes overhead. Must read the *Times* of yesterday or today; important.

21 November
<u>Fourth air raid warning.</u>
About 6.45 pm we heard ack-ack and I was just in time to see a B-29 travelling east over the Naval Base area. The Nip fighters were up but much too late to do anything. They're late every time.

Wolfe's Otway pits have had catches in the last few days – a dog, a cat that J.J. Porter promptly went down for and later ate, and today a mental patient jumped down the one into which the dysentery faeces are emptied. He was up to his neck in it and refused to come up – said he thought the top was a submarine.

23 November
The canteen is almost effete; it only seems to get in tobacco at about 3/- an ounce or more. Foodstuffs are, on average, far too expensive to purchase after the various cuts which the Japanese make before the stuff is put on sale. Our Sgt Yoshikawa takes 3% of everything sold. i.e. about $360/- a month. The Chinaman has to make a profit and also pay for the transport ($120/-) of the stuff out to us.

A few prices are:-

Coconut	$1.25
Towgay	$9.00 per lb
Sugar	$8.50 per lb
Coffee	$7.50 per lb
Red Palm oil	$2.00 per lb

<u>Fifth air raid warning.</u>
This was about 2.00 pm and lasted 1½ hours. Much local activity but we saw no raiding planes over our way.

27 November
I received five letters from Mother, all 1943, last dated 11/43, just a few words only and chiefly about that garden – I shall hate it yet. Isn't

there anything else Mother can tell me? Can't Mona, Stanley or Bess write? There's so much that can be put in a few words, important things we want to know – are all well, but what about finances, the house, work, insurances etc. Some letters are quite mad, ask[ing] for immediate replies.

I don't look forward to them so much now – dreadful thought. Want to know is Mother well and <u>what</u> has Mona produced.

Koromato (No.1 Korean) had me over today to explain the basis of blood groups and paternity tests, could we prove who the father of a child is! He was very keen on knowing the value of the tests. Subsequently we learn that he is probably a prospective father for a Eurasian girl in Singapore and the family must be bringing some pressure to bear on him

Later. At 9.00 pm I attended a discussion along with Julian Taylor, Collins, Harper and Davey. Koromato talked about many things but only the barest suggestion of what's on his mind. He served Asahi beer which tasted very good and a small fragment of sweetmeat, poor stuff. We think that he will ask more later.

Bob Davey also gave me 'brandy' later which almost knocked me out.

Back at the hut we found pro-British 'Goggle-eyes' waiting for D' to lead a party out to catch the fellow who is trading in drugs with the Koreans. ('Goggle-eyes' is going to double-cross him.) But at midnight they only caught the stooge seeing if the coast was clear. There seem to be no guards on duty round the camp after 11.30 pm, [when] they all turn in. The police were wondering what it was all about, as they know nothing of this plot. Of course 'Goggle-eyes' is trying to ingratiate himself with us because he wants us to persuade Nicholas to sell his waterproof watch to him and no one else – several Koreans are after it now. They all seem to be living on racketeering.

6 December

Reading *The Forsyte Saga* and looking at old Brown's map of London has caused an awful nostalgia for London to rise within me, and a severe wave of homesickness once more, shared with depression as to how much longer we have to stick this sort of life, things going so slowly. Chaps still dying but death does not seem so dreadful now; it's commonplace and threatens to become more so in the future.

11 December

Capt Richard de Grey has just finished giving us an excellent series of lectures on Norman and Elizabethan History and Party Politics.

Remarkably good speaker and has a really fine command of the English language.

We get lecturers over from Changi Camp to give us talks two to three times a week. They come as pseudo-patients and have a holiday at the same time, [then] go back after a stay of 20 days or so. Other lecturers who have visited here are Lt Morris 'Economic Geography' and Baron de Romsey 'Farming' and odd things; the latter was a pretty poor boy as a lecturer. Of course Padre Wearne hung around him like anything; he is fond of any suggestion of a title and advertising him much. Lionising him to excess.

14 December

Sent present to E. of one cake of soap, J's toilet powder and two small hankies. What a little to send her, poor girl, but we are getting a bit hard up now.

Another camp low – three boxes of *chungkol* heads are missing from the gardens' hut this morning. The gardens' Korean goes in to hospital today as a query TB and this deficiency was found, about three dozen heavy heads. Of course the blame has been put on the POWs by 'No.1' and we have to produce them or substitutes. Of course everybody knows that the Korean has probably sold them to the Chinaman nearby with whom he is very friendly. Yoshikawa has made dire threats. The whole camp and its vicinity have been searched, but no missing articles found – so all tools of every description have to be handed in to a central control store where they can be drawn for daily use only and then returned. Needless to say much has been retained – valuable things like pliers, files, hammers etc. – but it's surprising the amount of equipment that has appeared, gardening and in the RE base, enough for several workshops.

This is all to prevent sale to the Chinese and Yoshikawa says that this is on charge to him and he is answerable to higher authorities for it.

Several of the Korean guards have gone sick in the hopes of being boarded home. There has also been a sudden change and many Koreans have been transferred elsewhere; they were getting too friendly with us! Some were mandarins in the black market and others were news importers of the latest. Another one was a squealer in the drug trade.

21 December

At last, six recent letters from home and I hear that Mona has presented me a niece Elizabeth junior. Both well, dear Mona. Also lovely card from E. dated 5/10/44. We are not allowed to write to them at all. Mother's letter too are nicer than usual, one from Stanley, Olwen stopped writing?

Koronato and four rather pro-British Koreans have been sent away from this camp.

Canteen has a bit more in it than usual but very expensive, of course, lots of blasted tobacco – the CO and those who run it seem chiefly concerned with this.

23 December

Whilst on roll call parade Sgt Yoshikawa brought the internees presents, [and] made us go out in front and open them before everybody while he roared with laughter at the idea of my wife a prisoner and the simple presents she had sent me. It was disgusting. I was furious and he must have noticed my face and delivered me a lecture on the great generosity of the IJA to allow such presents to pass etc etc – said I was his friend, the swine. He likes to show off every now and again in a very childish manner. Later he got tipsy and went round the camp being a nuisance in the huts.

The IJA have given NO EXTRA rations for Christmas, but we have saved a little.

25 December

Our meals today have been good, my appetite quite satisfied. Last night Cooper caught the 'kampong bitch' in the trap. J.J. Porter cooked it and sixteen of us sat down to a terrific stew in the Lab, [which was] very, very good. This morning we had coffee with milk and sugar going in the Lab. Mess Christmas pudding and cake was super [illegible].

One more TB patient died.

Elizabeth, Mother, home – remember it all ....

Chapter 7

Jack's diary – 1945

5 January

Having used up all my diaries, I now have a makeshift one and hope that this will last me out with economy. Paper is not available at all now and I am very low. Popular substitutes are roughened X ray plate and glass surfaces to write on by Greer's method. He gives it a lovely surface and the two bits I have serve me well for scribbling notes in my efforts at study. If one uses a sheet of paper it is not cast away until it has been written on in three directions. Even blank space on newspaper is used, and of course the blank space and surface of home letters and envelopes are good material.

8/9/11 January [This entry in back of 1944 diary].

We have had air raids each morning. This last was a good raid on the Naval Base. Many B-29s over and much ack-ack, fighters and curious mushrooms appeared in the sky as well. Unfortunately I saw a B-29 shot down in flames over Johore and two fighters. It was quite a hot affair and my head felt very bare. Plenty of big crumps up the Naval Base way. The last Changi party say that many damaged Nip naval units are in the Base and I think so too judging by the number of personnel going in to town daily.

Many bits of paper floated down on the camp from the burning B-29, chiefly bits of catalogues and papers of his logbook. The Korean sentries went round collecting the paper; we thought at first they were pamphlets but no such luck.

This is the first real action we have seen out here since capitulation. Let's hope for lots more and bigger provided.

10 January

The rambutan trees have been prolific across Kranji and the antimalarial party have been returning with bags full after each weekly outing. The Chinese have been very good and allowed us to take as many as we want. Of course other vegetables – eggfruit, onions, papaya, and durian blondies are pilfered too. I think the latter is a delightful fruit, certainly the best I have tasted in Malaya. Never tasted it until the other day. Rambutan are now coming to an end; it's a short season for them.

At New Year, the Korean Sgt No.1 had a party over in the CO quarters, and when feeling pretty good, broached the question of this camp – behaviour in the event of heavy bombing or an attack being made in this neighbourhood. The reply was that as long as he played the game by us POWs, we would behave ourselves. He said that as long as he was here he would do his best for us.

Many of the Korean guard know the trend of recent events and tend to spill the beans now and again. A number of them with pro-British tendencies have been quite suddenly transferred away.

We all hope that it won't last much longer for us as we are coming to the end of everything – clothing, boots, towels, drugs, soap, razor blades and patience. Rags are common dress and pass without comment, and knocking about in bare feet. Bed linen for most is just a ragged worn blanket and a bundle of rags as a pillow. As far as drugs go, the Nips are not supplying anything now, and quinine S-figrioline group will soon be finished. The only way it is kept in stock is by half and quartering treatment.

Oh God how long!

20 January

Rats, rats all over the camp. They are getting very bad indeed, [with] no or very few cats to be seen as we have eaten them all. I have made a rat trap for our hut, but for the first five nights the rats have walked in and out of the mesh. At last I've caught one this morning and allowed 'Soda' to kill it after preventing a cat from breaking up the trap at night.

24 January

Started giving a talk [on] 'Malaria' in the camp wards. Judging by the numbers and questions it seems to be quite a popular subject. I give a historical point of view.

26 January

Disaster; at last my fountain pen has packed in, one iridium point has broken off. What now – I've had it since 1928.

Joe Birch has filed off the other point and made a new tip to the nib, reckons it will last about as long as I shall need it as a POW He is very handy with his hands, mends watches and other jobs, a likeable sort of American guy. The Lab is his watch-repairing shop; he uses it every afternoon.

As my Quink is very low in the bottle, I have had to dilute with water, hence the faintness of this script.

27 January

Saw Noel Coward's play *A Design for Living* put on by Bradshaw. Mackwood, Morrison and Backshall in the leads, the latter played the female part well and looks good too. Not so nice a play as *Private Lives* but we do enjoy them. The scenery is always excellent and lighting – one would not think we were in a POW camp. When I come out of the theatre I always feel so 'London-sick'; there should be taxis, crowds, pretty women in evening gowns and a snack at a restaurant. Instead, just back to the hut for some cold tea.

1 February

Our second big attacking air raid by B-29[s]. Was doing a post mortem on a pellagra and had to leave him in bits whilst I went to my Aid Post; very few showed their heads above ground while the shrapnel was flying about. Nips seem to have been using naval guns 5in or 8in size. Five huge bits fell in the camp.

Changi exchange took place as usual.

Fires went out suddenly in the evening, so we think it was a vessel that subsequently sank.

2 February

We have long discussions and arguments as to how the end is going to come for this term. Some think that it will be quiet and peaceful, others that we will be once more in the midst of fighting. Time alone will tell. The camp commanders, of course, have never bothered to try to visualise the terminal events which might occur in this camp – all they say is discipline must be maintained. 'Naafi Tea' Collins has little enough as it is, as witnessed by the events of New Year's Day this year when an uncontrolled mob ran wild in the camp ducking officers in the showers, including COs Middleton and MacDonald against specific orders. No orders are obeyed really except those of the Jap Sergeant.

We talk of Death now, not really fearing it except that if it should come it be quick, but my spirit would be intensely annoyed if, after lasting so long, I should die, and that seems to be the opinion of all in my room.

Events seem to be reaching a climax in Europe, let's hope very soon now, weeks not months to go.

6 February

Manila won at last. We are most optimistic here, wondering when the British are going to try and retake this part of the world. They are so painfully slow in progress.

There is a great craze in camp to put covers over slit trenches that one uses, as a result of all the shrapnel flying around on the 1st. Some trenches only have three to four inches of earth on wood rafters but some are solid with about three feet of clay. Wood is very short as roofing material and this demand happens to coincide with a 30% cut in the wood ration from 1000g per head daily down to 700g. As it is, fuel is insufficient, so wonder how we are going to manage.

Fragments of anti aircraft shells are still being dug up all over the camp; it's remarkable that no one was injured in that raid.

Apparently the local Chinese have to attend twice or three times a week when the Japs give them instruction in anti-invasion tactics and are drilling them.

Have not heard anybody talked of so much for last one to two years as Louis Mountbatten [admiral, Supreme Allied Commander, South East Asia Command] and Bruce Fraser [admiral, in command of British Pacific Fleet] without anything positive to their credit, all about what they intend to do – but when.

8/9 February

Much camp activity last night. One of the mental patients has broken out of the camp and vanished during last night. He was suicidal and forcibly fed for several days now.

Also Farwell (Junior) and a Eurasian boy called Peterson were caught trafficking in drugs with the Chinese cook in the Nip cookhouse. The Chink was found with Tab. Atibrine, Vit C, quinine and M&B powders such as we issue in the wards to try and prevent black marketing. We have suspected this leakage for months but did not know how it was going out. A most serious offence as we are intensely short of drugs and there are no fresh supplies coming in from the IJA. The Nip truck driver stumbled on them by accident in their kitchen after lights-out and Yoshikawa searched the Chinaman's kit. Peterson is also being charged with contacting his family in Singapore.

Later – Farwell Junior and Peterson, after many face-slappings, have been tried by Lt Tania and Sgt Yoshikawa and awarded 30 and 10 days respectively in the guardroom cells on a diet of rice only. As both are very friendly with the Koreans, I have no doubt that their diets will be considerably reinforced. The Civil Police refused to deal with the Chinaman so Y' has him back after much beating up and bashing.

11 February
Married three years, darling.

12 February
Search parties have been all over scouring the surroundings for miles looking for the 'loony' Gale. Y' took out a party of 100 of our chaps to look for him; they tramped for four and a half hours in the jungle, losing each other, but somehow all came back together correct after 6.00 pm.
Later – the mental patient was found by two Tamils down near Bukit Panjang village and has been brought back and is lodged in the guardroom cells too. Y' has not ill-treated him at all but is keeping him locked up there. The KEMPI [Kempetai] have been in on this loss, worrying Y' who has a healthy respect of them. They gave him orders that the body must be found dead or alive. Y' is delighted, and of course has recovered much face because of the find independent of the Kempi fellows.

13 February
Our perimeter is now surrounded by seven very well made ([by] our men) machine-gun trenches for the sentries use. The number of slit trenches about the camp is still increasing. This laterite soil makes good trenches, but holds rain water and breeds mosquitos.
There has been a big cut in the ration scales all over in the POW camps as from today. Three scales as before operate i.e. Heavy – Light – No Duty (patients)
The figures [in grams] in theory are:-

	Heavy	Patients
Rice	600	400
Tea	5	5
Sugar	25	15
Salt	20	20
Vegetables	500+	500+
Oil	25	25
Fish	50	25

Actually we never received these amounts as rations in this camp are pooled and redistributed to increase the patients' diet to make up for issue weight deficiencies, and also for local depreciation and loss in sacks etc. so that lately I have been having about 450g rice.

Present scale of rations – camp issue:-

	Heavy	Light	Patients
Rice	500	300	250
	(390)	(320)	(320)

Tea	4
Sugar	15
Salt	15 (14)
Vegetables	300 (+)
Oil	20 (18)
Fish	50 (35)

[Figures in] brackets represent actual issues to us from our store after pooling of rations.

15 February

Gosh what it is to be hungry and realise that one can't do anything about it, no larder to raid or nearby shop to buy from. Hunger pains are terrific and today we have started our lighter meals. Wonder for how long.

Squealer 'Goggle-eyes' – [says] that the island has a lot of aircraft now but very few troops to defend it. They have all gone upcountry and others are being withdrawn from Java and Sumatra too. The local population are all on edge and expecting things to happen. Goggle-eyes reckons that in two months the 'fun' will rightly start in this part and the Chinese will certainly rise in a body.

We have had a reinforcement of about 20 more Koreans posted here, some came from Java, others are some of those previously sent away from this camp.

1 March

IJA have informed us that a Red Cross ship with about 1200 tons of food and 13,000 personal parcels is expected shortly. This is said to be for 30,000 prisoners and internees on the island. Collins lost face badly today at the exchange with Changi. He was hoping to get rid of our extras and convalescents and reduce the patients by 250, but Niall and Newey are too savant and sent man for man, even though they are not really sick people. 'Where are your sick men?' said the Nips to Collins, and Davey (the interpreter). Niall threatens to send us all the old scroungers from there. They know we are doing this to try and increase the patients diet by pooling; no pooling of rations is allowed over in Changi but they can draw 'L' rations whereas we, as a hospital, can only draw 'H' or 'P'.

Once again Administration is using the hospital!

4 March

5th Postcard: "Fit at 142lb. Still occupied. Hope both Elizabeths well. Congratulate Mona. Am happier now. Keep well. Aching for home. Love to all.' Dated.

7 March

We hear that the Red Cross stores have been unloaded to Serangoon Road (Indian POW) camp and are to expect our share shortly.

10 March

IJA have further cut our rations to 'H' 300g, 'L' 250g, 'P' 200g [but] actual issues will of course be less than this because of the short weight in the bags. Vegetable issues are negligible now and fish about 30g a day. Diet has value of about 1600 cals for one and only about 1250 for patients. I work my basal metabolic rate out to 900–1000 cals/diurn in the Tropics and 1595 at home.

11 March

Davey has been told that the Red Cross stores at Serangoon Road camp have been partly looted by Indians and Koreans. We wonder if any of it will arrive to us eventually.

J.J. Porter and others are now eating rats as fast as they can catch them. Cooper, H' and Joe Bush eat an occasional one, but better still, we bait the cat trap with a caged rat and it worked successfully last night. Cat for lunch today.

Since the beginning of the month, no anti-malarial work has been permitted outside the camp so we expect the worst.

Not so many trains and road convoys going north these days, traffic has reduced considerably.

The hospital is getting full of Dutch civilians from Pulau Damar camp, and we have also had a few admissions from a party at Keppel Harbour, some of whom have come up from the Celebes islands where they have been working under appalling conditions and high mortality. Two shiploads of POWs sank on their way up to Java.

20 March

Rice ration reduced to 220g and we are given 50g of maize instead. Rumours about moves from Changi. No news about getting any of the Red Cross goods.

22 March

General Saito [commandant of Changi POW camp] and a news reporter came round the camp for the first time since we've been here – ten months.

30 March

We have evacuated the northeast quadrant of the camp for a 650 working party from Changi. It is a separate camp to ours by a single wire, no communication allowed whatsoever.

Sent 400 patients and discharges back to Changi today and tomorrow. Also ready – three medical parties of 40s, one Assistant Surgeon and 25 ORs to move out – where? Three work parties have left Changi for various places – to build fortifications in Johore and on the island.

Note that the sick from our neighbours cannot come to this hospital, they go to a special hospital at Changi. Saw some of the parties come in. Gosh they look dreadful – ragged, wasted, thin, depressed; 250 and their baggage arrived in seven trucks.

Y' made us strip the vacated area of all extras, fittings, pipes, taps, partitions, steps etc. and even the gardens have been devastated – shame.

1 April

Our neighbours have had an issue of Red Cross stores, about one parcel to 20 men, had it all as a big post on Easter Sunday. They are not being worked too hard at present and treatment by their Japs is quite good. They get 500g ration of rice and maize.

None of our parties moved yet.

The men speak badly of Col Newey; hate him and are glad to go anywhere from Changi away from him. He sent out this 650 party with five 6-gallon containers and three 3-gallon containers as their sole cooking utensils, yet there are materials in plenty and two welding outfits at Changi. He wouldn't let Harper bring a few engineering essentials to this camp and told Collins he was no longer interested in this hospital although we have some 600 Changi patients here.

10/11 April

Our three medical parties have moved to the new camps. Nicholas (Nick) is with one gone to Bukit Timah, another to Johor Bahru and the third to No.2 camp over the wire. What are they going to do! It's ridiculous that we cannot deal with the sick from over the way.

The men are engaged on building roads of a rough temporary kind towards the Naval Base and north-west coast of the island, and on anti aircraft positions up on Cemetery Hill behind us. They're getting much better rations than us. The medicals always suffer in this respect as, of course, we are not working for the Nips, though the work is just as hard physically.

13 April

At long last I've decided to sell my lovely pocket Omega with its sweep second hand – best watch I've ever had. 'MY FRIEND' has been given the deal to conduct in Singapore from my garden pitch. Handed over $1800, not too bad.

15 April

Disposed of this sudden wealth :-

Capt S. Campbell	$200/-	£20 cheque
Capt R. Taylor	$200/-	£20 cheque
J. Ledingham	$100/-	£10 cheque
Mr M. McCaul	$200/-	£20 cheque
Capt Huxtable	$20/-	for Cyma watch
Houghton and Cooper	$50/-	
Lt J. Strawbridge	$160/-	£20 cheque
Hodden	$10/-	
Nair	$5/-	
Capt Kingston	$105/-	£7 cheque

Increased E.'s sum to maximum allowed to pay.
Six months reserve at 50/- ($300)

19 April

At last 642 small Red Cross parcels have arrived at our stores, not issued yet, but the Sgt says 'though the Americans promised a safe return for the ship, it was sunk on the way back and for a time the IJA considered withholding these Red Cross goods from us. Now the spirit of Bushido has entered them and we have our stores' – after each gang of Nips who have handled them have taken a percentage. The small amount is being handed out as though it is a personal favour by Yoshikawa – but he has still not let any into the camp.

23 April

Brooks, our cook, caught a big cat last night, sold it to the Lab for 20/-. I ate a quarter share this evening and it was awfully good.

24 April

Issue of Red Cross stores begin to the various areas, it's a niggardly amount of goods – so far it will amount to half of a 'weekly' type of parcel. No cigarettes, and the chocolate is maggoty, mildewed and rancid. The sacking on the parcels was dated June '42 from England.

Later – the tinned M&U, puddings, biscuits were lovely. Gosh what are we missing.

More food has arrived at the stores but Y' is keeping it 'til he feels like issuing it or we go on our knees to beg him for it.

31 April

$2000/- was stolen from the hospital office between 4.00–5.00 pm yesterday. The CO has applied all kinds of restrictions on the camp, canteen closed, and all personal wealth has got to be registered, and then the canteen will re-open and check the amount each individual has to spend – so hope to catch the crook. Actually in the office staff are two ex-safebreakers of repute and other untrustworthy people whom the CO, for some unknown reason, keeps on.

Capt MacDonald has often left the safe open and probably did so on this occasion too as the lock was not forced. Cleverly only the small notes were taken.

I have declared $277 as my wealth though I own much more at present. Unfortunately this means that the sale of all articles must go through Capt M' and Pte Brody as official channels, as it is known that they take a big percentage each sale.

Later – Sgt Marsden RAMC convicted of theft and Cadet Norton of Merchant Navy for neglect of duty, but nothing happened to MacDonald who was responsible really for gross neglect – but everybody in the camp suffers, all money transactions, however small, to be registered, queue ages at the canteen to buy things and only once a day. Very, very tedious. What a Commander!

4 May

The latest act of Nippery is that we must wash our rice and send the washings to them – what for? We have no washings as they contain thyamine Hcl which we require. The camp next to us is getting terrific amount of extra food [with] 900g rice, fresh fish, jam, sugar, milk etc because they are a working party. The medical personnel who have worked steadily have never had such benefits and they certainly do as much work as a chap on a work party. Mouldy wet rice not accepted by our neighbours was issued to us – of course our QM Barber accepted it. Each time there has been a Red Cross issue, the medical staff have had milk, bully beef etc kept back for the benefits of patients in hospital who are, of course, nearly all combatant work party men.

Later: More food etc has arrived at the stores but Y' is keeping it until he feels like issuing it or we go on our knees to beg him for it.

A number of books, theatrical equipment sent with Red Cross stores won't be issued by Sgt Yoshikawa because he says they have not been censored yet.

8 May

This evening Steve bought a bottle of some poison '3 x brandy'. Seven of us celebrated at a cost of $11.50 each, sitting in the dark 'til midnight and thinking of home and our people ... will they think of us.

Mizina the medical Sgt of our camp, has handed over the Red Cross supplies to us. Plenty of vitamins and sulphonamide drugs, little enteric. It's noticeable that in each box the numbers of bottles or vials of certain useful drugs have been corrected to the reduced figures by Nips. Eg. Atibrine, B1, Emetine – they say that these had been destroyed in transit, ampoules broke etc! However, we're glad to get what's come, beautifully packed too.

Col Cotton-Harvey AAMC [Australian Army Medical Corps] who has the privilege of signing for drugs, has already taken away one bottle of multiple vitamin tablets (200) for himself. He and Charles Osborne have been extremely selfish; they get extra milk, bully beef, eggs, as they are convalescent patients.

Aussy OR from a Johor Bahru camp was buried this morning – he was killed by a fall of earth whilst digging an Iogawa igloo. These are being dug by our work parties all over the place, and minor accidents are constantly occurring. These are hasty defence works for the yellow bastards who seem to expect things any day now.

10 May

Another fatality on a work party due to blasting, brought in and buried very secretly. Many minor injuries are occurring on these parties, particularly due to falls of earth.

12 May

'Multiple Vitamin' tablets are very popular; all the influential people of the camp are on them besides C. Harvey, C. Osborne, Col Collins, Col Middleton, certain officer staff – they *had* sore mouths and deficiency evidence sometime back. True, there are about 60,000 of these tablets in.

16 May

Peak Freans canned puddings are delicious, must indulge in them after I get out of here.

22 May

Patience, wait a bit longer. Everybody at home seems to be resting, even Winston. No hurry to finish off the Nips and get us out of this captivity. Our dirt and conditions are so monotonous; the samples of Red Cross food only makes one feel all the more what is missing; how can anyone who has not been a Nip POW realise what it's like. I suppose volunteers only will come out this way! People still dying and working and being beaten by the Nips, and so we wait and wait.

3 June

Hear that John Diver RAMC died from beriberi at Normanton Camp working party. Yesterday there was a fall in a tunnel which our work party chaps were in, [with] one killed, two injured and one Nip killed too. Accidents like this are frequent – the Nips are having these funk holes dug all over the island.

4 June

Went out on a frond party. It was a most enjoyable outing, [but] rather hard work pushing the trailer; Col Taylor got boot 'bites' and hobbled back.

5 June

Four letters from home arrived, very old, last is 9/44. Only news is that Stanley is abroad and Mother's well. How we want to know things – Mona, Olwen, Bess, what about them? Can't my brother and sister write? What about some domestic news? Folk at home will never, never be able to realise what it's like being a POW.

23 June

Every Saturday night the camp 'Brains Trust' sit and answer questions for the curious in our Mess. Tonight I'm on invitation, joined to answer 'Physiological Questions'. J.T. was very poor in his answers and Graves equally so.

25 June

Eight men brought in from Keppel Harbour camp; three dead, one died soon after and others just alive. Had found a carboy of methanol and had a little each whilst on the scrounge. Most consumed was about 2oz, and symptoms came on about 36 hours later. Severe blindness predominant.

Still waiting patiently for things to happen.

2245hrs: Eclipse of the moon began and was all but total by about 0130hrs on 26th June.

2 July

We're getting more and more restive, impatient. Rations are getting really bad now, consist of rice 270g, sugar 14g, oil 17g, little salt and tea, some days no green vegetable, some whitebait 1–2oz. Patients only get 210–230g rice. Many more skeletons about the camp now. Dogs and cats have long since disappeared, rats are on the increase in all huts – but they are poor eating.

3 July

Wilkinson knocked down a carrier pigeon by his hut with a mess tin lid quite by fluke. In less than ten minutes, J.J. Porter and Joe Bush had it in the pot and its feathers down a borehole. Found its receptacle and a message in it dated 30.6, so the pigeon had lost its way. Y' gave a coincident yell when it was brought down and the guilty ones thought they were for it, but that was for something else.

For the last two weeks we have had Indian sentries all round the camp by day as several Koreans have been taken away to form a labour camp. Those that have shown us any sympathy have chiefly gone. My friend Hayashita is still here though I seldom see him now.

The Indians say that their camps are very badly constructed, [with] everything to benefit the officers. Col Chowdry at Nee Soon, they say, has been selling the drugs to the Nips. He was originally pro-Nip but has evidently tried to come back. Allagapia and Lagganadou are still with them. Jilani, Kopar and Manji are at a Seletar camp. The whole island is full of work party camps digging Iogawa igloos for the Nips, enlarging the airfields and humping stores. Health at most camps is very poor indeed, especially of those fellows come up from Sumatra.

6 July

Rumours that we are going to move north, so is Changi? And the internees camp? Hope we're together. Sent Elizabeth extra money and Harty $10/- this month. Nips are going to fight hard for this island it seems. All unnecessary population, says the *Sinbun*, will begin to move out after 15th July.

10 July

IJA now say that the supply of vegetables (leaves) is going to fail and have <u>ordered</u> that we have to produce and use 30 buckets of night soil on our outside gardens daily. They offer no material with which this can be carried out so they are going to make us eat our own shit at last. Up will go the dysentery and worms rate again.

14 July

Wolfe, hygiene officer, has the above order in hand and not hurrying matters. I have to examine all the Nip and Korean stools, 37 [of them], and all but five have helminthic infection; I thought we were pretty bad!

How much longer have we got to wait??

21 July

Am celebrating Mother's and Elizabeth's birthdays today, eating a tin of meat tonight with Robin and Steve in the room, and a big curry for lunch tomorrow, coffee and flan cakes with Kingston and QM this morning at 11.00 am.

Yoshikawa ordered that we are to get no more produce off the big garden until we get this faeces business going – anyway we only get red amaranth off it. All the good vegetables – tapioca, sweet potatoes, cucumbers, beans, papaya etc – are taken by the Nips as their share of it. The rest worthwhile is eaten on the garden by the workers on it who get a big stew everyday – perhaps as well as they are convalescent patients.

Very little vegetable comes in from outside.

24 July

Vegetable and fish issues of the camp have been stopped for two days until we get the night soil on the garden regularly.

Received four letters from home, the last dated Christmas 1944.

All lectures and camp entertainment at night has been stopped, a general order for all camps. Most unfortunate for us, [as] a play was about to go on and several good lectures.

Later – all band instruments have been put under lock and key, the stage dismantled and Yoshikawa has taken the wood to build his air raid shelter near his office.

Nips are going through the camp at night to see that no lectures etc are in progress.

25 July

My birthday.

There are more skeletons walking around the camp than ever before, and others, just lying on their beds from one scant meal to the next – rations are very low.

Everybody is very optimistic, though if we are not relieved or killed in a few months, death will come on a great percentage anyway. Extra food for the worst is almost exhausted now and our medicines are again very low.

In the meantime tunnels and trenches are being built all round us using POW labour, [and] several gun positions on the hill above us. The hills in Mondai forest are being turned into rabbit warrens, as is Mount Faber and other hills about the island.

31 July

Our canteen purchases are now restricted to $50 a month because Y' has suddenly asked how it is that, although only $8000 in pay comes into the camp monthly, yet last month we spent $11,000 through the canteen. We had been steadily mounting to this new figure. Of course it does not mean much because goods are so expensive. Whitebait $32 per lb, tapioca flour $12 per lb etc. In JB a coconut costs $7, a small cheroot 90 cents or $1.00 each, so anyone who does out the black market is in a poor way.

Of course Y' gets a 6% cut off canteen subs, but I guess he wants to try and cut down the huge amount of money the Koreans are making. Several have run away and are hiding from various camps, waiting for the relief of Singapore.

How long have we to wait for Lord L' and M' [Lord Louis Mountbatten and Major General Robert Mansergh, British commanders of Operation *Tiderace* to retake Singapore]; if we had to depend on the Yanks something might have been done about us already as they are more go-ahead.

3 August

Fortification and tunnelling work goes on all around us; at night we hear the underground reverberations of underground blasting. More march out daily to dig those trenches etc.

In this camp, old Pearson and others gather and eat rubber nuts still. Others are going in for rats in a big way; I've tasted some roasted – but it's still 'rat'. Food is very bad – no wonder all this being resorted to – yet there's a great feeling of optimism throughout.

8 August

Went over the wire to the next camp and had a talk with Mitchell, Bradshaw, Findlay and others. Whilst there a patient was brought in at 9.15 pm with four stretcher-bearers, MO and Korean escort. They had been made to walk all the way from north of Jurong Creek since 2.00 pm. Hitchhiked a part of the way only, but no food or drink, distance of about 19 miles. The Jap in charge of the camp said he could provide no transport although it was for a seriously injured man (whilst digging a tunnel mouth fell in on him).

Normanton Camp is brutal these days. The patients only come in here to die.

However things are going well elsewhere, and we reckon at most four to six weeks and have done. Y' does not think we are so well informed; he is very behind us. Most estimate it in days but I am more pessimistic in times.

9 August

Well two further developments [atomic bombs dropped on Hiroshima and Nagasaki] – should now clinch Japan's decision. Absolute hammer blows they are. I should like to know how the nuclear energy is liberated and so devastating too. Further it is pleasing to know that Russia is doing her bit too.

11 August

Now six years in Malay and what a day this is! Optimism reigns supreme, coffee parties everywhere, and hidden tins of food are being opened all over the place. Folk are beginning to crop their gardens and take up root vegetables all over. I heard the gist of the news last night about the Japs submission and our quibbling but managed to sleep. All day we have been watching the guards and Sgt Y' for a sign that they have heard of this capitulation offer, but none forthcoming. At 3.00 pm in Johore Palace, a big gathering of Nip officers took place – but what for?

At dawn about 30 fighters flew over in a due east direction.

Wouldn't Y' be wild if he knew that we have been hearing the news all along and he knows nothing of what is going on.

12 August

Hardly slept last night, though heard that negotiations are not much further. Was up at 7.00 am and looked at the stars; they are beautiful, and the *kluangs* [fruit bats] flying towards their day roosting place.

Still watching the guards for a sign. We think the Indians know, and the Koreans know, but one won't tell the other – just laugh nervously when the other laughs etc. The working parties still go out, and our labour gang is still working on the underground fuel store for Y'.

August 13

After Ted Harper told us the news at 11.05 pm I hardly slept a wink, restless – and full of wind because of the artichokes we ate last morning. Up at 7.00 am again.

We all hope to be away in five to seven days.

The various stores are emptying themselves, handing out stuff, and the canteen is giving away 1lb of red palm oil and one ounce tobacco <u>free.</u>

About 2.00 pm air raid siren sounded and the fighters went up as usual. We all thought negotiations had broken down. None of our planes came over.

No signs yet that the Nips know what is going on. Rations as usual – rice 230g, maize 40g, dried fish ¼oz, vegetables 4oz, tea, sugar, oil, salt.

14 August

The tension continues.

Went for a swim with the saltwater party and, on the way back, a Malay on a truck tried to tell us something – the first sign.

Our gardens are being pulled up everywhere, but for the Nips work continues as usual, digging tunnels and earthworks, and every night we listen to see if blasting operations have ceased or not.

[At] 10.00 pm the Koreans and Nips had a party and Lt Naga addressed them [and] told them to expect the worst. One made a feeble attempt at suicide by stabbing his throat; he was stitched up.

They seem to think invasion is at hand, says our friend 'Goggle-eyes'. They still do not know the truth of what is going on.

15 August

The Emperor broadcast that they had surrendered at 12 noon today, but at 2.00 pm the air raid sirens went here in Singapore and fighter planes went up as usual.

16 August

Went on saltwater party. Out on the road, the locals looked at us in astonishment. Fatigues and working parties continue as usual. Yoshikawa as arrogant as ever.

The Indians heard the news today and are terribly excited.

17 August

Our miserable condition continues as before. The Korean guards have heard the news today for the first time; they have not been allowed out of camp since the 14th, and one who went to Changi on the 15th to hear the Imperial script has been sworn to secrecy.

Wonder how long this farce is going to continue.

18 August

Went up to the Cemetery Hill this morning; this looks very beautiful from up there.

A Dutchman was buried, the last we hope.

At 1245hrs one of our bombers came over low, [and] he was heavily fired on from all over, north and north-east of us. Fighter planes went up after him.

Koreans lined up by Y' at 2030hrs and told that the War was over, but 'Japan had not surrendered unconditionally', she was back to her 1941 position. The Koreans were not to tell us – but within ten minutes they were over, one after another, to inform us, Bob Davis and Collins, bringing presents to the last two. Collins is doing well at the expense of the Koreans.

19 August

Our camp is being filled up with sick from the various labour camps; about 380 more are coming in.

Work parties have ceased, and Lt Naga has informed the CO officially that War is over and we will be relieved very shortly.

No let-up in restrictions as yet.

The Indians are very worried about their position and I intend to help them all I can and told Maj Hay HKSRA [Hong Kong and Singapore Royal Artillery] to do so as well, as most of them are his men.

20 August

Indians have been seeing me and Hay all day as to what they should do!

Nips have sent a lot of cheap boots into the camp which are being issued ad lib. Also some Red Cross clothing.

Indians went and saw Y' this afternoon – saying they would not do any more guard duty.

21 August

Indians are overjoyed because they have handed in their arms and are now fraternising freely with our people. Steve Campbell and I were entertained at 6.00 pm in their hut to a wonderful chicken curry and *halwa* sweet by the *havildar* [sergeant] and all of them. It was a big 'do'.

Last night in our room we had to entertain a Korean (plus beer) and two P.M.s; a very amusing and awkward party. Languages spoken were Jap, Urdu, Punjabi, Malay and English.

The Col' and several others of our camp administration dined with four Koreans in his bunk last night – Kim, Kim K. Dak, Toyahara and Nishyama (the 'basher'). The guard system on the camp has fallen through and hundreds are going out every night to kampongs all round, and bartering their new clothing, boots etc for chickens, ducks, and eggs. We are getting plenty of rice now and the other rations are being increased too.

The 380 party have moved to Changi, leaving 15 sick behind over here.

Still wondering about the state of the internees – where is Elizabeth now? Been trying like anything to persuade Collins to ask for a visit to their camp.

22 August

More clothing came in, with boots. Also half a Red Cross parcel each so we are having big eats this evening.

Indians left at 5.30 pm.

9.00 pm. Big party in our room (given by two Koreans) consisting of biscuits, bully, butter, coffee with milk and sugar. Later some cheap brandy was served too, I took my share up to the Lab staff.

11.15 pm. Steve came over looking for me to go out as Kim had a car ready in the corner Tamil *kampong*. Quite a surprise. Davy lent me an alpaca jacket. Went through the wire led by K' dressed in white. Morris '8' saloon parked there. Down to Adam Road work party camp, picked up one of their Korean guards, rifle, bayonet and all. I took over driving to Sime Road Internment Camp, parked car about 100 yards away. All went to main gate, met a Malay armed guard who shivered with fright – begged us not to go in because of Nips around the camp and inside, but told us to write a note. (12.15 pm) Drove back to Adam Park camp and the sentry took us to the main guardroom where the Koreans sat us down and gave us cold tea, while Kim told them all the latest news. One produced a satchel, and Steve wrote to his brother enclosing my message to E. The Korean said it would be delivered today by Sgt in charge of Internee Camp. I then drove back; it was lovely although the car steering was pretty bad.

Back by 1.00 am in camp. Noticed Mondai village was very lively as was Bukit Timah. Passed several Korean guards, and, at Ford Works, about 25 Nip patrol, this place was heavily guarded.

23 August

Much food and clothing (very cheap stuff) all over the camp. I'm eating very little rice these days.

All very expectant. Blakang Mati camp and their sick are now here; Capt Frankland RAMC came in with them.

24 August

Most of us have eaten up our half box of Red Cross eats and Collins won't issue the rest.

Gen Saito called at 6.15 pm to tell us that supplies will be dropped by air tomorrow and asked Collins if we had enough food. The latter replied 'yes' – this is incorrect. Told Collins to ask for anything, [but] he only asked for Y' to be sent away from this camp for his own safety!!

Did not ask about visiting the internees.

Had a long visit from Hayashita last morning; he is worried that he is going to be interned for 15 years and asked that I get him a job in a hospital; was very amusing.

26 August

Another half parcel issued to us, less milk and some bully beef. The radio keeps telling us that food, drugs and MOs are going to be dropped but nothing materialised as yet. There have been two issues of 4oz meat in the last three days. Any amount of cigars and cigarettes in the camp now.

It's awful remaining cooped up so much longer and apparently nothing happening.

28 August

At 1430hrs a B-24 came over at 500ft and, after three and a half years, dropped us pamphlets in Japanese. The men were mad about it. Patients who had been in bed for months staggered out and malarias at 104°F, we cheered first – but groaned later and what foul language. This, after waiting two days since Gen Saito told us that our planes would be over dropping us food etc. – how disappointing. We could even see the faces of the crew and one taking a movie of the camp.

2100hrs Gave Kim a note for Elizabeth (no. 2) says he'll deliver it himself tomorrow. The internees are still at Sime Road.

29 August

Been expecting planes over all day but none even heard.

Black Jack Galleghan AIF and Neale came over, just full of themselves, not for any public benefit whatsoever, though they have been to other camps as well, including internees. Neale only saw a QM to talk to, and Black Jack gossiped with AIF, telling them how he was going around in a big car and Nip officers were bowing to him etc. No help to us – what the hell are they doing!

How much more of this are we to put up with?

30 August

Two officers RAMC, two Para Lieutenants and two ORs were dropped at Changi. They know little or nothing, but brought the POW classification for evacuation.

Token medical supplies and Red Cross comforts also dropped by plane parachute. We have been issued with more Red Cross parcels, about one each so far in the last seven days.

31 August

Long talk with Sutor, the Swiss Red Cross representative, who promised to see Elizabeth. Sent a brief note by him.

Later – four Red Cross chaps came round and looked at the hospital. Talked much. Saw Nash who told me all about Elizabeth.

We are still prisoners, feeding on masses of butter.

1 September

Open-air concert on the *padang*, first since the ban was enforced. Thousands attended and people came in off the road to look on – Chinese, Tamils etc. All joined in. Ron Morrison was on form. Ended by singing 'God Save The King' very lustily so that the [illegible] rang.

We all feel better now.

2 September

Still prisoners.

Went out this morning to see if a food dump made in 1942 at Woodlands Camp could be found, Lt Col Webster, I and four NCOs. We all got a lift down and back. Met 5/2 Punjabi men under Sub Ahmed Khan and Jen Sarwar Khan, both fine fellows. The food dump was empty. But it was a good outing.

Dr Campbell arrived from the civilian camp at 4.30 pm. Hitch hiked up here. Told us much.

3 September

Went to Nee Soon Indian Hospital with Col Taylor who operated on Capt Awara's cholecystectomy. Spent the day there with 12 IGH people led by Siva? Tears came to my eyes. All the old faces, thin and grey. What a time they've had. Pleased to meet all the IMD personnel, Fairy Mohindra, Maluk Singh and all the others. Batman Khan Moh' is a bit mental.

On way back noticed that Chinese and Malays had been scrapping. Gosh what preparations had been going on in Mondai forest; it would have been a frightful battle for us.

4 September
    Still prisoners.
    The Changi fellows have been allowed to see their relatives, not us. We in Kranji are being left out of things a good deal. Collins is hopeless and ill. McDonald thinks he is too good but is incompetent, and the men are all very dissatisfied. One radio set in the camp, but M' has hidden it in the canteen and nobody is able to hear anything but his select circle.
    Our own 'Canary' [radio] which has served us so well was on show; only three valves with transformers and local made coils. It had been fixed under the boards of the canteen floor. Three headphones served.
    The Changi crowd are allowed to Sime Road to see their relatives today, but not us. Collins and his staff have no interest in us. I and others keep worrying them.

5 September
    Two trucks are crossing after much worrying of the COs today.
    At last I see Elizabeth again – but what a short time, three hours, and I was rushed from one place to another to see Hugh [Wallace] and Rob [Scott] and all the others – but I only wanted to see you, darling. Am I jealous?

6 September
    Went to Nee Soon 11.00 am then to Seletar. Saw Col Muthatra, Hussein, Jilani and Col Chowk then back round, Raffles Quay and the Royal Singapore Yacht Club. Saw our troops, Gurkhas and the transports out at sea.
    To Sime Road. Saw E. for five minutes but she seemed awfully busy. Very little time for us, and that's after three and a half years.
    Sent a cable home today.

7 September
    Fed up, fed up, still not allowed out. Collins scared stiff.

We've had FANY [First Aid Nursing Yeomanry] and Red Cross round, Press etc, but where do they get us – we're still prisoners.

Nobody can tell us anything or when we're likely to go, where and how. Don't know whether I can travel with E. yet. Was hoping to get to Sime Road but C' said 'no' again.

E. has just sent a message to say she has gone on night duty – a fine time to start now.

Two air letter cards sent – Mother and Ruth. Sent a letter by Joe Bush via Calcutta.

The Americans were flown away today.

8 September

Any number of visitors to the camp, but they are not helping the poor bloody prisoners much. Whatever they bring in is hopelessly inadequate. Three thousand in the camp and enough comforts, fags, tobacco etc. arrives for 300–400 only. The airmail letters went to Changi but RAPWI [Recovery Allied Prisoners of War and Internees] had no planes laid on to take them. Yet planes are arriving, bringing one to two women who are joining the crowd already at Goodwood Park Hotel.

ENSA [Entertainments National Service Association] representative around the camp, but she does nothing, looks sweet and coffees with the officers!

Nip labour gangs have already begun work clearing up Singapore, *padang* etc. Chinese looking on and gurning at them. Indian troops keeping order.

Cars are being looted and taken off the Japs ad lib. There are a large number of people (eg. RAPWI and administrative staff) touring around doing nothing.

Afternoon – Visited E., Ken Morrison brought in Tom Fields of Rajput for tea. Hugh Wallace said good-bye, flying with Lady Shenton-Thomas early tomorrow morning.

Came back to camp in Lady S-T's lovely car.

9 September

Fifty to sixty patients taken to hospital in Civil General and Field Ambulance, CCS and GH unit, but none of them ready for reception of really sick cases, poor fellows kept waiting about in ambulances in the hot sun.

Evacuation???

In the hospital work continues as usual, and we are still prisoners except for good diet, and those of us allowed out.

<u>R</u>etain <u>A</u>ll <u>P</u>risoners of <u>W</u>ar <u>I</u>ndefinitely

<u>S</u>upreme <u>E</u>ast <u>A</u>llied <u>C</u>onfusion

Had a break' party down at Sime Road Camp in the evening – present were E., Joan Veysey, Ken M', Vivien Wemsby, Tom Field, Steve and brother Sam Campbell, Robin T', self and one Derby. We tasted our first gin and rum. Ken Morrison was sick on the way back and lost his patch of one central upper incisor. Back at 12 midnight.

Hear that we may sail on the 11th.

RAPWI is in awful confusion.

10 September

Packing up at last. Today huge RAPWI vans are setting up on the *padang* and chaps are saying that it looks as though they are going to be in camp a long time more.

2.30 pm to 6.00 pm. Saw E. at Sime Road. Final arrangements made.

Chapter 8

Elizabeth in captivity, Changi Gaol then Sime Road camp

Initially housed in internment bungalows at Katong, on 8 March 1942, the women and children were ordered to Changi Gaol. Built only six years previously and designed to hold 600 men, the gaol now held around 3,000 civilian prisoners, including about 400 women and children. Outwardly it is still a forbidding place: grey concrete with high, almost windowless walls. Although their hearts must have fallen as they approached the dark sinister gateway, determined not to appear cowed of their Japanese captors, the women marched into the gaol, heads held high, defiantly singing 'There'll always be an England'.

Years later, Elizabeth remembered the terrible circumstances of some women and children who had been rounded up by the Japanese with no warning whatsoever, no time to prepare for the unknown conditions that they now faced:

> 'Some women had no possessions other than the clothes they wore. Some had managed to bring in what they treasured – sometimes useless items like stamp collections or gorgeous evening dresses; some had brought in extra food and clothes. I am sure that it was due to our Guide games that when I was taken to Changi gaol I had a case containing a few extra clothes, toilet requisites, sewing kit, First Aid kit, writing materials, enamel mug, plate, cutlery and four books.' (Extract from *The Guide*, 25 October 1963, article by Elizabeth Ennis)

Unknown to Elizabeth, Rob Scott, her former employer, had also been captured. Having closed his office in Singapore on 11 February, the following day, Rob secured passage on a Chinese coaster, HMS *Giang Bee*, for himself and the last few of his staff as the ship sailed for Java.

On 13 February, some 170 miles from Singapore, the ship suffered several air attacks and then a long stand-off with two Japanese destroyers. The crew of the *Giang Bee* tried in vain to explain their wish to surrender but were unable to communicate clearly to the Japanese destroyers. There followed a long period of anxious waiting.

On the *Giang Bee*, the Captain, growing ever more uneasy and fearful, ordered the women and children to the lifeboats – distressingly, there were not enough for all, and many of those that were launched had been damaged in the air attacks. As a Japanese speaker, Rob volunteered to try to make contact with the Japanese, and, with three others, set off in a small dinghy to row over to the nearest destroyer. For two hours in heavy seas, they tried in vain to reach the destroyer, which even though it held the little craft in the searchlight, stayed out of reach. Suddenly, about 10.30 pm, without warning, the Japanese fired on the *Giang Bee*. The ship sank in a few minutes; the Japanese destroyers moved quickly away.

In the dark, those in the dinghy managed to pick up a few survivors from the stormy seas. Eventually, exhausted after five days at sea, the survivors reached the coast of Sumatra. At first they were given food and shelter in a small village near Palembang, but local people, terrified of the repercussions for harbouring Westerners, turned the fugitives over to the Japanese. Rob was kept in a civilian camp and then a local prison. Finally, having been identified as one of the wanted 'black list', on 15 July 1942, he was taken back to Singapore, where he was kept in solitary confinement for seven months.

Of the some 300 passengers and crew on the *Giang Bee*, only seventy survived.

In Changi Gaol, living conditions for the women and children have been well documented. The gaol was severely overcrowded, with no privacy, few toilets and only basic cooking facilities. Unlike the military POW camps, where Forces personnel kept their ranks and hierarchy, the civilian internees quickly had to organize committees and representatives to negotiate with their Japanese captors. Before the war, many of the women had had little contact with Asian or Eurasian women on equal terms. As the wives of Government officials, civil servants, tea or rubber planters and bankers, most households had at least three servants – a cook/houseboy, *amah* (nursemaid) and *syce* (driver). While servants ran the households, memsahibs enjoyed the social life of clubs, golf courses and tennis courts. Class distinctions, feuds and friendships were now enclosed in the overcrowded area that was Changi Gaol.

A camp commandant was chosen and a committee elected. This was followed by the organization and representation of each floor of cells. Posts and duties were allocated.

Once again, Elizabeth returned to nursing shifts. As well as the common medical ailments, there was a rise in cases of dysentery and malaria. One patient nursed by Elizabeth was Marion Walker, who suffered recurring bouts of malaria.

Initially, food was very poor. Gradually mealtimes improved when cooking was organized for the men's and women's sections together, and could be supplemented by a little fresh fruit and vegetables. Supply of protein remained very low. At mealtimes, Elizabeth's books provided her with an excuse to sit apart. With her small serving of rice on her plate, she would sit away from other women and children, focussed on reading so that, as she ate, she did not actually look at the weevils and grubs that were also cooked up in the rice. Immersed in her book, she would try to avoid the 'continual screams of disgust' from other women as they ate. Her books were her escape.

In October 1943, the Kempetai took over the camp. From then on, food became seriously lacking in both quantity and quality.

Elizabeth wrote later: 'The Japanese were very cruel, they really were. One thing that affected the whole camp was "No food today" – and we got no food. Something had annoyed them, and especially when they started losing battles. "No food" and we just had nothing. It was very sad; quite a number of women died.'

Resourceful as ever, Elizabeth, after talking with some of the older girls who had been keen Girl Guides before internment, now set about providing some structure and occupation for them. The girls were enthusiastic but had no Guide uniform. It was agreed that as everyone had a white dress, common wear in the Tropics, that would be the basis, with Guide badges sewn from scraps of navy material and embroidered with yellow thread. The designs for the patrol emblems were chosen by vote, and were Malayan wild flowers; these too were embroidered by every Guide.

A small white handkerchief became one of Elizabeth's few treasured possessions in those days of captivity. Neatly embroidered in the centre of the handkerchief is the gold Girl Guide trefoil, with the names of the helpers Trudie Van Roode, R. Reilly and Anna Silberman below.

Trudie was Dutch, a school teacher before internment, and Anna, a Romanian, had been a typist. In each corner was the patrol emblem (a Malayan flower) together with the names of the girls in that patrol:

1. The red Hibiscus – Nellie Symons, E. Harris (later Eileen Page), O. Morris (later Olga Henderson) and O. Hancock;
2. Helen Harris and P.N.G. S. Summer;
3. Queenie Smith, C. Smith, S. Sager and T. Walters;
4. Mary Trevor, J. Davidson, B. Harris, S. Harris, N. Cumming and M. Gilfinnan.

(This handkerchief was donated to Changi Museum in 2013.)

The first 'official' meeting of the Guide Company took place on 12 June 1942. Below the high concrete walls, the Guides met once a week in a corner of an exercise yard. Elizabeth had to be very careful that their activities did not arouse the suspicion or hostility of the watchful guards. Whistles and hand signals were not allowed, so several games were modified so the Guides could not be accused of trying to send secret messages. Handcrafts included macramé and patchwork. At last the Guides were ready to be enrolled. As Elizabeth wrote some years later:

'20th July 1942

'Also interned in Changi was Lady Thomas, wife of the former Governor of Singapore, and as she had been a former Colony Commissioner for Guides, it was with great pleasure that we invited her to enrol the Guides, and we were all tremendously thrilled when she agreed to do so. She came to our little meeting in the corner of the yard, and performed the ceremony as graciously as if she had been doing it on the lawns of Government House. When you realise that we were forbidden by the Japanese to display the Union Jack or sing the National Anthem, it was a wonderful moment when, led by Lady Thomas, the new Guides made their promise.'

The Guides were very fond of Elizabeth and, unknown to her, found out the date of her birthday. Secretly, they met together and sewed a patchwork quilt which they presented to her on her birthday. Elizabeth was very touched. She explained later: 'I ... believe that because of my early training I was able to pass on something of the aims and ideals of

Guiding, and out of the grimness and misery of that internment camp, something so beautiful could be made by the Guides who had lost all their possessions – but still had courage.'

Many years later, this quilt was loaned to Sheila Allen (formerly Sheila Bruhn), who used it on lecture tours in Australia. Finally, in 2006, the quilt was presented to the Imperial War Museum, London.

To return to events in Changi: inspired by the idea of a patchwork quilt, Ethel Mulvaney, self-appointed Red Cross representative, organized the collection of rice bags that were washed and cut into 6in squares. Threads and scraps of material were also collected. Each square was individually embroidered by an internee with their signature and unique design, with sufficient squares embroidered to make three quilts.

Elizabeth recalled: 'Fortunately the Japanese didn't insist we stayed in separate cells and we could meet. We usually gathered together and sewed the squares from the bags the rice came in. You just had to think of something beyond the prison walls. That was the whole idea.'

Elizabeth stitched a picture of an ocean liner sailing away from a tropical scene, with a banner headline 'Homeward Bound', and signed it 'M.E. Ennis'.

The first quilt to be completed was dedicated to the 'wounded Nipponese soldiers with our sympathy for their suffering'. The embroidery in the squares is conciliatory and pleasing: many patches decorated with flowers and garlands, others with a Japanese touch – a traditional garden, the Rising Sun or Mount Fuji. After this quilt was diplomatically presented to the Japanese guards – and accepted – for the Japanese Military Hospital, two other quilts were completed for the hospitals of the British and Australian casualties.

Now the quilts took on a much more important role, both as a way of getting messages to loved ones in the other camps and as a show of spirited defiance; the signature on each embroidered patch identified a woman who was alive and well. Many patches celebrated the nationality of the internee – a Union Jack, a shamrock for Ireland, thistles and heather for Scotland or a maple leaf for Canada. 'Heroes' were embroidered too: St George and the dragon, a 'Tommy' with a wide grin and 'thumbs up', a Scottish piper complete with kilt and full Highland dress. Some squares reflected the sense of longing for home, nostalgia for well-loved country gardens and familiar landscapes, while others described the inescapable harsh reality of life in internment, the stark black bars of the prison cell a contrast to the more colourful stitches of other patches.

In September 1942, the completed quilts were sent to a craft fair organized by the civilian men in their section of the gaol. Later, the Japanese authorities gave permission for the quilts to be delivered to the hospital in the military camp.

Jack took up the story:

> 'We had had no information about the women at all. We thought there would be correspondence allowed, notes would come through and we would know they were well, but this never happened. We began to worry. Then one day Australian Red Cross Captain Wright called me, and I can remember, even now, standing in a lower corridor of the hospital, and he said "Look at this" – and he opened out the quilt.
>
> 'And there it was – the bows of a boat in black thread outline, and beneath it "Homeward Bound", also in black writing. I could see it straightaway, that that was her. It immediately expressed her personality, that she was a woman of determination, and that we were going to make it together eventually.'

In spite of the severe penalties for being caught passing notes, some did pass between the men's and women's camps. Elizabeth remembered: 'I was walking past and one of the men suddenly flicked, and a tiny note, the size of a postage stamp, fell on my rice so I promptly put my soup cup on top of it and walked past the Japs. It had a woman's name on it and I delivered it to her.'

At great risk, Jack and Elizabeth exchanged notes, never knowing whether their 'postman' would be discovered or the letters fall into Japanese hands. Perhaps for this reason, but also not to cause worry or alarm to the recipient, letters were often innocuous, taking care to be mild and inoffensive.

The following letter, closely written lines of tiny script covering both sides of a single sheet of paper, was written by Elizabeth towards the end of June 1942 and folded neatly to fit into a cigarette packet. It was safely delivered to Jack who kept it hidden away until the end of captivity.

> 'Darling,
>
> 'It looked as if our "express delivery" had failed at last but after many months an opportunity presented itself and I'm hoping it will work. However erratic the system may be nowadays it cannot

prevent our thoughts going out to each other and not a day passes but I wonder what you are doing, with whom you are spending leisure hours and what your thoughts are. You are so near to the familiar scenes of January that I can guess what some of your thoughts will be and I bitterly regret that I cannot be with you to re-live those happy moments.

'Joan and I continue to find life quite amusing; there are sufficient idiots in this place to provide unconscious humour for as long as we're likely to be here. The lady who still bemoans the loss of the family silver is a typical example.

'Life is inclined to be very lazy after the hectic days of my former job but it has not become boring, thanks to the good library and Joan's bright presence. She has suddenly started sewing the most exquisite baby garments cut out of extra silk underwear and of course that provides a grand excuse for my teasing but she says she is only preparing for my future!! Gosh she is looking far ahead! One day I made a dreadful faux-pas about having "missed" my wedding (actually meaning the discarding of the traditional veil etc) but Joan has never ceased to tease me about you and I having been immoral!! There are hundreds of humorous episodes which we are saving up to tell you one day.

'Weight is normal now (126lb) and with the daily siesta is likely to remain so.

'Food is sufficient if somewhat monotonous but is often supplemented by extras from Joan's husband. He has been awfully good to me for he always sends double of any gift to her. I have promised them a long holiday with us in Kashmir one day!

'Our "flat" is very comfortable and just large enough to hold ourselves and luggage with an extra clear space christened the "lounge" because of the straw mat and arm chair. I shall never forget the excitement when we acquired that chair and our very special friends' invitations to call on us so that they could sit in a real chair! After weeks of sitting on tiny campstools, I thought the chair was the last thing in luxury.

'We have all the necessities of life and a little extra. For example I still have my emergency supplies of Eau de Cologne, Johnson's powder, face cream etc. and of course there is much less demand on the Dettol nowadays!! It has been an experience finding out just what were the necessities of life. My ideas on the subject have changed somewhat since pre-war days and I find that I can do without lots of believed necessities.

'Although we manage along very well I doubt if I could continue this existence indefinitely for I miss you more than it is possible to describe. Darling Jack, I long for the day – the marvellous day of reunion when I shall be able to tell you everything and listen to everything, to laugh and love as we used to do. It may be a long time in coming but it must surely come one day, and it won't find me much older in spirit. For your sake I hope I won't have changed much. I try not to in spite of a different up-swept hairstyle encouraged by Joan.

'You will not recognise Victoria (the doll) for now she's a very grand lady, dressed in pink silk (all from the same underwear), but she still squeaks and objects to being pitched out of bed, so she occupies the space next to your photo on the book shelf.

'It's unnecessary to say that my best wishes will be with you on two days in the near future – the anniversary of our meeting and your birthday. I know you'll be with me on the 21st – wonder if the home folks will have sherry as usual that day or if they have already put my name on the family tombstone!

'I have just finished sewing a locker curtain for "Harty" and after I finish this note I shall continue the Scottish book I'm reading. It is wonderful being able to transport oneself back to the bens and the glens, the pine trees and the heather, and forget these grey walls for a little while. Joan has been almost hilarious over the word "toorie"; she didn't know its meaning and uses it on all wrong occasions. Ledingham will be able to translate it for you! (By the way, it's an old Scottish custom to make two cigarettes out of one!!)

'Darling, I do so wish you could drop in for tea this afternoon. It would do you good to see our table set with the dainty tea cloth, the glass cup and saucer I had in IMGH, Joan's enormous enamel mug and in the centre a full tin of Ginger Nuts. They, by the way, are the answer to a Maiden's Prayer!! In fact I feel we should invite Gibb, Ward, Stratton, Lads and all the rest. Gosh, what a party but as it isn't possible, Joan and I will have to be content with the biscuits and leave all the delightful male company to another time.

'Don't worry about me, darling, for I'm awfully fit and having the happiest time possible with Joan. Now don't be jealous of her for you know you'll always have first place in my affections but I've grown very fond of her and it does say something for both of us that after four months of living like this we have not scratched each other's eyes out. We've decided that we must both be good-natured!!

'Take care of yourself, darling, and get out of immediate surroundings through the medium of books, music etc as often as you can, and our future life will be all the richer from the experience. Do you want to hear a whispered secret? I love you more than ever Jack, and believe I shall keep loving you always.

'Lots of kisses xxxxxxxx
Elizabeth'
(The letter was not dated but it must have been sent in mid-July 1942.)

The internees were also concerned that word of their capture and wellbeing had not been received by their families back in the UK. Finally, on 1 November 1942, the Japanese allowed each prisoner to send a card home – Elizabeth's card to her mother in Edinburgh was received two years later. The first few sentences more than amply illustrate Elizabeth's resilience and sense of humour:

'Dear Mum
'All my wishes for unusual experiences came true! Don't worry. I am a trifle slimmer but general health very good. The days pass quickly with studying, sewing and good books.'

Meanwhile, Rob Scott had been kept in solitary confinement in 'the Tower'. From a small window in his cell, he was able to see the monthly parade of women and children with Japanese guards as they walked from the prison to the seashore a mile or so away. An extract from his post-war report describes how his spirits were lifted:

'At the end of November (1942), watching the women's parade, I suddenly saw Elizabeth Petrie. She was looking hard at the various windows, and I guessed she knew I was there but didn't know in which cell. I sent out an urgent message by Hoppy (C.E. Hopkins) for her, and was very much taken aback when a few days later back came the answer that there was no such person in the women's camp. I insisted – described her, and finally traced her as Mrs M.E. Ennis. I had not 'til then known of their marriage just before capitulation.'

The sight of Elizabeth lifted Rob's spirit. At a time of such hardship and deprivation, small acts of kindness also did much to raise one's mood. The following extract is from Freddy Bloom's diary entry for 20 December 1942:

'Delightful surprise today – Elizabeth Ennis had invited me to morning coffee. When I arrived found table all decorated and little presents. She said I had missed out on a bridal shower [Philip and Freddy Bloom had married on 6 February in Singapore] – so here it was.'

These little tea or coffee 'parties' helped raise the spirits of women internees. Even with a ragged or faded cloth over the table and an assortment of chipped or cracked china or tin mugs, the women could recreate the social gatherings of life before captivity.

There were more brief moments of intense happiness – then heartache – when on Christmas Day 1942, wives with husbands also in captivity were allowed to meet. Elizabeth and Freddy were allowed to see their husbands for thirty minutes.

There were no such happy intervals for Rob, who remained in solitary confinement with no visitors until, according to his post-war report,

'On 11 February [1943] – her wedding anniversary – my cell door opened and in walked Elizabeth with a sentry. She came up to me, winking hard, and saying "Very glad I am at last able to visit my guardian". I tumbled to what she meant, and asked my "ward" how she was and all the news. It appeared she had made a cake to be sent to me to mark her wedding anniversary, but when she tackled the women's office about it, it so happened that everyone was in a particularly amiable mood. They suggested that she should deliver it herself – so here she was.

'I was delighted to see her: my first visitor for seven months (not counting the Japanese police who visited a couple of times).'

On this visit, Elizabeth was allowed to stay for fifteen minutes. Her visit to see Rob had been audacious and coolly undertaken. After leaving the women's camp, Elizabeth had to bow twenty-three times passing Japanese guards before she was allowed to see him. A few days later, on 14 February, Rob was removed from solitary confinement in 'the Tower' and returned to the civilian camp.

Improvement in the conditions of his internment lasted only a few months. Rob knew he had to be careful. In the summer of 1943, the Kempetai, wary of an anti-Japanese conspiracy, began to tighten up their control of the camp. By December, they hoped to find enough evidence of illegal activities such as radios and phone tapping to be able to identify and punish ringleaders. This Kempetai plan was completely thrown out of gear when, on 26 September, six Japanese oil tankers were sunk or seriously destroyed in Singapore Harbour. The raid took the Japanese authorities completely by surprise. They assumed the raid must have been carried out by local saboteurs, most likely pro-Communist Chinese guerrillas, and if internees had not actually arranged the attack, they must at least have been involved in its planning.

The raid, code-named Operation *Jaywick*, had in fact been a special operation by commandos of Z Force operating out of Australia.

The Kempetai plan was now accelerated. On 10 October (the 'Double Tenth'), in the men's camp, internees were ordered to parade. When all had gathered outside, the doors and passages were closed. Around a dozen names were called out for immediate arrest. Rob's name was first. Meanwhile, a thorough search was made of the entire camp.

In the women's camp too, roll call had been ordered for 9.00 am. Under armed guard, the women and children were kept waiting in the open area known as the Rose Garden. After several hours in the rising temperature and burning sun, and after some women fainted, they were eventually allowed to go to 'A' compound where at least there was a tap and two toilets, and some very limited shade could be made by draping blankets over the drying lines. A thorough search was again undertaken by the Kempetai and guards. Late in the afternoon, prisoners were allowed to return inside to find their possessions scattered across the floor, photographs removed from frames, hems of dresses ripped open and so on. Many books and personal papers had been removed.

All Elizabeth's books had been taken. Having identified herself as a friend of Rob, during the following weeks she was searched and interrogated on several occasions by the Kempetai. Later in life, she never spoke of these times, but the deep mental scars remained.

On the same day, about fifty other internees – including Freddy Bloom from the women's camp – had been rounded up for questioning. Sumida, chief of the Singapore Kempetai, was convinced that Rob was the ringleader behind the sabotage of the ships. He began by interrogating the other internees, hoping to build up a mass of evidence which, when revealed to Rob, would persuade him to make a full confession. Internees were alternately bribed and tortured, cajoled and beaten, until by the end of November, Sumida was able to conclude that there were several radios in the internment camps, that a committee of internees were planning for the time when British forces would reoccupy Singapore, and that espionage had been going on.

Sumida now turned his attention to Rob. According to Japanese law, Sumida explained, Rob had to make a confession before he could be tried. This first interview lasted over fifteen hours.

By the end of the interview, Sumida had learnt nothing – and Rob had refused to incriminate himself or others. For some weeks, Rob was left in peace, but for others, the situation worsened as the Kempetai resorted to more beatings and torture. At the end of February 1944, Rob was interrogated under torture continuously for seven days and six nights. When this did not produce the required 'confession', the treatment continued on and off for another three weeks, still without the result required by the Kempetai. Indeed, as the months dragged on, Rob, despite his suffering, realized the Kempetai were becoming unsure of their ground, and that much of the evidence they had obtained from internees by torture was unreliable. As Rob wrote in his post-war report: 'It became a race with time; could I so discredit the evidence collected as to shake their faith in it before I collapsed? I won, but only by a short head.'

Despite suffering from dysentery and beriberi, Rob was taken by the Kempetai to stand trial on 7 November 1944, accused of the only crimes to which he had confessed: anti-Japanese propaganda he had carried out before the invasion and his work with the wireless receiving set in Changi. He was sentenced to six years' imprisonment in the civilian prison in Outram Road.

By now, Rob's weight had dropped to just 7 stone 10lb. He was suffering from dysentery, oedema, beriberi, scabies, dizziness, blackouts and the effects of torture. Due to exposed ligaments and bones in his feet, he was unable to walk. In late February 1945, the Kempetai, convinced that Rob was about to die, sent him to Sime Road Civilian Internment Camp Hospital.

In early May 1944, all the women and children had already been moved to Sime Road Civilian Internment Camp, a former British military camp. It was on the outskirts of Singapore, on a hillside overlooking the city. Although the huts were dirty, dilapidated and in need of much attention, the fresh air and freedom to walk outside, the overgrown vegetable patches and small groves of trees were appreciated by many – a contrast to the concrete walls and closed yards of Changi. Inside the huts, however, there was no privacy. Elizabeth shared a small room with sixteen others.

There had still been little news of Jack, but in July, she received a message saying 'Jack at Kranji Camp'.

By mid-March 1945, Rob was deemed to have recovered enough to receive visitors once a week.

Still unable to walk, he would be carried out of the dysentery ward on a stretcher and Hugh Wallace, a friend and doctor, arranged for Elizabeth to visit them. These visits, kept up right to the end of the war, developed into, in Rob's words, 'very pleasant Monday afternoons. Hugh provided coffee, donated by wealthy Jewish patients or acquired by other means, and sometimes sugar as well.'

Unlike Jack, who maintained a continuous diary in captivity, Elizabeth kept no record of her experiences in internment.

Chapter 9

Homeward Bound

For Jack and Elizabeth, their journey home finally began on 11 September 1945. Again, Jack recorded the events in his diary.

11 September
Left Kranji at 0700hrs [and] aboard SS *Monowai* by 0900hrs. E came aboard little later.

Impressions – small vessel 11,000 tons, 1189 aboard, about 800 POW and internees from Sime Road camp. On SMO instructions we are on very little to eat, [so] very, very hungry first day. Ship, or its MOs have no idea as to our health state. Water shortage aboard. Very crowded, 16 to a cabin is usual, very hot and stuffy. No cold drinks or water available to satisfy our craving. No deck space, no deck chairs, no cosy corners.

Elizabeth, as usual, is awfully cheerful about it all.

Sailed at 1300hrs [and] went round St John's Island, passed [HMS] *Rodney* and [Free French battleship] *Richelieu* in the outer roads. Third in a long line. All day in a line up a busy marked passage. Occasional destroyer passed and huge convoys going the other way.

12 September
Very calm sea; leave line tonight and make our own way as we are a fast vessel. Passing much shipping going the other way.

Many discomforts on this transport but it's taking us home first of all.

16 September
Sunday – about 2100hrs sailed into Colombo harbour [Ceylon]. Wonderful sight, full of ships, Navy and Merchant. What a greeting of sirens, searchlights, yelling, whistling and singing. Red Cross and Press came aboard, FANY etc.

Picture show at midnight, not a great success.

17 September

Allowed ashore at Colombo, [in] landing barges at 1000hrs. Taken in hand by FANY to United Services Club, coffee, civilisation, a lovely room, sofa, fans, cold drinks.

To Echelon Barracks, got some money and a little clothing. E. to Red Cross place where she had a shower and fitted out with some clothing. Back to United Services Club for lunch, then I went to try and shop. No deck chairs, no book shops open, things very expensive though cheap and nasty looking; wonder what home is going to be like?

Back on board ship by 4.30 pm, feeling very tired and full of a sore throat and cold.

23 September

Passed Socotra [island off Yemen] early this morning.

24 September

Night – saw the outer lights of Aden about 10.00 pm. E. was disappointed that we didn't put in.

27 September

Came into Suez Gulf by 11.00 am. And alongside pier of Adabia at 12.30 pm. Went ashore about 2.30 pm and on to the Ondurman depot for fitting out of warm clothing for both of us. Done very well indeed. Masses of brass hats around the ship, WAAF [Women's Auxiliary Air Force], Red Cross etc. We still queued and stood about a long time at each place.

Not allowed to Suez to buy things.

28 September

Went ashore again to NAAFI and had a fight to buy a few things. Very little for sale and poor quality at that. Back by 11.30 am. And sailed about 12 midday while the HT *Corfu* put in immediately after us.

Entered Canal about 1.30 pm. What a lot of buildings and garrison now, Naval vessels and aerodromes all along it.

29 September

E. and I sat up on deck, it was chilly, and saw Port Said at about 2.00 pm. We halted in the Canal for one hour and again at Port Said for about two hours.

How the weather has changed – cool, and cold at night.

2 October
   Saw the North African coastline, Cape Bon and Tunisian peninsula.

3 October
   About opposite Algiers at 6.00 am this morning.

4 October
   At 7.30 am, Gibraltar appeared in the east, looking magnificent. Four destroyers passed us out.
   Stopped at 8.10 am to pick up some mail and off again in ten minutes.

7 October
   In evening stood off entrance to the Mersey.

8 October
   Put in slowly to Liverpool Dock at 1.00 pm.
   Much confusion amongst Disembarkation staff.
   We were off at 3.00 pm, [with] tea by the Red Cross folk.
   Hung about in the Customs Shed.
   Then to a Reception Camp at Maghull where they did not know what to do with families – the worst in-coordination and lack of intelligence that I have ever seen. The Army folk are hopeless.
   Hung about 'til 2.00 pm. Slept at a boarding house – people very nice to us. Managed to collect all luggage and get train.

9 October
   Train at 9.50 am. London at 2.30 pm. HOME met by Stanley and Mother. Again the Red Cross helped with a car.

Back in Singapore, even before he had left Syme Road camp, Rob was very conscious of the role Elizabeth had played in his recovery, both physical and psychological. As soon as he could, he wrote to Jack expressing his gratitude:

> 'Letter to Captain J.E. Ennis, IMS Hospital, Kranji Camp
> 'Sime Road Civilian Internment Camp Hospital
> 'Saturday September 1st 1945
>
> 'Dear Jack
> 'May I add my voice to the chorus of praise you must be hearing about Elizabeth?

'She has been simply grand all through – as of course you and everyone else who knew her would expect. Cheerful, sane, balanced, sensible, active, useful and in every way.

'To me especially she has been more than a friend – I have had a bad time, one way and another, and Elizabeth has been a stout support and staunch unfailing help in time of trouble. Perhaps a tonic (which when required would and did turn into a much needed dose of castor oil to deflate my silly flatulence – but it usually took the form of bucking me up when I had to be bucked up) would describe it best.

'In Changi, I wangled (actually Elizabeth had the bright idea first) official recognition by the Japanese as her "guardian" (though God knows the boot should have been on the other foot – I should have been the ward and she the "guardian"). This entitled and enabled me to go over to the Women's Camp once a week, on Monday mornings, where I sat and guzzled her coffee and biscuits whilst she chatted of the doings of the women.

'Then I was removed to another place, as they say in Parliament. When I came back to Camp sixteen months later, she fixed, with the help of Hugh Wallace (who had also been a splendid friend) to come and visit me in Hospital weekly, and few things contributed more to my recovery than those visits; we drank Wallace's coffee and Elizabeth reassured me about Rosamond (my wife), about myself, and about anything else I seemed to need reassuring about. (Not forgetting, as I mentioned above, to deflate me when I was well enough to take it and seemed to need it.)

'I think that about covers it. I could expand a lot on the subject, but the main points are that I am immensely and immeasurably grateful to her, and that you are a very lucky man.

'Sorry I was not there to be present at your wedding; and delighted to know you are alive and well. Hope we shall meet again soon.

'Yours
'Rob Scott'
(Written on the back of a Requisition Form)

As soon as he was fit to travel, Rob was moved to 114th British General Hospital at Bangalore, Mysore, India, for recovery and convalescence from 25 September until mid-October.

While there, Rob began to document his experiences for the official reports and a separate account for his family. Despite his horrific treatment at the hands of the Kempetai, he showed no malice in his writings. His calmness and steadfast inner strength shine through his writings, as shown in the following extract, on his move to Sime Road Civilian Internment Camp Hospital (provoked by 'collapsing' while carrying planks during a work party): 'I was so full of glee at having fooled the Japanese into thinking I was dying that it didn't occur to me that in fact I might be dying. So I didn't die. I honestly can't think of any other reason why I didn't die last February, excepting that it never occurred to me.'

When fit enough to travel further, he was repatriated by hospital ship to Southampton and continued his recovery at the Military Hospital, Osborne House, on the Isle of Wight. There, he and Rosamond were finally reunited. A full family reunion with his children Susan and Douglas finally took place. Susan, by then aged 10, recognized her father, although gaunt and limping, as soon as he spoke. Douglas, had only been 5 years old when he had last seen his father, was initially more guarded.

The family spent their first Christmas together in Selkirk, Rob's home town. Susan later remembered the hotel as cold and bleak. Wartime rationing continued.

Chapter 10

Post-War

For Jack and Elizabeth, the joy of being together and back in the UK was dampened by their reception in London. There, Jack's mother could not accept that any experience, even as long as three-and-a-half years as a POW, could be nearly as bad as the Blitz. One also suspects that she never forgave Elizabeth for marrying her favourite son. Jack and Elizabeth did meet Olwen in London but, apart from one short diary entry, there is no further mention of Olwen. It is to be hoped that she met someone else and lived happily ever after.

In London, Jack's family had celebrated VE Day and then returned to a grey life of rationing and job concerns. They had been 'told' not to ask about Far East experiences, and seemed not to know how to approach returning FEPOWs. Elizabeth felt most bitterly that in some way they were being blamed for the Fall of Singapore, and were indeed the 'Forgotten Army'.

Jack's reception by Elizabeth's mother in Edinburgh was much more welcoming. Despite rationing and food shortages, she had saved an egg for her new son-in-law. However, while preparing his breakfast she was distracted by the chatter, and on returning to the kitchen, was horrified to find an inedible black crisp in the pan!

In 1946, Jack, now promoted to Major IMS, was recalled to India for specialist pathology duty. Postings included Meerut and Poona – Jack and Elizabeth had many happy memories of these times. Their bungalow in Poona was encircled by a shaded terrace with hanging baskets of orchids.

Also in 1946, there was time for a belated honeymoon – one month in Kashmir, trekking in the Himalayas, then a stay in a houseboat on Dal Lake, Srinagar.

However, in 1947, as calls for Partition grew louder and civil unrest increased, they made their way back to Delhi. As on their wedding day five years earlier, this journey would be under live gunfire, an eventful journey with their train ambushed by Sikhs. Terrified, the engine driver stopped the train and ran away. In their compartment, Elizabeth hid the train guard (a Muslim) under coats and luggage as gunfire could be heard around the carriages. Eventually, the attack ended. Cautiously, Jack made his way through the now-empty train to the engine, and spent the rest of the journey stoking the boiler. In darkness, the train finally pulled into a remote platform at Delhi Station – in eerie silence. Jack wrote later: 'Station rooms wrecked, burned out, shrapnel damage. Piles of bodies at each end of long platform. No station staff.'

Jack and Elizabeth went over to the deserted main platform. There, Jack went to find out information, leaving Elizabeth sitting on the microscope case with their luggage. He returned to find her surrounded by silent terrified Moslem women with their children. Eventually, a British officer arrived with a truck 'to pick up strays', and they were taken to the safety of a transit camp until evacuation could be arranged.

Settling back in England, Jack began work in Durham, eventually becoming Director of Pathology for the Durham Group of Hospitals. He also lectured at King's College Medical School, Newcastle, and worked on many (often high-profile) forensic cases throughout the north-east of England. Friendships, such as that with Dr Bill Frankland, were maintained with regular meetings in London.

Friendships that had formed during years of internment or before remained strong. Frequent visitors included Harry Cooper, Jack's Lab technician in Robert's Barracks. Indeed, Jack almost certainly owed his life to Harry. In February 1942, just before Singapore fell, they had been working in the Lab when Japanese soldiers attacked the hospital. Alarmed, Jack and Harry hid under a table. They became even more alarmed when a grenade was thrown through the window and rolled across the floor towards them! With great presence of mind, Harry picked up the grenade and threw it back out of the window. It immediately exploded outside – then there was silence. After some time, they cautiously emerged to find that all was quiet – the Japanese soldiers had left.

Then there were the Cummings. Robert, Squadron Leader, RAF Medical Branch, had been captured in Java in 1942 and was first held in Java No.1 Camp, Bandeong. On 25 February 1942, as part of Java Party 15, he was taken to the docks in Batavia and two days later sailed on the *Kinta Maru* for Singapore, arriving at Changi on 2 March. On 14 March, he left with 'D' Force on Train 1 to Ban Pong, the transit camp at the start of the Thai–Burma Railway. There he was allocated to Work Group 4, the largest on the Railway consisting of 11,200 men in thirty-one work battalions.

Robert survived the war and was reunited with his sweetheart, Marion Walker, whom Elizabeth had nursed in Changi Gaol. They married in 1947.

Jack and Elizabeth made their family home in Durham. Their daughters, Jacqueline (Jackie) and Patricia (Tish), grew up accustomed to many friends from Singapore days coming to stay. Indeed as a very young girl, Tish thought it was just part of growing up, that everyone's parents spent some time in prison! However, it must have raised a few eyebrows in the school staffroom when Tish, as a Kindergarten pupil, wrote in her daily 'news book', 'My Mummy was in prison' – at that time, Durham Gaol was a High Security Category 'A' prison for dangerous prisoners (including murderers, train robbers and London gang members).

Elizabeth resumed her interest and work with the Girl Guide movement. In 1947, she had been awarded a certificate for her 'Gallantry under Enemy Occupation', and now the Girl Guide quilt, often put on show at fundraising events, inspired younger generations. The Girl Guide quilt was later loaned to Sheila Bruhn (née Allan), who took it with her on lecture tours around Australia, using the quilt not only to inform audiences of her life as a young POW in Changi, but perhaps also to come to terms with her own personal experiences.

Elizabeth rarely spoke of her experiences as a POW, and often only to those who had shared internment. Jack maintained that she had suffered more than he had. Jack had had his work, his interest in wildlife and the recreational and entertainment opportunities of the large military camps, while conditions inside the bleak concrete walls of Changi Gaol had been very different.

Although Elizabeth rarely showed any outward signs, the deep mental scars remained – occasionally to catch her off-guard.

One day in 1988, on holiday in Sydney, Australia, she was walking with her younger daughter along crowded pavements near the Town Hall. As they followed a group of young Boy Scouts in uniform, Elizabeth noticed they had the Japanese Rising Sun emblem on their lapels. She casually remarked to her daughter that she hoped these young Japanese were learning different values to the previous generation. Suddenly, the Scout Leader turned to ask directions – Elizabeth gasped, turned ashen white and collapsed against the shop window, looking extremely unwell. The young man was most concerned and stretched out a hand to support her, whereupon Elizabeth shrank back, crying out, 'No, don't let him touch me!'

She recovered a little, and quietly explained that, with his uniform, he had appeared to her like a Japanese guard. The young Scout Leader was most apologetic and sympathized with her bad memories.

This was only the second Japanese person she had spoken to since her days in Singapore.

By contrast, Jack was able to talk of his experiences and was a popular and entertaining speaker at many clubs and societies. Audiences appreciated his often humorous tales from prison camp – of keeping sea-snakes in an outside bath-tub and being asked if the snakes came down the tap; of racing frogs across the yard (only to discover the Australian team always won as they had managed to wire a small pin under each frog to make it jump further); of the mystery of the beans stolen from his garden (and then a couple of days later four soldiers being admitted to hospital with 'food poisoning').

Of course, one person who did relate to Changi was Rob Scott.

Rob resumed work with the Foreign Office as Assistant Under-Secretary of State in charge of the Far Eastern and South-East Asia Department, then moved to Washington as Minister at the British Embassy. This was followed by his appointment as British Commissioner-General in South East Asia, as Commandant of the Imperial Defence College at Sandhurst (the first civilian to hold the post) and finally Permanent Secretary at the Ministry of Defence. It was a distinguished career, during which he was awarded a GCMG and CBE. After his retirement in 1963, Rob and Rosamond finally settled at Lyne Station, a beautiful house overlooking the River Tweed. At last he had time to fish, to garden, to keep bees and plant trees. As Lord Lieutenant for Peeblesshire and later for Tweeddale, he still contributed much to life in the Borders. He and Rosamond never forgot their friends from Hong Kong and Singapore days, including Jack and Elizabeth. As granddaughter Sarah noted many years later, '(In the Visitors' Book) Ennis signatures appear almost every year at Lyne'. On one occasion, after receiving a thank-you note (in verse) from the Ennis family, Rob replied in kind:

> <u>The Knight Errant makes reply to the Baltal Gang</u>
> Where Tweed hath 'guiled her son to stay
> To dig and delve the live long day,
> How sweet it is to flay the water
> Where salmon leaps but n'er he caught her.
> The walls run long, the weeds grow high,
> The rooks they clamour in the sky.

> And while the cook her pots doth clatter,
> The blessed peace from cocktail chatter
> Enfolds with balm her wandering son,
> Relaxed with pipe when day is done.
> Waiting to welcome with good cheer
> From Baltal, Durham our good friends dear.

When Jack retired from the NHS, he and Elizabeth moved to Edinburgh. They bought a modest house, intending to take their time to choose a house with a stream running through the garden; Elizabeth's love of gardening had never diminished. However, still with a love of travel and work, Jack took up various locum posts, including Broken Hill and Darwin in Australia.

Edinburgh eventually became their permanent home.

Over the years, the exchanges and visitors from Singapore days gradually dwindled and ceased as old age took its toll. Elizabeth died in 2003 and Jack in 2007. Each funeral service was brightened by the flowers on the coffins – purples, pinks, creams and white, orchids from Singapore.

Appendix 1

Captain Jack Ennis – Changi Pathologist

By Geoff Gill and Meg Parkes
Liverpool School of Tropical Medicine

In the sources relating to medical matters in the Far East imprisonment under the Japanese, the work of pathologists rarely features. But as well as his diary, Dr Jack Ennis kept meticulous notes and records of his pathology work as a prisoner of war in Singapore from 1942–45. Here we review this unique source, with quotations and extracts, to hopefully provide an insight into the remarkable and vital work which supported clinical care in conditions of extreme adversity and difficulty. As writers of this appendix, we come from both medical and historical backgrounds, and are part of a longstanding project of Far East POW research at the Liverpool School of Tropical Medicine (LSTM). We are grateful to Jack's daughter, Jackie Sutherland, for allowing us access to these records. It has been a rare opportunity to scrutinize such a valuable historical archive. Thanks are also due to Dr Jonathan Sheard, a Liverpool consultant pathologist (now retired), for technical advice.

Unsurprisingly, much of the source material contains specialist medical jargon and abbreviations, and we have done our best to explain these so that the records can be understood by non-specialist readers. However, even without these explanations we believe that the contents of these documents reveal a remarkable attention to meticulous record-keeping, consistent with good military and medical practice.

Background

Jack Ennis was born in Rawalpindi, India, in 1911. He was a British national and studied medicine at St Bartholomew's Hospital ('Barts') in London between 1931 and 1937. Having qualified, he undertook house physician and surgeon posts at Barts, in Plymouth and (very usefully) the Hospital for Tropical Diseases in London. He returned to Barts to a junior pathology job, but in late 1938 transferred to his homeland to work as part of the Indian Medical Service (IMS). After a short period of general clinical duties, he was moved to the Pathology Service, and in 1939 was posted to Malaya to run a Command Laboratory and later a Mobile Bacteriology Laboratory. With his unit, he was captured by the Japanese at the Fall of Singapore in February 1942 and remained a POW in Singapore for the next three-and-a-half years until the defeat of Japan in August 1945.

As was the case for many other doctors qualifying shortly before the start of the Second World War, his early career had been unconventional, but by the time of his capture he had three years of intense general pathology experience, mostly in a tropical setting – an invaluable asset in his role as Head of Pathology Services in the POW hospitals in Changi, Selarang and Kranji.

POW disease and pathology services

Changi POW camp was huge (in the beginning over 90,000 men), and sanitation was variable but usually sub-optimal. The area suffered malarial transmission, and the diet was deficient (mostly rice-based) and particularly short of B vitamins. The diet did improve significantly in early 1943, but deteriorated markedly in 1944 and continued so until the prisoners' release. Overall, conditions of diet, work, and general treatment were significantly better than for example in the jungle camps of the Thai–Burma Railway – but Changi was certainly no holiday camp. Particularly prevalent diseases were malaria, dysentery (a severe bacterial gastro-enteritis) and a variety of syndromes of malnutrition – notably beriberi (due to thiamine or vitamin B_1 deficiency). More will be said of these and other diseases later. The medical burden was significantly increased from late 1943 when numbers of POWs from the Thai–Burma Railway returned to Changi – many extremely sick.

As Head of Pathology Services, Captain Ennis faced significant problems of shortages of equipment, laboratory facilities and personnel. The huge numbers with sickness, and frequent deaths, also strained the service. Despite this, a relatively complete range of pathological support was provided for the clinical staff. This included basic haematology (eg haemoglobin estimation), some biochemical estimations (mainly glucose and urea), bacteriology (particularly testing for diphtheria) and parasitology (such as examination of blood films for malaria, and faecal smears for the larvae of worms and other parasites). Post-mortem examinations appeared to be carried out on most, or possibly all, deaths. More details of all these activities will be discussed later.

The archives

Jack's pathology archives are extensive and meticulous in detail. Mostly they are handwritten, some occasionally typed. His writing is small, possibly to conserve paper which was in very short supply.

An example of this is a series of autopsy reports handwritten in a deposit book of the Hong Kong & Shanghai Banking Corporation! In terms of content, the main documents are post-mortem records, and also three annual reports of laboratory activities (more details of these are given in sections below). A selection of documents have been transcribed for the purpose of this appendix – only the occasional word has proved impossible to make out, and in these cases we have put [illegible] in the extracts used.

Standard laboratory reports were allowed by the Imperial Japanese Army, but other material may have been recorded secretly and at considerable risk from reprisals if found. This probably included post-mortem reports, as the causes of death (particularly when due to malnutrition) are likely have been an indictment of the IJA treatment of POWs.

Range and volume of laboratory work

One typewritten document in the archive gives a useful insight into the type of laboratory work undertaken and the very large amounts of such tests. This is a report on activity in the first six months of captivity (March–August inclusive, 1942), supporting the clinical work at Roberts Hospital, Changi. It is signed 'Capt J Ennis IMS, Officer in Charge, Laboratory, Robert Hospital', and records a remarkable 15,769 tests in the six-month period (between approximately 2,000 and 3,000 per month). The main investigations with numbers are shown below, and demonstrate the high numbers of suspected malaria, dysentery, tuberculosis (TB) and diphtheria. As well as these main investigations, others included urine examinations, biochemical blood tests, blood counts (for haemoglobin) and even tests for syphilis (contracted before imprisonment presumably!)

TEST	TOTAL NUMBERS
Sputum for TB microscopy	465
Malarial blood slides	9731
Stool microscopy	1158
Throat swabs for diphtheria	1298

Annual reports

Captain Ennis wrote three annual reports of the laboratory activities – the first for the period from 15 February 1942 to 14 February 1943 (handwritten), the second from 15 February 1943 to 14 February 1944 (also handwritten) and the third from 28 May 1944 to 31 July 1945 (typed). The reason for the three-month gap between the second and third reports is unclear. All the reports follow a similar pattern – outlining general aspects of the pathology service (staff, accommodation, equipment issues etc) and then detailing the numbers and types of investigations undertaken.

The first report discusses the formation of the main laboratory on 3 March 1942, using equipment from various sources, but in particular from the Command Laboratory of Malaya at Alexandra (which Jack had led before captivity), though he notes that 'several of the boxes from Alexandra went astray'. He also describes giving some equipment to groups of POWs moving up to Thailand, as well as a shortage of supplies from the Japanese. Staffing was limited, and for the first part of the period summarized the laboratory had no running water or electricity. Despite this, an enormous amount of testing was done – for example, 13,790 malarial blood films, 2,273 throat swabs, 2,217 faecal smears, 1,893 urine tests and 1,435 haemoglobin measurements.

The second report is given below in full, transcribed as handwritten. The only additions are explanations of medical and scientific terminology (bold print, in brackets). Of particular interest and concern, Jack notes a 'marked depreciation in the equipment' – particularly affecting microscope lenses – as well as continuing short supplies from the IJA – 'hardly any addition to our stocks of reagents'. Under the section on stool examinations, he refers to an increase in the findings of intestinal worms and other parasites – attributed to the return from Thailand of F Force survivors, after completion of the railway. The groups sent from Changi to Thailand and Burma were all known as 'Forces', and F Force were sent to remote up-country camps under particularly harsh conditions.

The final part of the document gives an interesting breakdown of the causes of death from sixty-five autopsies carried out during the period of the report.

Subject: Annual Report of Lab and Post mortem work 15/2/43 – 14/2/44

Officer Commanding Changi Hospital

The work of the Hospital laboratory has continued this year much the same as last year, though there has had to be considerable reduction in the number of investigations which M.O.s would like to have had carried out on cases owing to shortage of materials, chemicals, slides, etc. Work was much reduced when the various parties left for 'up country' during March and April last year, but this reduction was compensated for, as we supplied a fair share of reagents and apparatus for the provision of small laboratory outfits which accompanied the parties, to enable the M.O.s to carry out simple diagnostic investigations. Unfortunately in many cases they failed to get this equipment which included microscopes. There has been a marked depreciation in the equipment during the year through fair (excessive) wear, the effects of the humid climate and the spoiling of lenses etc by fungoid growth over their surfaces. The seriousness of the latter is not fully realised by those looking after microscopes and several 1/12 and other lenses are now useless. If this damage continues there will be a serious shortage of necessary lenses in a further twelve months.

There has been hardly any addition to our stocks of reagents from I.J.A. sources during this year; and chemicals they have supplied e.g. Ab [Ab = absolute, or 100 per cent] alcohol, [illegible] acetic acid are far from chemically pure, the small quantities of methylated spirit would not burn without treatment. Only when the I.J.A. have required parasitic surveys to be carried out have they supplied prepared [illegible] stain, cedar wood oil of poor quality, and slides. There appears to be no prospect of fresh supplies of stains and reagents, so very strict economy has been practised this whole time.

The lack of suspensions of the Salmonella group, B proteus and the cholera vibrios [these are three bowel bacterial pathogens –

use uncertain] has again been felt, and a small amount of cultural work has been continued at the Australian laboratory.

Records have been maintained as far as the shortage of paper would allow, but under most headings only positive findings have been recorded. An analysis of the period 15/2/43 – 14/2/44 follows:-

1. Smears for M.P.s [**malarial parasites**] – 4,152. As previously, these have all been examined by Fields Thick Film technique, using any other method we would have been soon short of reagents (and the standard of diagnosis would have been much lower). In a small percentage of cases resort has been made to Leishman thin film technique for special diagnosis. In addition to the above figures 11,500 smears were stained and examined at this laboratory when parasite surveys were carried out on parties going up country and returning later on.
2. Stools – 1327 specimens were recorded as containing pathological findings. These include all tests viz microscopic occult blood tests, and cultural investigations. There has been a slow increase in helminthic [**worm**] infections, and since the return of 'F' Force a remarkable increase in infection with Strongyloides stercoralis [**an intestinal worm**], but not the reported increase in amoebiasis [**a protozoan organism causing amoebic dysentery**]. In no cases has a cholera vibrio been isolated from the British sick.
3. Urine tests – 446 pathological specimens were encountered during this period. The routine examination of urine had to be abandoned on account of the shortage of reagents, but full investigations were carried out when considered necessary.
4. Blood counts and Hb [**haemoglobin**] estimations – 635. This figure includes as a single test, whatever the M.O. requested, be it an Hb estimation or a full blood investigation.
5. Throat swabs and other smears for K.L.B. [**Klebs-Loffler Bacillus – the bacteria causing diphtheria**] – 157 smears were recorded as showing 'morphological K.L.B. present' a considerable decrease on the previous year. These smears were from faucial [**throat**] and cutaneous [**skin**] lesions, and the bacilli seen did not differ in appearance from classical K.L.B. or from those seen in the previous year when their virulence was evident by the number of deaths and at least

25% showed paralysis. In cases where this infection was suspected but bacilli were not seen in direct smears, cultures on egg medium were made, but it is emphasised that this got one no further in deciding the actual virulence of the bacilli under consideration, and therefore all such positive cases have been treated with due regard to this and the clinical condition.

6. Sputum for T.B. [tuberculosis] – 141 positives recorded. Most of these were from the monthly test carried out in the T.B. ward, only 7 fresh cases were diagnosed this year.
7. Sedimentation rates [**a blood test to indicate infection or inflammation**] – 626 were performed, the test maintaining its popularity as a diagnostic aid, and also as a prognostic guide in the cases of Tuberculosis etc, or where it is carried out at monthly intervals.
8. F.T. meals [**fractional test meals – to measure the acidity of the stomach**] – 107 meals have been analysed. It is noted that though wards have been employing this test for two years now, there is much carelessness in the taking of specimens. A ground rice meal forms an admirable substitute for gruel and there is little difference in the acid curve resulting.
9. Kahn Tests [**a test for the presence of syphilis**] –248 were performed this year. During the last four months the tests have only been carried out once a month in order to economise on antigen. There is just about enough Kahn antigen to last a further 12 months. Positive results are still occasionally met, occurring amongst those on [illegible], or rarely on old inadequately treated cases (chiefly Dutch Forces).
10. Miscellaneous tests 120. Includes routine C.S.F. [**cerebrospinal fluid**] tests, pleural and other fluid investigations, van den Burghs [**a test to measure bilirubin in the blood – an indicator of the presence and severity of jaundice**], urea concentration tests [**a test of kidney function**], blood sugars and curves [**to test for diabetes**], pus examinations, a few cultures and carrier test etc.

Accommodation. The hospital laboratory moved over from Roberts Hospital on 24th August 1943 and occupied almost the same accommodation as before with water, light and power plugs fitted.

Staff. The laboratory staff consists of an As/surgeon, two laboratory technicians (a S/Sgt and a Sgt) and an R.A.M.C. private. This number has been varied according to the amount of work in hand and demands elsewhere in the hospital. One of the N.C.O.s also assists at Autopsies, looks after the mortuary and carries out the duties of 'undertaker'.

In conclusion of the laboratory part of this report I must add that a steady reduction in the diagnostic facilities of this department must be expected because of wear and breakage of apparatus and deficiencies of stains, reagents and materials, although every attempt is being made to eke out what remains here and in the medical stores.

Autopsy Report 15/2/43 – 14/2/44

During this period 64 autopsies were carried out, and there were 65 deaths on the British side.

Of them, 52 were British and 13 were Dutch Forces, and of the British deaths 15 have occurred amongst patients returned from Thailand.

The following is a summary of the causes of Death:-
Bacillary Dysentery, directly responsible for.........................16
Pulmonary Tuberculosis...9
Pyaemic conditions, Prostatic abscess etc 6
Malnutrition, Deficiency Diseases and complicating
diseases (eg. Malaria, Broncho Pneumonia).............................6
Lobar pneumonia and Malaria...5
General peritonitis, acute appendicitis, peptic ulcer.................5
Amoebic Dysentery and its complications 3
Acute encephalitis 3
Neoplasms 3
Chronic Nephritis, Uraemia..3
Cardiac and Vascular Degeneration 3
Fractured Bones of skull (accident)...................................1
G.S.W. **[Gunshot wounds]** Face [illegible] in antral abscess 1

The figures for the Dysenteries show a notable decrease and only one death due to Diphtheria (myocarditis) occurred. The high figures for Pulmonary Tuberculosis may be associated with the loss of 'extras' in their diets owing to the exhaustion of stores. The appearance of Lobar Pneumonia amongst 'down country' patients is also to be noted, as it was rarely met last year. Only in two cases (26335 and 26063) were the autopsy findings unsatisfactory viz chronic B.T. [**benign tertian – a type of malaria**] Malaria, but I feel that even in these cases the precipitating cause of death was Avitaminosis [**lack of vitamins**].

The Mortuary and Post Mortem facilities for the hospital are excellent, thanks to the cooperation of the R.E.s who fitted up the present room, there being a proper slab, set of instruments etc. It is unfortunate that [illegible] cannot be carried out to complete investigations.

20.2.1944   signed J.E.

In the final report, there is an impression of more severe equipment and reagent shortages, as well as generally deteriorating camp conditions. The microscope and lens situation had become critical, and it is mentioned that there is a 'lack of apparatus and materials', and 'the maintenance of records has of course suffered for lack of paper'. There was also a 'rapid rise in the incidence of ascariasis' (intestinal roundworm infections), which was attributed to 'a lack of adequate treatment facilities, a rising reservoir of infections, and an unavoidable breakdown in hygiene'. Significant rates of malaria, tuberculosis and diphtheria are also referred to. Despite the clear difficulties, the continued high levels of laboratory testing were maintained.

Autopsy reports

Of the many autopsy reports in Jack Ennis' pathology archive, the causes of death can be divided into two groups: those that are clearly related to imprisonment and those likely to be unrelated. The latter group includes deaths due to trauma, cancers, stroke, septicaemia, appendicitis, post-operative complications, pneumonia and rheumatic heart disease. Though these deaths may be regarded to some extent as 'incidental', it is certainly likely that the poor nutritional status of POWs may have predisposed them to infective mortality; and when surgery was necessary, it made post-operative complications more likely.

Many deaths, however, were clearly a direct result of imprisonment – exposure to tropical infections and syndromes of malnutrition. The likelihood of death was worsened by the often inadequate supplies of appropriate medicines. Tropical infections recorded as causes of death in Jack's reports were mainly dysentery, tuberculosis, and less frequently malaria and diphtheria. The major nutritional disease causing death was beriberi. An explanation of these diseases follows:

Dysentery. As has been mentioned, this is a severe gastroenteritis, usually with abdominal cramps and the passage of blood in the stools. It is either 'bacillary' – caused by bacteria of the *Shigella* group – or 'amoebic' – caused by the protozoan amoebic organism *Entamoeba histolytica*. The latter is a particularly protracted and severe form of the disease, and was particularly common in the jungle camps of the Thai–Burma Railway.

Malaria. There are several different sub-types of malaria, and in Changi most cases were due to *Plasmodium vivax* – causing what was known in those days as 'benign tertian' (BT) malaria. As the name suggests, though very debilitating, this rarely caused death on its own, though could be a contributory factor.

Beriberi. This is due to deficiency of the B vitamin thiamine and exists in 'wet' and 'dry' forms. The dry type is characterized by damage to the peripheral nerves, particularly in the feet and legs – causing numbness, tingling and sometimes pain. The wet type leads to weakness of the heart muscle, and passage of fluid from the blood vessels into the surrounding tissues, abdomen and pleural spaces of the lung. As may be expected, this was the more serious form of beriberi, and could lead to death.

In one case of cardiac beriberi, Jack's post-mortem report mentions that 'both pleural cavities contained about 1 pint of transudate' – referring to fluid surrounding the lungs. Also, 'the pericardium contained an excess of fluid' and 'the abdomen contained an enormous volume of transudate' – again indicating the massive fluid retention which occurred in this disease. The heart was enlarged and 'the myocardium looked atrophic … and hypotonic', meaning that the heart muscle was weak and thinned. This fatal disease was essentially due to the rice-based diet and could have been prevented by the supply of reasonable amounts of fruit and vegetables.

An autopsy report of a fatal case of amoebic dysentery records that 'the large bowel was found to be the site of extensive amoebic ulceration'. This patient had suffered a known complication of this disease where the infection spreads to the liver, causing abscess formation, which in this case had ruptured into the abdominal cavity. He reported that the abscess was 'about 250cc capacity containing thick yellow pus' and that it 'opened directly into the peritoneal space'. Jack also noted that the patient was generally malnourished. The death occurred in late 1943, and with such advanced pathology, it seems likely that the man had been evacuated from Thailand – perhaps part of the ill-fated 'F' Force.

Incidental findings in several autopsies included evidence of malarial infections, round worms (*Ascaris*) and *Strongyloides* worms. The latter is of particular interest, as many years later, research at the Liverpool School of Tropical Medicine was to show that a substantial number of ex-Far East POWs carried this Strongyloid worm infection long-term (about 15 per cent), and that under conditions of reduced immunity (particularly related to steroid drug treatment), the infection could rapidly spread and be potentially fatal (the so-called 'hyperinfection syndrome'). Other aftermaths of Far East imprisonment were relapses of malaria, tuberculosis and amoebic dysentery – as well as significant psychological ill-health in at least one-third of cases (later recognized as post-traumatic stress disorder or PTSD).

Conclusions

These pathology records of Captain Jack Ennis represent a highly unusual and useful primary source.

There are a number of contemporary accounts of clinical disease and its management, written by medical officers during Far East imprisonment, but very few pathology records have come to light. To our knowledge, the Ennis files are by far the most detailed and complete. His information complements clinical records and gives a very different insight into illness and mortality under Japanese imprisonment. We owe a great debt of gratitude to Jack Ennis, who, by his specialist expertise, organizational skill, meticulous record-keeping and raw courage, has left behind such valuable and unique records.

Appendix 2

Changi Gaol, Block 'A' Fourth Floor

At the time of capitulation, the civilian population of Singapore was largely Chinese. There were just over 10 per cent Malays, slightly fewer Indian and the remainder (just over 4 per cent) was classified as 'Others'. Most of the latter were British, but there were also Irish, Australian, Canadian, Polish, French, Italian and Dutch, as well as other European and Eurasian. It was men, women and children in this last category who were now interned.

After temporary detention in former private houses in Katong, on 8 March 1942, civilian women and children were moved to Changi Gaol. The oldest women (in their 80s), the youngest, the sick and the few pregnant women were taken by truck along with all their limited possessions while the rest of the women walked.

The women were housed in Block 'A', where Elizabeth shared space with unmarried women who were nurses, teachers, secretaries or buyers for commercial businesses, and married or widowed women who often assumed the perceived social status of their husbands. A mixed bag indeed, from rubber planters and tin miners, merchants, engineers, solicitors and bankers, judges and members of the Colonial Office to police and prison officers and many other occupations. Inside the gaol, no such distinctions were made.

Compiled by Elizabeth at the time, the following list of names records the occupants of the fourth floor:

AINSLIE, Mrs Murray	DRAPER, Mrs Joan*	MOIR, Mrs R.G.
ALLEN, Mrs Lucy	EISENGER, Mrs Maureen	MOUBRAY, Mrs de
D'ALMEIDA, Miss	ENNIS, Mrs Elizabeth	NEW, Mrs Pat
BECK, Mrs Helen	FERGUSON, Mrs	RENTON, Miss

BENTLEY, Mrs
BLOOM, Mrs Freddy*
BOLTON, Mrs
BRISK, Mrs
BYRNE, Mrs

BYRON, Mrs
CHOWNS, Mrs
CORLEY, Mrs
CRONYN, Mrs

CUTLER, Mrs
DALTON, Miss

DALY, Mrs
DAVIES, Mrs
DAWSON, Mrs

DICKINSON, Mrs
DIXON, Mrs

GOTTLIEB, Miss
GRAAF, Mrs de

HADLEY, Miss
HAGT, von, family
HARRISON, Mrs

HOPKINS, Dr E.*
JONES, Miss Griffith
KING, Mrs
KINNEAR, Mrs Gwen

KIRKBRIDE, Mrs
LINDSAY, Mrs

LOVERIDGE, Mrs
McIVOR, Miss
MacKENZIE, Mrs Kate
MACKIE, Mrs
MITCHELL, Miss

ROEPER, Mrs
ROGERS, Mrs Bess

ROODE, van, Mrs*
SILLEY, Mrs Sylvia
THOMAS, Lady Shenton*
THOMAS, Miss Mary
TOBY, Miss
TOSTEE, Mrs
WALTON, Mrs

WARREN, Mrs
WILLIAMS, Miss Marion*
WILLIAMS, Mrs Toby
WILLIS, Mrs
WOOTTON, Mrs

WRIGHT, Mrs J.
YOUNG, Miss M.

Further Notes (*)

Mrs Freddy BLOOM
A former journalist, Freddy was married to Major Phillip Bloom RAMC.

Mrs Joan DRAPER
Jack's cousin. Married to John Francis Draper, a barrister.

Dr HOPKINS
Wife of a doctor with the Government Medical Service, Dr Hopkins was the first elected Commandant of the Women's Camp.

Mrs van ROODE
A school teacher, Trudie helped run the Girl Guide company in Changi.

Lady Shenton THOMAS
Wife of Shenton Thomas, Governor of Straits Settlements.

Miss Marion WILLIAMS
Later married to RAF Squadron Leader Robert J. Cummings, who had been captured in Java and sent to work on the Railway. Lifelong friends of Jack and Elizabeth.

Appendix 3

Post-war Compensation Claim and Correspondence

On 11 February 1942, Tyersall Hospital, Singapore, was bombed. The resulting fire destroyed the building with the loss of many lives, both staff and patients. On that day, Jack had been working at the Combined General Hospital and returned to Tyersall to find, as he wrote later that day, 'everything gone'. Literally all his possessions had been in Tyersall.

While a POW in Roberts Barracks, he compiled a list of his losses to support a claim for compensation following his release at some future date.

His list of 'Private Chattels' indicates the comfortable lifestyle of a British officer working in the Tropics. There are many items of military dress, from the daily working uniform (mostly khaki) to evening Mess kit and a dinner suit with tails for formal evenings. For recreation and leisure, he notes his tennis and squash racquets, swim trunks, a radio, binoculars and a camera, as well as riding clothes.

The final items ('Miscellaneous') reflect his enthusiasm for the country, the peoples and wildlife. In remote settlements in the rain forest, the Temiar and Senoi indigenous peoples were famed for their wooden carvings. Largely dependent on traditional agriculture supplemented by hunting, tools and weapons such as blowpipes and darts were made from bamboo. Baskets and fish traps were made of rattan. Perhaps in these hills and dense forests he learned to track and identify animals, expanding his knowledge of snakes (Ophidia) in particular. Interested in snakes since his childhood in India, as a pathologist, Jack was often called upon to prescribe a serum when a patient had been bitten. Identification of the species (particularly those most venomous – krait, cobra or coral snake) was vital in determining the most effective serum.

A. Private Chattels

Pair of brown leggings
Pair of riding breeches
Sword, scabbard and knot
Raincoat, light khaki
Set of leathers
Spurs
Mess jacket and overall, warm
Cap, Mess dress
Boots, Wellington, patent
Mess spurs
Dress shirts, white
Dress collars
Dress ties, socks etc
Sets of cufflinks, studs (gold)
Gabardine khaki shirt
Shirts, khaki drill (9)
Shoes, 8 pairs
Helmet, Wolseley
Shirts, various (20)
Stockings, various (20 pairs)
Gumboots, 1 pair
Military Mess dress, white
Sets of boot and shoe trees

Cabin trunk
Wooden tin-lined trunk
Leather suitcase
Revelation suitcase
Attaché case
Oil compass
Binoculars, Ross
Blankets, Whitney (4)
Travelling rug
Eiderdown quilt
Sheets bed linen (8)
Pillows
Pillow slips
Face and bath towels
Mosquito net
Pyjama suits (6)
Dressing gown, warm
Dressing gown, light
Lounge suits, warm (3)
Lounge suits, light (3)
Fitted holdall
Trousers (3)
Tweed jackets (2)

Pullovers, Jaeger (3)
Shirts, sports (12)
Hats, Trilby (2)
Ties, various (12)
Overcoat, warm
Slippers, 1 pair
Suit, dinner dress
Suit, evening wear tails
Shoes, black dress (1 pair)
Braces, suspenders etc
Crockery
Cutlery
Trays (2)
Typewriter, Royal Port.
Car, Morris 8
Camera, Rolleicord
Additional camera lenses
Wireless set, Pye
Tennis racquet
Squash racquet
Swim trunks, Jantzen

B. Business equipment (Medical Practitioner)

Medical diagnostic set
Lovibond Universal Comparator
Sahli-Hellige Haemoglobinometer
Neubauer Counting Chamber
Set of B.D. Syringes
Aural Head Mirror
Direct Vision Spectroscope
Baumanometer
Assorted surgical instruments
Personal medical library, mostly recent editions

C. Miscellaneous

Collection of Temiar and Senoi Implements
Collection of Malayan Ophidia
Collection of photographs

In 1945, as experienced by many other returning POWs, money was a pressing need, as evidenced by Jack's file of correspondence.

In 1946, questioning the settlement of his account with FCMA, he pointed out that he had not been credited with the married officers separation allowance in full, despite the fact that he had arranged for money to be paid to Elizabeth.

In early 1947 he questioned deductions from his pay: 'For period from 1/8/39, Rent of Rs.685/1 deducted without explanation – this is extraordinary as for much of this period [sapper camps throughout India] I occupied a leaf-roofed hut or nothing at all.'

His rate of pay had been restored on 15 August 1945. Years later, Jack wryly noted that from 15 August to 11 September, 'rent' had been deducted although he was still effectively held in a POW camp. Rent was also deducted for the repatriation voyage.

Given the unique circumstances of his marriage in Singapore, it is not surprising that the next file of post-war letters (confirming his marriage) is substantial. In February 1942, notification of his marriage had been published in 2nd Echelon orders from the unit order and a copy sent to CMA Lahore. In 1946, upon his return to London, Jack visited the India

Office, where his marriage certificate was examined and accepted by the Accountant General.

The paper trail became more complicated following partition:

'25 August 1947
  'Letter from Supreme Commanders HQ, New Delhi
  'As a consequence of the partition of India resulting from the transfer of power MZ-17704 Major J. E. Ennis will be compulsorily retired.'

For the next two years, Jack sought to establish the arrangements for his pension fund. In early February 1947, when the Controller of Pension Funds wrote again asking for proof of marriage certificate, Jack's reply this time – having already written at length – was a little more terse: 'The Civil Post system had broken down in Singapore at the time of my marriage and I was taken POW four days later.'

Now the matter was bounced between the Commonwealth Relations Office, UK, and the equivalent department in India, eliciting this reaction on 9 April 1949, when he wrote to The Under-Secretary of State for Commonwealth Relations, Service Dept.: 'I do not recall being in the service of the present Government of India who, I feel, in arriving at a decision in the matter under consideration would naturally have a bias in favour of their own Dominion.'

Despite correspondence having continued throughout 1949, the question of his pension was eventually resolved – and paid.

Perhaps more welcome at the time, he received a chit stating:

'Clothing coupons on returning to civilian life.
  'Form RH591 to be issued with 90 civilian clothing coupons – military officer returning to civilian life (collect from Board of Trade, Victoria Street, London).
  'Further certificate L.S.7 for 63 additional civilian clothing coupons.'

Bibliography and Suggested Further Reading

Allan, Sheila, *Diary of a Girl in Changi*, 2nd Edition (includes the Changi Quilts) (Kangaroo Press, 1999).
Archer, Bernice, *The Internment of Western Civilians under the Japanese 1941–1945* (Routledge-Curzon, 2004).
Barber, Noel, *Sinister Twilight* (Collins, 1968).
Bell, Leslie, *Destined Meeting* (Odhams Press, 1959).
Bloom, Freddy, *Dear Philip* (Bodley Head, 1980).
Bradley. James, *The Tall Man Who Never Slept* (Woodfield Publishing, 1991).
Dunlop, E.E., *The War Diaries of Weary Dunlop* (Viking Books, 1986).
Gill, Geoff and Parkes, Meg, *Burma Railway Medicine* (Palatine Books, 2017).
Huxtable, Charles, *From the Somme to Singapore* (Costello, 1987).
Laird, Rory, *From Shanghai to the Burma Railway* (Pen & Sword, 2020).
Ledingham, Capt. J., Private papers, Catalogue No. Documents 1621, IWM.
Manson-Barr, Phillip H., *Manson's Tropical Diseases* (Cassell & Co. reprint, 1941).
Marshall, Captain G.K., *The Changi Diaries, Singapore 1942–1945* (Private publication, 1988).
Parkes, Meg and Gill, Geoff, *Captive Memories* (Palatine Books, 2015).
Radio 4 Broadcast 3, 'Threads of Hope' (13 September 2001), presented by Mike Thomson, produced by Helen Weinstein.
Scott, R.H., War diary and various papers. National Library of Scotland. Acc. 8181 Box 2.
Sleeman, Colin and Silkin, S.C. (eds), *Trial of Sumida Haruzo and Twenty Others (The 'Double Tenth' Trial)* (William Hodge, 1950).
Tretchikoff, Vladimir and Hocking, Anthony, *Pigeon's Luck* (Collins, 1973).
Watkins, Paul, *Hay Fever to Hell Island* (Brown Dog Books, 2018).
https://fepowhistory.com.
www.cofepow.org.uk.

Index of Names

The following list of names is compiled from Jack and Elizabeth's records of their time in Singapore. Spellings have been transcribed as per their writings, but may be incorrect.

Ackhurst, ('Akki'), xiv, 84
Ainslie, 270
Alagappa/Allagapia 15, 223
Alford, 14, 158
Allen, 74, 239, 270
Anderson, 73
Andrews, 195–7, 199
Aubrey, 105
Arimura, 180–1
Awara, 231

Backshall, 176, 212
Ball, 147
Band, Lt, 34
Bangs, 50, 52, 54, 56, 61–2, 77, 88
Barber, 119, 125–6, 128, 220
Barrowman, 109
Bassett, 90
Bassett, 163
Bates, 100, 119
Baxter, 189, 197
Beck, 118, 270
Beadnell, 161
Beckwith–Smith, 94
Bell, 63, 70, 114
Bennet, 20, 30, 32, 36, 38, 55, 59, 62–4, 70

Benson, 63, 87–8, 140–1, 152–3
Bentley, 271
Benton, 187
Best, 46, 48, 52, 54, 66, 80, 83, 88, 90–1, 93, 130, 131
Bevan, 103, 117, 123, 140, 186–7
Birch, 211
Black, 41, 57, 120
Blackburn, 107
Blackhurst, 91
'Black Jack', *see* Galleghan
Blakeman, 85
Bloom, 15, 31–4, 36, 38, 46, 48, 50, 53, 55, 58, 62, 89–90, 100, 103, 119, 129, 132, 187, 244, 246
Bloom (Mrs Freddy) 35, 187, 271
Bolton, 271
Bradshaw, 162, 176, 201, 212, 225
Brahan, 86
Brennan, 30
Brisk, 271
Brody, 219
Brooks, 219
Brown, 140
Bull, 110
Burton, 193, 195

Bush, 216, 222, 233
Byrne, 271
Byron, 271

Caldbeck, 139, 153, 191–3, 199
Calder, 15
Calderwood, 49
Cameron, 74
Campbell, 88, 122, 148, 156, 172–3, 181, 187, 218, 228, 231, 234
Campbell–Paterson, 150
Carlisle, 22
Chapman, 45, 141
Chatterjee, 72
Chawla, 203
Chiltern, 110, 120, 133
Chopping, 116, 151, 160
Chowdry, 203, 223
Chowk, 232
Chowns, 271
Clarkson, 140
Collins, 88–9, 114, 126, 185, 188–93, 195–9, 207, 212, 215–6, 218, 221, 228–30, 232
Cooke, 134
Cooper, 16, 29, 36, 38, 61, 91–2, 131, 175, 190, 193, 195, 209, 216, 218, 254
Cordiner, 99–100
Corley, 271
Cortini, *see* Crustyen
Cornelius, 57, 129, 136
Court, 5, 9–10
Cousins, 36
Craigie, 84
Cranshaw, 72
Craven, 31–2, 41, 62, 75, 153

Crawford, 140
Cronyn, 271
Cruikshank, 54, 59, 94, 114
Crustyen, 108–9
Cummings, 118, 254, 272
Currid, 63
Cuthbert, 134
Cutler, 271

Dak, 228
D'Almeida, 270
Dalton, 271
Daltrey, 162, 176
Daly, 271
Daniels, 125–6
Darwell, 192
Davey, 199, 202, 207, 216
Davies, 271
Davis, 34, 48, 60, 140, 228
Dawe, 153
Dawson, 115, 131, 136–7, 140, 271
de Graaf, 271
de Gray, 64
de Moubray, 46, 55, 56, 107, 112, 117, 119, 270
de Romsey, 91, 180, 185, 208
de Soldenoff, 41, 60, 80, 90–1

Denaro, 138
Deverill, 186
Dewar, 33, 53, 56–7, 63, 99
Dickinson, 271
Dillon, 69, 183
Diver, 107–108, 132, 221
Dixon, 271
Dowling, 120
Doyle, 13, 40, 88, 120, 148

Draper, 24, 56, 103, 270–1
Dunn, 35
Durrell, 140

East, 51, 57, 66
Eastwood, 120, 140, 186
Eisenger, 271
Elliot, 176, 201
Euston, 67
Evans, 140

Fairway, 56
Falk, 119, 136
Farmer, 169
Farrant, 182
Farwell, 124, 131, 213
Field(s), 54, 233–4
Feinhols, 83
Ferguson, 271
Findlay, 178, 180, 225
Finlayson, 96, 109, 157, 173
Flanner, 31
Frankland, 60, 89, 115, 138–9, 143, 153, 167, 175, 179, 229, 254
Franks, 34, 83, 117, 140, 186
Fukuye, 74

Gale, 214
Galleghan, 107, 180, 195, 230
Garlick, 43, 67
Garrard, 140
Garrett, 112
Garry, 145
Gasper, 176, 179
Gass, 40
Gavin, 25, 48, 73, 76
Gawn, 31, 37, 74, 93, 104, 123–4, 127, 133, 152–3

George, 61, 92
'George', 141
Gibbs, 13, 20, 60–1, 63, 70, 88
Gibson, 35, 61, 140
Glancy, 139
Gledding, 56
Glendenning, 38, 50, 59
'Goggle Eyes', 207, 215, 227
Goodall, 71
Gordon, 37, 183
Gottlieb, 271
Graham, 38, 47, 53, 72, 78
Graves, 47, 51, 64, 222
Griffs, 117
Guest, 160

Hadley, 271
Haigh, 57, 66, 121, 126
Harper, 188, 193, 207, 218, 226
Harris, 169, 171, 238
Harrison, 44, 271
Harty 17, 44, 63, 223, 242
Harvey, 86–7, 191, 198, 220–1
Harwood, 86
Hay, 228
Hayashita, 223, 230
Hayward, 39
Heath, 31, 46, 55, 64, 86, 95
Henderson, 105, 140, 186, 238
Hewitt, 19, 25, 46
Hind, 51
Hodden, 218
Holmes, 75–6, 130, 149, 160, 180, 184, 195
Hopkins, 243, 271
Houghton, 55, 61, 91–2, 131–2, 139, 144, 218
Houston, 34

Hunt, 94, 111
Hussein, 232
Hutchins, 141–2, 179
Hutchison, 111
Huxtable, 218

Jain, 5, 10–11
James, 75, 107, 119, 147, 158
Jamieson, 63
Jenkins, 65–6, 86–7, 101, 103
Jibani, 72
Jilani, 223, 232
Johns, 103, 163
Jones, 141, 271

Kanomitsa, 202
Kennedy, 43, 53, 62, 166
Kent, 186
Khan, 21–3, 231–2
Kim, 228–30
King, 271
Kingston, 43, 48, 126, 185, 218, 224
Kinnear, 271
Kirkbride, 271
Kopar, 223
Koromoto/Koronato 199–200, 209

Lads, 20, 52–3, 242
Lawson, 123
Laycock, 67
Ledingham, xvi, 42, 59, 101, 153, 160, 162, 167–8, 176, 203, 218, 242
Lennon, 85–6
Lennox, 15, 26, 29–31, 34–7, 41, 55, 79
Lewis, 154
Lillico, 44
Lindsay, 271
Litton, 17

Loveridge, 271
Lucas, 32–3, 52
Lyndsey, 37

MacDonald, 139, 141–2, 144, 191, 196, 199, 212, 219–220, 232
MacFarlane, 36, 44, 49, 62, 89–90
MacGarrity, 101, 113–4, 131, 135, 142–3
MacGregor, 69, 91, 102, 105, 116, 123, 134, 139, 141–2
MacKenzie, 76, 271
Mackie, 144, 271
Mackwood, 201, 212
Malcolm, 89, 91
Malhotra, 203
Maltby, 108
Manji, 223
Markby, 137, 149, 192–3
Markowitch (Markowitz), 74
Marriot, 155, 168
Marsden, 118, 220
Marsh, 44, 107–108, 121
Marshall, 15, 140, 169
Matheson/Mathieson, 65, 101, 149
Maynard, 35, 46, 58, 73, 101, 179
McCaul, 200
McConachie, 63
McCrae, 66
McDonald, *see* MacDonald
McFarlane, *see* MacFarlane
McGarrity *see* MacGarrity
McGavin, 19
McIvor, 271
McLaughlin, 68
McMahon, 50
McMoran, 94
Menon, 95

Middleton, 42–3, 53, 135, 153, 185, 212, 221
Ming, 133, 137–8
Mitchell, 56, 225, 271
Mizina, 220
Moir, 270
Molesworth, 150
More, 200
Morgan, 193
Morris, 15, 19, 46, 201, 208, 238
Morrison, 169, 176, 212, 231, 233–4
Mulvaney, 16, 25, 37, 55–6, 59, 64, 75, 79, 84, 86, 120, 136, 239
Munro, 144
Murray, 100
Muthatra, 232

Nagusaki, 37
Nair, 218
Nardell, 71, 133, 137, 151–3
Nancy, 53–5, 132
Neale/Neill, 33, 36–7, 75, 126, 185, 230
 (*see also* Niall)
Neave, 38
New, 270
Newey, 195–6, 216–7
Newman, 110
Niall, 216
Nicholas, 191, 207, 218
Nishyama, 228
North–Hunt, 20, 24
Norton, 220

Oberman, 59
O'Donnell, 70
O'Neale/O'Neill 31, 41, 129, 144
Osborne, 191, 198, 220–21

Painter, 81
Pearson, 68–9, 198, 225
Pemberton, 63, 67, 88
Perrera/Pereira, 73, 92, 132
Peterson, 213
Petrovsky, 122
Phillips, 73, 75
Pigot, 67
Pitt, 60, 81, 87, 91–2, 113, 115–8, 121, 124, 133
Porter, 156, 191, 206, 209, 216, 222
Purvis, 109

Quarant, 195

Rahill, 56
Reid, 57
Rendle, 103
Rennison, 66
Renton, 270
Richards, 62
Riddell, 169
Rigby, 30–2, 38, 52, 64, 70
Rivers, 130
Roberts, 26, 28, 84, 93, 105–106, 111, 144, 151
Robson, 60
Roeper, 271
Rogers, 104, 271
Rose, 11, 34, 51–2, 63, 127
Ross, 43, 67
Rye, 162

Saito, 217, 230
Sandy, 180
Scott, 43, 49, 62, 186
Scullion, 81
Sefton, 118
Shaw, 150, 203

Shepherd, 93
Silley, 271
Simmons, 37, 105–106, 108
Simpson, 118
Singh, 232
Sitwell, 107–108
Smiley, 96, 136
Smith, 80, 94, 238
Smythe, 55
Snell, 130
Spedding, 56, 111, 120
Spooner, 51
Stephens, 198
Stewart 25–6, 34, 53, 152
Stillwell, 188
Stone, 53
Strachan, 48, 54, 72, 77, 94–8, 101, 163, 169
Stratton-Christenson, 50, 66, 242
Strawbridge, 218
Stringer, 25–6, 32, 35, 38, 40, 44, 48
Stuart, *see* Stewart
Sullivan, 65–6, 71, 80, 90, 123, 127, 138, 169
Summons, 14
Sutor, 231

Takahashi, 183, 196, 200
Tania, 202, 213
Taylor, 17, 22, 37, 47, 63, 72, 129, 144, 152, 190, 202, 207, 218, 222, 231
Thomas (Shenton), 23, 66, 233, 238, 271–2
Thomas, 271
Thyer, 132
Tidd, 86, 99–100, 174, 196
Toby, 271

Todd, 29, 32
Tomlinson, 140
Toraka, 177
Tostee, 271
Toyahara, 228
Tretchikoff, 12
Tucker, 51
Turner, 120

Ullman, 197, 199

van Roode, 237, 271
Vardy, 34, 36, 42, 44–5, 51, 55, 60, 67, 77, 79–80, 86–7, 89–91
Veysey, 234
von Hagt, 271

Wallace, 23, 86, 108, 117, 140, 184, 232–3, 247, 251
Walsh, 127, 199
Walter(s), 152, 238
Walton, 271
Ward, 32, 37, 40, 69, 178, 242
Warren, 271
Waters, 126
Wearne, 97, 102, 109, 115, 139, 188, 208
Webster, 86, 231
Welch, 119, 151
Wemsby, 234
West, 58
Wharton, 16, 38, 50, 53, 61, 63–4, 88, 92
Wheeler, 16
White, 54, 56, 71, 98, 107, 142, 169, 172, 186, 188
Wild, 109, 175, 197
Wilkinson, 222
Williams, 85, 119, 202, 271–2

Willis, 271
Willy, 118
Wilson, 126
Withers, 64
Wolfe, 53, 134, 142, 145, 206, 223
Wood, 176
Wooller, 161

Wootton, 271
Wright, 14, 142, 240, 271
Wyatt, 16, 61, 63, 105–6, 111

Yoshikawa, 203, 206, 208–9, 213, 219-20, 224, 227
Young, 76, 111, 154, 271

General Index

45 Anti-tank Company, 37, 58, 163
13th Australian General
  Hospital, 60
17 CGH, 13, 16, 21, 41, 120, 178
20 CGH, 14, 16, 20, 100, 120
12 IGH, 9, 17, 231
19 IGH, 19
11th Division, 43, 55–6, 59, 63, 67, 70, 72, 74, 87, 93, 100, 102, 107, 145
13th Division, 67, 183
18th Division, 68, 74, 82, 87, 90–2, 94, 96, 102, 104, 113–14, 117, 121, 125, 127–31, 135–36, 144, 148, 166
114th British General Hospital, Bangalore, 251
198 Field Ambulance (FA), 30
137th Regiment, 43

A Force, 195
  see also Forces leaving Singapore
Accidents, 36, 111, 164, 213, 221
Adam Road, 189, 229
Aerodrome construction, 168–9, 174–5, 184
Alexandra Hospital, 99
Alor Star, 13, 68
Amoebiasis, 32, 111
Anaemia, 43, 83, 86

Anaesthetics, 13–4, 17, 21–3
Anti-malarial squads, 34, 46, 54, 111, 134, 203, 210, 216
A&SH (Argyll and Sutherland Highlanders), 4, 49, 155, 168, 183
Artificial limbs, 174
Avitaminosis, *see* Vitamin deficiency diseases

B-24 aircraft, 230
B-29 aircraft, 204–6, 210, 212
Black market, 39, 43, 48, 53, 81, 107, 111, 190, 195–6, 208, 213, 225
Blakang Mati, 167, 175, 179, 229
Beriberi, *see* Vitamin deficiency diseases
Bronchitis, 115
Broncho-pneumonia, 38
Bukit Panjang, 214
Bukit Timah, 20, 188–190, 218, 229
Burma Railway, 171, 254, 260, 262, 268
Burning feet syndrome, *see* Vitamin deficiency diseases

Cats, eating, *see* Diet
Cemetery Hill, 218, 227

Changi Balls, *see* Vitamin Deficiency Diseases, scrotal dermatitis
Changi Medical Society, 37, 41, 65, 97, 101, 109, 111, 118, 135, 138, 142, 161, 175, 177, 179
Changi village, 19, 37, 39, 48, 135, 138
Cholecystectomy, 231
Cholera, 57, 120, 128, 141, 144, 151, 153–4, 163, 171
Corfu HMS, 249

D Force, 195, 254
  see also Forces leaving Singapore
Deaconess Hospital, 7
Death, causes of, 164, 266
Dengue fever, 52, 87, 94, 132
Dentistry (treatment), 96, 109
Diarrhoea, 24–5, 32, 46, 123
Diet, extra protein sources
  cat, 193, 195, 202, 206, 211, 216, 219
  dog, 109, 111, 187–8, 193
  ducks/ducklings, 117, 124, 139, 142, 146, 149, 151, 153, 160–1, 170, 179, 185, 229
  egg/hen (combines), 153, 157, 159–60, 162, 163, 166–7, 170, 175, 192–3
  fish, 115, 144–7, 150–1, 157, 159
  monkey, 138
  pigeon, 222–3
  rats, 216, 222, 225
  rubber nuts, 225
  snails, 113
  snakes, 160

Diphtheria, 30, 33, 71–3, 75, 94, 109, 169, 261–2, 264, 266–8
  See also KLB
Dogs, eating, *see* Diet
Double Tenth, 14, 245
Ducks/ducklings, *see* Diet
Dysentery, 3, 25–33, 36, 38, 43, 47, 64, 71, 111, 130, 145, 156, 161, 165, 167, 171, 206, 223, 237, 268

Egg/hen combine *see* Diet
Empress of India SS, 8
Encephalitis, 35, 56, 94, 164
ENSA (Entertainments National Service Association), 233
Entertainments
  concerts/plays, 34, 44, 51–2, 57, 59, 64, 66, 69, 72, 94, 104, 123, 126, 138, 142, 156, 159, 178, 191, 198, 231
  'Great Cortini', 109
  classes (German language), 48, 63, 110–11
  film show, 74, 84
  horse racing, 113
  lectures, 200–1, 207–8, 224
  Spelling Bee, 53, 55
Escapes, 31, 73, 75–6, 90, 106, 145, 155, 168–9, 171

F Force, 171, 175–6, 185, 262, 264, 269
  see also Forces leaving Singapore
FANY (First Aid Nursing Yeomanry), 233, 248–9
Far Eastern Bureau, 11–2

Film/photograph unit (Japanese), 108, 180–81
Flies, 25–30, 61, 116, 156, 165
FMSVF (Federated Malay States Volunteer Force), 34, 44, 76
Forces leaving Singapore
 1942 May to November, 56, 62, 70, 85–7, 89, 91, 95
 1943 January to November, 109, 114, 121–2, 126, 129, 131–2, 141, 147, 158, 168
Ford Works, 229
Fort Canning, 15, 20
Fullerton Buildings, 15, 21, 28, 33, 43, 76

G&W (Garden and Woods Camp), 135, 137, 145, 147–9, 162, 165, 167–8, 171
Gemas, 15–6, 46–7
Giang Bee HMS, 235–6
Gillman, 17, 19–21, 140
Girl Guides (Changi), 13, 237–9
Glycosurias, 86, 100
Growing vegetables, 34, 36–7, 42, 102, 130, 144, 200, 224, 226
Gurkhas, 232

H Force, 171, 185
 see also Forces leaving Singapore
HKSRA (Hong Kong and Singapore Royal Artillery), 228
Hookworm, *see* Skin diseases
Houston USS, 86

INA (Indian National Army), 198
Indomitable HMS, 12

Indian General Hospital, Tyersall Park, 20
Interpreters, 39, 75, 107, 110, 140, 147, 158, 175, 192, 195–9, 216

Johore 15, 47, 59, 204–5, 210, 217, 226
 causeway, 18
Kahn tests, 33, 35, 92, 94, 120, 265
 See also syphilis
Katong, 28–9, 235
Kedah, 13
Kelantan, 13
Kempetai, 14–5, 155, 214, 237, 245–7, 252
Keppel harbour, 55, 57, 59, 65, 75, 204–5, 217, 222
Kidney disease, 133, 155
Kinta Maru, 254
KLB, (Klebs-Loeffler bacillus), 76, 167, 169–70, 188, 264
 See also diphtheria
Korean guards, 189–91, 193–6, 199–203, 207–11, 214–6, 223, 225–9
Kranji Camp, 188–9, 194, 201, 203, 210, 232, 247–8, 250
Kuala HMS, 21
Kuala Lipis, 4, 9–11, 17
Kuala Lumpur (KL), 4–5, 13–4, 73, 82–3, 85, 99

Larva migrans, *see* Skin diseases
Leishmaniasis, *see* Skin diseases
Lexington USS, 54
Lisbon Maru, 84
Lizard, 88, 146, 194
Lymphangitis, 55

Malaria,
  cases, 3, 29, 31, 38, 64, 83, 88, 99, 141, 230, 237, 260, 268–9
  deaths/post-mortems, 38, 50, 98, 164, 171, 216, 266–8
  lectures, 36, 38, 94–5, 97, 104, 161, 211
  tests, 25, 31, 77, 94, 118–20, 125, 128–9, 169, 261–2, 264
  See also anti-malarial squads, mrps
Malaya Command (MC), 32, 76, 83, 85, 93–4, 102, 105
Mondai, 203, 224. 229, 232
Monkeys, *see* Diet
Monowai HMT, 248
Mrps, 27, 64, 121, 169, 172

NAAFI, 102, 153, 195, 212, 249
Narkunda SS, 8
Naval Base, 29, 33, 35, 39, 41, 65, 165, 167, 204–6, 210
Nee Soon, 203, 223, 231–2
Night soil, 223–4
Normanton Camp, 221, 225

Oedema, 29, 41, 45, 47, 78–9, 168, 181, 246
Operation Jaywick, 245
Otway pit (liquid waste disposal) 201, 206
Outram Road Gaol, 106, 145, 155, 168–9, 171, 246

Pathology, reports and records, 259–69
Pearl Harbor, 13, 98
Pellagra, *see* Vitamin deficiency diseases

Perth HMAS, 86, 89
Phagedena, 171
Pigeon, *see* Diet
Pig farming, 27, 91, 170
President Adams SS, 9
Prince Eugene (Prinz Eugen), 47
Prince of Wales HMS, 13
Pulau Panging, 205

QAIMNS (Queen Alexandra's Imperial Military Nursing Sisters) 11, 48
Queen Mary RMS, 29
Quilts
  Girl Guide quilt, 13, 238–9, 255
  Red Cross quilts, 239–40
Quinine, 73, 94, 121, 128, 211, 213

RAPWI (Recovery Allied Prisoners of War), 233–4
RASC (Royal Army Service Corps), 34, 52, 90, 104, 185
Radio sets (in camp), 109, 132, 149–51, 158, 175, 182, 230, 232, 245–6
Rations (scale of rations as POW), 214–6, 222, 227
Rats, eating, *see* Diet
Repulse HMS, 12–3
Rice polishings, 60, 80, 110, 124
Richelieu, 96, 248
River Valley Road Camp, 47, 53, 62, 79, 109
Rodney HMS, 248

Saratoga USS, 47
Scabies, *see* Skin diseases

Scrotal dermatitis, *see* Vitamin deficiency diseases
Selarang incident, 74–6
Seletar, 18, 99, 204–5, 223, 232
Serangoon Road Camp, 216
Skin diseases
   larva migrans (hookworm), 79
   Leishmaniasis, 45, 77
   scabies, 73, 82, 145, 182, 246
Smallpox, 172
'Smokey Joe's', 136, 139, 143, 147–8
Snails, eating, *see* Diet
Snakes, 145, 162, 256, 273, *see also* Diet
Spastic diplegia, *see* Vitamin deficiency diseases
Sport,
   hockey, 52, 129, 131, 135, 137, 139, 145, 149, 156, 172, 181
   rugger, 72, 107, 116, 128, 161
   soccer, 60, 70, 96, 104, 107, 112–4, 127, 129, 156, 161, 172, 180–1, 183
   tennis, 180–1
Spotted fever, 64
SSVF (Straits Settlements Volunteer Force), 44, 107, 121
Suicide, 111, 164, 171, 227
Syme Road Camp, 229–30, 232–4, 247
Syonan Sinbun (*Times*) 94–5, 98, 105, 111, 116, 118, 121, 132, 136, 143, 145–6, 152, 158–9
Syphilis, 33, 73, 261, 265

Taiping, 11, 14
Tanjong Malim, 11, 14–5
Tower, The (Changi Gaol), 245

Tropical ulcer (*see* phagedena)
Tuberculosis (TB), 28, 97, 100, 130, 208–9
Tutuka Maru, 78
Typhoid, 10

Vitamin deficiency diseases,
   avitaminosis, 267
   beriberi, 36, 39–42, 82, 95, 105, 200, 221, 246, 268
   burning feet syndrome, 80, 86, 97, 268
   pellagra, 72, 79, 82, 118, 183, 188, 200, 212, 183, 188, 212
   scrotal dermatitis, 59–60, 66, 72–3, 76, 78, 118
   spastic diplegia, 78–80
Vitamin tablets
   multvitamins, 83, 170, 220–21
   vitamin B, 40, 43, 45, 48, 73, 77, 79

WAAF (Women's Auxiliary Air Force), 249
Woodlands Camp, 186, 188, 231
Worm infections, 32, 88, 100, 105, 223, 264, 267, 269

X-ray, 22, 36, 68, 118

Yeast
   Brewer's Yeast, 38
   growing yeasts, 40–1
Marmite, 60, 76, 86, 191
Vegemite, 66, 76, 80
   Yeastivite, 39

Z Force, *see* Operation Jaywick